SEX, ATTACHMENT,
AND COUPLE PSYCHOTHERAPY

The Library of Couple and Family Psychoanalysis
published and distributed by Karnac

SEX, ATTACHMENT, AND COUPLE PSYCHOTHERAPY

Psychoanalytic Perspectives

edited by
Christopher Clulow

KARNAC

First published in 2009 by
Karnac Books Ltd
118 Finchley Road, London NW3 5HT

British Library Cataloguing in Publication Data

A C.I.P. for this book is available from the British Library

ISBN: 978 1 85575 558 1

Edited, designed and produced by The Studio Publishing Services Ltd,
www.publishingservicesuk.co.uk
e-mail: studio@publishingservicesuk.co.uk

www.karnacbooks.com

CONTENTS

ACKNOWLEDGEMENTS

The original idea for this book was suggested to me by Susanna Abse, Director of the Tavistock Centre for Couple Relationships (TCCR), with the thought that it might form part of celebrating the sixtieth anniversary of the Centre in 2008. The proposal was to invite new work and bring together existing papers on sexuality and couple psychotherapy written by current and past members of the TCCR and its professional association, the Society of Couple Psychoanalytic Psychotherapists (SCPP). This seemed to me like an excellent proposal, which I was delighted to accept. Those of us who have worked in, or studied at, the TCCR owe a huge debt of gratitude to our mentors and colleagues who, over the years, have brought the best of psychoanalytic thinking to bear on our understanding of the interior of couple relationships, and have applied this understanding to the practice of couple psychotherapy. With their inspiration and energy, and the focus provided by the formation of the SCPP in 1988, psychoanalytic couple psychotherapy has established itself as a distinct discipline in the United Kingdom, with its own particular identity and training, and a formidable track record of publications.

Anniversaries, while celebrating past achievements, also pro-vide an opportunity to take stock. So it seemed to me that the six-tieth anniversary of the TCCR (and the twentieth anniversary of the SCPP) provided an opportunity not only to assemble what we have learned about sexuality in couple relationships but also to reap-praise the state of our knowledge. The fresh challenges that come from reviewing what we know in the context of a wider body of knowledge and experience provide an impetus to extend the fron-tiers of our understanding about this most intimate aspect of adult partnerships and to hone our skills as clinicians.

In this developing process we are and always have been hugely dependent upon the couples who have consulted us for help. They have allowed us into the most private part of their lives and entrus-ted us with their invaluable experience, challenging our assump-tions and helping to shape our responses to their distress. They are our teachers, to whom we owe an immense debt of gratitude. We offer our deepest appreciation to those who have consented to their experience being written about, and we have taken great care to protect confidence and anonymity when using the experience of couples to illustrate our thoughts and ideas.

Discussion with colleagues is an indispensable part of the process of developing ideas, and while all the contributors to this book take sole responsibility for what they have written, they do wish to acknowledge the people and groupings that have provided the milieu in which their thoughts have been formed and found expression. In this context, Joanna Rosenthall particularly wishes to acknowledges and thank Dr Karen Nash for her helpful comments during the writing of her chapter.

Two of the chapters in the book have been published in an ear-lier form. We wish to acknowledge our appreciation to Karnac Books and Joseph Schwartz, Editor of the journal *Attachment: New Directions in Psychotherapy and Relational Analysis*, for permission to reuse a paper by Susie Orbach that first appeared in March 2007 as "Separated attachments and sexual aliveness: how changing attachment patterns can enhance intimacy" (*Attachment*, 1(1): 8–17). This paper was based on a lecture delivered at the Summer Conference of the TCCR on 26 May 2006. We are also grateful to Blackwell Publishing for permission to reproduce a paper written by Mary Morgan and Judith Freedman (also generated from a

TCCR conference) that first appeared in the *British Journal of Psychotherapy* in 2000 as "From fear of intimacy to perversion: a clinical analysis of the film *Sex, Lies and Videotape* (*British Journal of Psychotherapy*, 17(10): 85–93). Warren Colman's chapter was first presented as part of a series of lectures called "The labyrinth of sex", organized by Confer at the Tavistock Centre, London, on 14 November 2001. Although some of the material has been developed into subsequent papers (Colman, 2005, 2007; see chapter references) this original version has an overall unity that has not been published before. The lines from Elaine Feinstein's poem "Getting older", which originally appeared in a collection entitled *Selected Poems*, are reproduced with permission from Carnacet Press.

Finally, the cover illustration, "Adam and Eve", is from a wood sculpture by Piotr Woroniec (photographed by Damian Wojtowicz), and appears with his kind permission. I would like to thank him, and also Bozena Ingram for acting as interpreter in arranging consent.

Christopher Clulow
Editor, January 2009

Susanna Abse is Director of The Tavistock Centre for Couple Relationships. She is a full member of the Society of Couple Psychoanalytic Psychotherapists, registered with the psychoanalytic section of the United Kingdom Council for Psychotherapy. She is a past Programme Leader for the MA in the Psychoanalytic Study of the Couple Relationship, and past Vice Chair of the SCPP. Currently, she is developing a new intervention that aims to diminish destructive inter-parental conflict over parenting styles and issues. She has published several practice papers on work with couples and lectures and teaches on a range of related subjects.

Andrew Balfour studied English Literature before going on to train as a clinical psychologist at University College London and then as an adult psychotherapist at the Tavistock Clinic. He works at the Tavistock Centre for Couple Relationships, where he undertook further training in couple psychotherapy, and is now Head of Clinical Services. He is also a consultant clinical psychologist at the Tavistock Clinic, where he teaches in the area of old age.

Maureen Boerma worked in the sexual and reproductive health field before training with the London Marriage Guidance Council as a psychodynamic couple counsellor and psychosexual therapist. She has since qualified as a psychoanalytic couple psychotherapist with the Tavistock Centre for Couple Relationships, where she is a staff member and Programme Leader for its Postgraduate Diploma in Psychodynamic Couple Counselling. She is also in private practice. She is accredited with the British Association of Counselling and Psychotherapy, a general member of the British Association for Sexual and Relationship Therapy, and a full member of the Society of Couple Psychoanalytic Psychotherapists.

Christopher Clulow is a Senior Fellow of the Tavistock Centre for Couple Relationships, founder member and Vice Chair of the Society of Couple Psychoanalytic Psychotherapists, honorary research psychotherapist at the Tavistock Clinic, and a Fellow of the Centre for Social Policy at Dartington. He is a patron of Hertfordshire Central Relate and a trustee for several charitable bodies working in the field of family support. He is the author or editor of nine other books and over a hundred published papers that consider marriage, partnerships, parenthood, and couple psychotherapy, most recently from an attachment perspective. He was Therapies Editor of the international journal *Sexual and Relationship Therapy*, 1996–2008, and Chair of the International Commission for Family and Interpersonal Relationships, 1987–1994. He teaches in this country and overseas, and lives with his family in St Albans, where he has a private couple psychotherapy practice.

Warren Colman is a training analyst of the Society of Analytical Psychology and Editor-in-Chief of the *Journal of Analytical Psychology*. A founder member of the Society of Couple Psychoanalytic Psychotherapists and a former senior staff member at the Tavistock Centre for Couple Relationships he is now in full-time private practice in St Albans. He teaches and supervises in England, Sweden, Poland, and Russia, and has published many papers on diverse topics, including couples and sexuality, the self, the therapeutic process, and symbolic imagination.

Peter Fonagy is Freud Memorial Professor of Psychoanalysis and Director of the Sub-Department of Clinical Health Psychology at University College London. He is Director of the Menninger

Clinical Outcomes Research and Effectiveness Centre and the Child and Family Centre, both at the Menninger Foundation, Kansas. He is also Director of Research at the Anna Freud Centre, London. He is a clinical psychologist and a training and supervising analyst at the British Psychoanalytical Society in child and adult analysis. He has published over 200 chapters and articles and has authored, co-authored, or edited several books, including *Attachment Theory and Psychoanalysis* (2001).

Judith Freedman is Consultant Psychiatrist in Psychotherapy at the Portman Clinic, London, which is a forensic psychotherapy service. She is a Fellow of the Royal College of Psychiatrists and is a psychoanalyst. She frequently prepares reports on parents and families for family courts, where couple relationships, sexuality and perversion, lies and the truth continue to be issues that are of interest to her.

Laura Green trained as a psychodynamic counsellor and psychosexual therapist at the London Marriage Guidance Council. She currently teaches the Introductory Course at the Tavistock Centre for Couple Relationships and runs a psychosexual case discussion group. She sees individuals and couples in her private practice in North London, and is an accredited member of the British Association for Counselling and Psychotherapy and a general member of the British Association for Sexual and Relationship Therapy.

Francis Grier is an associate member of the British Psychoanalytical Society and a full member of the Society of Couple Psychoanalytic Psychotherapists. He has been a senior couple psychotherapist, clinical lecturer, then visiting research lecturer, at the Tavistock Centre for Couple Relationships. He has a private practice for individuals and couples. He edited *Brief Encounters with Couples: Some Analytical Perspectives*, published by Karnac in 2001, and *Oedipus and the Couple*, published by Karnac as part of the Tavistock Clinic Series in 2005.

David Hewison is Reader in Couple Psychoanalytic Psychotherapy and a senior clinician at the Tavistock Centre for Couple Relationships. He is Programme Leader for the Centre's MA in Attachment,

Psychoanalysis and the Couple Relationship and he is a full member of the Society of Couple Psychoanalytic Psychotherapists. He is a Jungian analyst and a professional member of the Society of Analytical Psychology, and he has particular interests in qualitative research, film, and clinical and organizational supervision. He publishes, lectures, and teaches widely in this country and abroad, and he has a private practice of individual analysis, supervision, and couple psychotherapy.

Brett Kahr is Senior Clinical Research Fellow in Psychotherapy and Mental Health at the Centre for Child Mental Health in London, and a visiting clinician and lecturer at the Tavistock Centre for Couple Relationships. Since 2007, he has been the Chair of the Society of Couple Psychoanalytic Psychotherapists, the graduate body of qualified couple psychotherapists who trained at TCCR. He is the author of six books, including *D. W. Winnicott: A Biographical Portrait*, which won the Gradiva Prize for Biography, and, most recently, *Sex and the Psyche*, newly published in paperback from Penguin, which has already appeared in American, Canadian, Dutch, German, and Italian editions. A registered practitioner with the British Psychoanalytic Council and the United Kingdom Council for Psychotherapy, he works in full-time private practice in Hampstead, North London, with individuals and with couples.

Mary Morgan is a psychoanalyst and associate member of the British Psychoanalytical Society, a couple psychoanalytic psychotherapist and full member of the Society of Couple Psychoanalytic Psychotherapists, and a senior clinician at the Tavistock Centre for Couple Relationships, where she is currently the Programme Leader of the Clinical Training and Professional Doctorate in Couple Psychoanalytic Psychotherapy. She has a particular interest in the psychoanalytic theory and technique of working with couples, and has published a number of papers: for example, on the "projective gridlock" and the "creative couple" states of mind. She teaches widely in the UK and abroad, and has a private analytic practice in North London that includes couples.

Susie Orbach has worked with individuals and couples for over thirty years. During this time she has written widely both for the profession and the public, including *Fat is a Feminist Issue, Hunger Strike, What's Really Going on Here*, and *The Impossibility of Sex*. For many years she also wrote a regular column for *The Guardian* newspaper. She is Visiting Professor at the London School of Economics, a consultant to the Kings Fund and the National Health Service, and to various businesses. She co-founded The Women's Therapy Centre in New York and London. She is an associate member of the Society of Couple Psychoanalytic Psychotherapists and currently practises in London.

Sandy Rix worked originally as a social worker in a psychiatric hospital specializing in the therapeutic community, where she was a co-therapist in a married couples group. Later she trained in Relate as both a couple counsellor and a psychosexual therapist. She submitted a paper, "Inhibition of sexual desire and the menopause" for her Relate Diploma, which was later published. She completed her MA at the Tavistock Centre for Couple Relationships, in which her original research focused on the difficulties for therapists in working with loss of sexual desire in couples. She works in private practice as a couple and psychosexual therapist.

Joanna Rosenthall was a senior staff member for many years at the Tavistock Centre for Couple Relationships, where she ran the Clinical Training and Professional Doctorate programmes in couple psychoanalytic psychotherapy. She now runs the clinical service for couples in the Adult Department of the Tavistock & Portman NHS Trust, and is in private practice. She teaches and lectures both in Britain and abroad on the psychoanalytic theory and practice of working with couples. She has published a number of papers in this area. Recent papers have focused on couples who function as if they are fused, violent couples, and couples who hate each other. She is currently training at the British Association of Psychotherapy.

Jane Seymour trained at London Marriage Guidance as a psychodynamic couple counsellor and psychosexual therapist. She is an accredited member of the British Association for Sexual and Relationship Therapy and the British Association for Counselling and Psychotherapy. She is a staff member at the Tavistock Centre for

Couple Relationships where she supervises on, and is the Organizing Tutor for, the MSc in Psychosexual Therapy. She works in private practice and as a Relate licensed counsellor.

Avi Shmueli originally qualified as a clinical psychologist before training as a psychoanalytic couple psychotherapist and subsequently as a psychoanalyst with the British Psychoanalytical Society. He has always been interested in combining clinical work with research, and completed a PhD at University College London. After working for many years at the Tavistock Centre for Couple Relationships, he now works at the Anna Freud Centre and also has a private practice for individuals and couples.

FOREWORD

Peter Fonagy

Let us be frank. This book is a bit obvious. I mean, would the man in the street be surprised that problems in romantic relationships have a sexual dimension? Isn't attachment and sex what coupling is all about? And why shouldn't people talk about it when they go for therapy? After all, sex is one of the main reasons why we form relationships, and when it goes wrong we talk about it in the hope of sorting it out. Indeed, it would be quite surprising if the process of offering psychological help to couples in trouble did not involve addressing sexual difficulties as a major component of the therapeutic work. As Christopher Clulow aptly notes, "sex permeates every fibre of the dating couple". So why do we need this book? And why do we need it particularly from a psychoanalytic perspective?

The answer is simple. Because there are no other books like it!

Why is it that the profession that discovered that sex was a key organizer of psychological function has done so little focused work on this key facet of relational problems? Why is it that it is behaviourists, rather than psychoanalysts, who have tended in the past to provide key descriptions of the phenomenology of sexual relationships? As Clulow's magisterial introduction to the field reveals, sexuality has been little enough studied by psychoanalytic clinicians over recent decades, even in the context of individual psychotherapy. Freud's great discovery, that the study of the neuroses through treatment could teach us a great deal about normal functioning and normal development, certainly opened the door on a broader understanding of human sexuality. But that door appears to have been at least partially closed by various alternative concerns with aggression, the mother–infant relationship, and perhaps the prudishness of psychoanalytic clinicians.

One would have thought that psychoanalytic couple therapists have a unique opportunity for studying sexuality, particularly in relationships that are, at least in some respects, dysfunctional. We might hope that couples therapists would be able to construct a profound and subtle picture of both normal and abnormal patterns of sexual relationship. They could do so on the basis of the comprehensive accounts they elicit from the troubled relationships about which they sensitively gather detailed information in the course of their daily work. Yet, as this book testifies, very little has so far been written from a psychoanalytic perspective about the subject of sexual relationships from a couples' perspective. This is surprising, given that sexuality lies at the evolutionary heart of all romantic encounters.

In some way, it is tragic that this book is almost alone in taking as its focus the sexuality of the troubled couple in the context of psychoanalytic psychotherapy. Giving this observation a positive reframe, I believe the reader is very fortunate to be holding the most important psychoanalytic book on the sexuality of the troubled couple—ever. The essays in this volume take very different points of view, but are held together by a strong intellectual and emotional commitment to understanding sexuality in the context of couple relationships and psychotherapy. In the developmental psychopathology tradition, the book as a whole provides a fresh perspective on sexual behaviour, which may be seen in clearest relief through the struggles of the troubled couple who are sufficiently distressed to seek the help of a "third".

Achieving what psychoanalysts like Ron Britton (2004) or Tom Ogden (1994) refer to as the "third position" in relation to the couple requires something akin to what we all need to understand in relation to our unconscious awareness of our parents' intercourse. The "primal scene" (whether of our imagination or of our memory) is a necessarily immensely ambiguous chaotic mental experience. The therapist's task in considering the patients' sexual life is to mentalize, to fill with intentional states, their physical coupling. Being able simultaneously to give mental life to both the sentimental connection between a man and a woman and the drive-dominated selfish passion and often aggression-filled encounter is the challenging task that gradually emerges from the chapters.

Attachment and sexuality are linked by a paradox. Attachment may inherently preclude the experience of sexual excitement. Some, including Ruth Stein (1998), Georges Bataille (1957), Peter Fonagy (2008), and Mary Target (2007), have argued that sexual excitement necessarily entails obliterating the genuine mental image of the partner. By contrast, attachment pivots around coming to understand oneself through interaction with the other, learning about who one is from the reactions of a trusted informant, the figure of attachment and affection (Fonagy, Gergely, & Target, 2007). Attachment is constructed through contingent responding (mirroring). Sexuality is arguably the only aspect of the infant's emotional repertoire that reliably remains unmirrored by the caregiver (see Fonagy, 2008 for the mirroring deficit theory of sexual functioning). The relationship of the romantic couple is unique in creating a context for all of us where our sexual excitement can finally be adequately contingently responded to by the other. In this context we are not only allowed, but also called upon, to mirror the excitement of the other so that the other can find their alien subjective state finally within. This is not dissimilar to Susie Orbach's argument that careseeking and care-giving behaviours can adversely affect the sexual dimension of a couple's relationship. Some have argued from an evolutionary perspective that attachment relationships exist in part to enforce an incest taboo. It is certainly striking that children brought up together in the arbitrary families of the classical kibbutz show a strange reluctance to form sexual partnerships, despite the absence of legal or biological counterindication and the presence of ample opportunity (Erickson, 1993). Forming early attachments appears to preclude the possibility of a sexually infused romantic relationship. If couple relationships call on the same mechanism of interpersonal bonding as early attachments, and if the latter stand as behavioural markers of a biological risk of excessively constraining genetic variability, then it is hardly surprising that the sexual relationships in romantic partnerships are a fertile source of problems.

As Clulow notes, Bowlby was quick to recognise that sex and attachment had little to do with one another. The biology of sex and attachment, as well as their psychology, are incompatible. The best animal model for human couple relationships is found in meadow voles, who once they have identified a partner will huddle together selectively when threatened (Lim et al., 2004; Young, Lim, Gingrich, & Insel, 2001). However, studies of the DNA of their offspring have revealed that they are as promiscuous as the pine voles, who do not huddle selectively. Couple relationships, in the voles at least, turns out to have little to do with sexual fidelity. But, of course, the problems of the human couple cannot be reduced to that of a primate, let alone a rodent. Nor can they be reduced, as Brett Kahr points out, to the pseudo-objective facts and figures that surveys of sexual behaviour yield.

Human sexuality may be thought of as a phenomenological "zone of catastrophe". Our experience of ourselves is profoundly altered during sexual encounters. We are excited by seeing the excitement of our partner because our excitement becomes *real* when we perceive it, externalized, outside of ourselves. Bataille, Stein, Fonagy, and Target all describe how in sexual excitement the individual disappears, and reappears to himself as the other. He is simultaneously no longer responsible for, or even connected to, his actions, and momentarily in control of the least well-integrated and least contained aspects of his experience. So, sexuality crucially involves the fragmentation of the self. As Fairbairn taught us, the splitting of self can become the convenient host for neurotic conflict. This is why, in the course of the journey between self and other, sexuality attracts to itself as a magnet so much that we on other counts wish to disown. Clulow and Boerma also argue that sexual desire is inherently disorderly, because it invariably contains conflicts that lie at the core of our relational and psychological being. No wonder, then, that sexologists and psychoanalysts have been treated with suspicion by the rest of the scientific, and, broader still, the cultural, community. If the individual is primed to use their sexual experience as a vehicle for carrying repudiated aspects of the self such as aggression, envy, grandiosity, derogation, contempt, or plain selfishness, it is inevitable that sexual interpersonal relationships will eventually become a problem. It is also clear that within the disruption of a phenomenological sense of agentive selfhood created by sexual experience, a unique window is created by the therapist's countertransference on the couple's experience. This is why psychoanalytic therapy is so helpful in understanding the romantic couple in trouble. Colman's chapter argues strongly that the couples therapist needs to maintain evenly hovering attention if she or he is to understand the personal meanings contained within sexual fantasy. Abse provides a wonderful illustration of how tolerating not knowing what is going on in the therapeutic relationship facilitates an attitude of risking sexual curiosity and can transform the couple's sexual relationship.

From this perspective, the common experience of lost desire is a signal that the crisis of the phenomenological self brought about by sexual excitement has not been possible to integrate and the avoidance of excitement is the only solution. This is strongly implied in Rix and Shmueli's excellent chapter. The loss of desire can protect from a potential loss of selfhood in an encounter that would normally risk the disappearance of an agentive sense of self. The countertransference to this experience can be equally deadening for the therapist. This also hints at the unique connection between the destabilization of selfhood, emphasized by Clulow and Boerma, and the presence of sexual excitement in a relationship. We often wonder why the mere longevity of a relationship can serve to diminish sexual excitement. In so many other contexts, after all, we seek the familiar. However, if sexual excitement is rooted in the discovery of one's own excitement in the other, the gradual internalization of that particular form of seeing oneself in the mind of the other will inevitably lead to an integration of that alien experience into the self and thus, sadly, the loss of excitement. The clinical implication, of course, is that on most occasions this condition is untreatable, although by no means incompatible with a secure attachment bond if the motivation for the relationship is balanced in terms of these two drivers (sex and attachment), and if the rate of internalization is comparable in both partners. Balfour's chapter in this book beautifully describes how shared alterations of subjectivity can mimic loss of desire, with the declining sexual interest of mature years being driven as much by changes of intrapsychic constellations as shifts in hormonal status.

There is a clue here about why so-called perverse sexual desire persists longer than "normal" sexual desire. By its very nature, abnormal sexuality is less likely to be adequately mirrored, and the range of contexts in which it can be experienced in the other will be profoundly restricted and often far from genuine. Sadomasochistic relating is often accompanied by a perverse stability. Green and Seymour and Hewison, in their chapters, illustrate this wonderfully in the context of a fantasied bisexual relationship. "Perversion" retains its potency to excite because the attachment part of the couple's relationship does not create a genuine context for mirroring. Rosenthall's chapter warns us that perversion should be located in a technical context as a compulsive violation of personal boundaries and should preclude the colloquial association of censure.

There is much in this important book that will give the reader an enriching opportunity to reconsider their view of the developmental unfolding of sexuality through the lifespan and in the context of interpersonal relationships. As invariably and theoretically predictable in the case of sex, we try to find ourselves in the representations of sexuality in others. The scopophilic instinct is born of our universal incomprehension in the face of our subjective experience of our sexual feelings. This is why books on sex tend to sell. I truly hope that the present volume is no exception.

References

Bataille, G. (1957). *Erotism: Death and Sensuality*. San Francisco, CA: City Lights, 1986.

Britton, R. (2004). Subjectivity, objectivity, and triangular space. *Psychoanalytic Quarterly*, 73(1), 47–61.

Erickson, M. T. (1993). Rethinking Oedipus: an evolutionary perspective of incest avoidance. *American Journal of Psychiatry*, 150(3), 411–416.

Fonagy, P. (2008). A genuinely developmental theory of sexual enjoyment and its implications for psychoanalytic technique. *Journal of the American Psychoanalytic Association*, 56(1): 11–36.

Fonagy, P., Gergely, G., & Target, M. (2007). The parent–infant dyad and the construction of the subjective self. *Journal of Child Psychology and Psychiatry*, 48(3/4): 288–328.

Lim, M. M., Wang, Z., Olazabal, D. E., Ren, X., Terwilliger, E. F., & Young, L. J. (2004). Enhanced partner preference in a promiscuous species by manipulating the expression of a single gene. *Nature, 429*(6993): 754–757.

Ogden, T. H. (1994). *Subjects of Analysis*. Northvale, NJ: Jason Aronson.

Stein, R. (1998). The poignant, the excessive and the enigmatic in sexuality. *International Journal of Psychoanalysis, 79*: 253–268.

Target, M. (2007). Is our sexuality our own? A developmental model of sexuality based on early affect mirroring. *British Journal of Psychotherapy, 23*(4): 517–530.

Young, L. J., Lim, M. M., Gingrich, B., & Insel, T. R. (2001). Cellular mechanisms of social attachment. *Hormonal Behaviour, 40*(2): 133–138.

The facts of life: an introduction

Christopher Clulow

"They fuck you up, your mum and dad . . ."

(Philip Larkin, 1971)

What, from a psychoanalytic point of view, constitute the "facts of life"? What are the stories that our professional mentors tell us about the psychological equivalents of the "birds and the bees"? How useful are these stories, and in what ways do they help those of us who work with couples understand and change the sexual difficulties that they present us with? Do these stories, indeed, have anything to say about sex, or might they, like the inventions of embarrassed parents, deflect our attention away from what we really need to know in relating to the sexual lives of our patients?

In framing these questions, it is immediately apparent how metaphor and symbolism creep into communications about sexual behaviour. Like Larkin's jaundiced take on family life, the "facts" can be infused with ambiguity and meaning. So, when we talk about "fucking" from a psychoanalytic perspective, we are not simply talking about the interpenetration of bodies, but also the intermingling of minds and affective states. It can be hard to hold bodies, minds, and feelings together when considering sexual matters. Present a urologist with a man suffering from erectile problems and the relationship context within which these problems occur may not receive attention. Present a psychotherapist with a woman who has lost sexual desire and the biochemistry of her circumstances may go unconsidered. Connecting the dimensions of psyche and soma, male and female, individual and social, in order to form a holistic understanding of sexual experience is no easy task, involving, as it does, working with different but interconnected factors that combine to make up the whole. As with couples, so, too, with therapists: effective sex therapy requires therapists to engage with professional differences, not only between, but also within, disciplines.

Sex, for couple psychotherapists, is an unavoidable part of their psychotherapeutic brief. The defining feature of marriage and adult partnerships is sex, even when there is no sex. Sex permeates every fibre of the dating couple. It forms part of their identity as a couple, defining a boundary of exclusivity and constituting a powerful private and public symbol of intimacy between the partners. It is the precondition for creating a child together. Through sex, partners have opportunities to connect with each other and themselves, not just physically, but also emotionally, and from the deepest part of their being. Through sex, they can also disconnect from each other: witness the betrayal of intimacy when one partner has an affair, or when sex becomes depersonalized and insular. Whichever way it takes us, sex is a means of communication as well as a bodily encounter.

This book explores sexuality in the contexts of couple relationships and psychotherapy. It presents a range of psychoanalytic and psychodynamic perspectives from which problematic sexual behaviour—that is, sexual behaviour that has troubled couples sufficiently for them to seek outside help—might be understood. With very few exceptions, the focus of attention is on heterosexual couples, or, to be more precise, couples in which there is a male and female partner. An important limitation of the book is the absence of experience that draws on work with same sex couples, preventing the testing of an implicit assumption made by many of the contributors: that the dynamics of sexuality, from a psychoanalytic perspective, can translate directly from straight into lesbian, gay, and bi-sexual relationships.

The roots of sexuality have formed a tangled web that has embroiled psychoanalytic debate since Freud (1924d) famously declared that anatomy was destiny, that development was driven by the presence or absence of a penis, and that the basis of sexual pathology was to be found in attempts to block or divert the expression of libidinal drive through oral, anal, and, ultimately, genital pathways towards its object. Put simply, sexual desire was conceived by Freud as a pleasure-seeking instinctual energy—libido—that sought expression through a progression of bodily zones. The infant's primary instrument for gratification was the mouth, through which a physical link with mother was possible. Later, the development of anal and sphincter muscles afforded new delights of autonomy through control of bodily functions. Finally, libido was expressed through the genitals. For Freud, the pinnacle of infantile sexual development was reached between the years of three and five years with mastery of the Oedipus complex, the child relinquishing sexual longing for the parent of the opposite sex and identifying with the parent of the same sex (Freud, 1905d). These, from a Freudian perspective, were the key developmental "facts of life". Resolving the Oedipus complex was the key to achieving psychological maturity and laid the foundations for fulfilling sexual and emotional relationships in adult life.

There has been much critical comment about this phallocentric view of human sexuality, its emphasis on a linear developmental model of drive satisfaction and pleasure-seeking that is disconnected from relational origins (for example, ignoring the part parents actually play in encouraging or discouraging the sexuality of their children), and the assertion of a universal childhood complex from experience of clinical work with adults undertaken in an age and culture that has long since passed. Oedipus, it is argued, is only one of many metaphors and complexes, only one constellation of meaning, that can be brought to bear on our understanding of sexuality.

Those who have followed Freud have increasingly used the body as a metaphor for intrapsychic states and interpersonal ways of being with others. Erikson's (1950) substitution of modes of relating for erogenous body zones emphasized the psychosocial implications of Freud's theory. Orality, he argued, can express need or greed; it can also express the mutuality of the feeding relationship in which giving and taking find expression through mutual trust. Anality can symbolize the conflict between holding on and letting go in relationships, including sexual relationships. Genitality can symbolize the potential for intrusion and exclusion in patterns of relating. Representations of the insides of bodies—messy or sepulchral—communicate attitudes towards and feelings about sex. What Erikson emphasized was the capacity of the body to provide metaphors for psychological and relational conflicts in childhood that could be replayed in adult relationships.

Object relations theorists such as Fairbairn (1952) emphasized the influence on development of real relationships rather than instinctual drives. Where libido formed part of the language of this new emphasis, it tended to be de-eroticized. Crucially, attention was drawn to systems of social relating that can be split off from consciousness because of the overwhelming affect or trauma associated with them. Such repressed systems are held to be constantly seeking expression in relationships, especially those that most closely approximate the context within which the unconscious fantasies were originally generated. Fairbairn's work has had a significant influence on the development of object relations-based sex and couple therapy in this country and the USA (Dicks, 1967; Kaplan, 1979; Pincus, 1960; Scharff, 1982; Scharff & Savege Scharff, 1991).

The repressed system that has received most attention in relation to sexual problems is that relating to the anti-libidinal object, with hate being the affect that is suppressed. This focus has sometimes been in the context of defining and understanding what might constitute perverse sexuality. For example, Stoller (1979) proposed that in the absence of special physiological factors or direct bodily stimulation it is hostility that generates and enhances sexual excitement, without which there is only boredom. He suggested that sexual excitement was a relational dialectic involving hostility, fantasy, the partial dehumanization of the object, risk, illusion, secrecy, frustration, and the hope of ultimate triumph. His clinical project was attempting to differentiate between ordinary and perverse sexuality. Kernberg (1995) understood sexual excitement as aggression in the service of love, and its charge as emanating from emotional conflicts surrounding intimacy in childhood that carried over into adult sexual relationships.

Psychoanalytic theory since Freud's day has been affected by changes in time, place, and culture. Contributors to Harding's (2001) edited collection of papers on psychoanalytic perspectives of sexuality make this point very clearly. As non-medical, female analysts became a match for their medically trained male forbears, theories changed: the timing of the Oedipus complex moved from the early years to the early months of childhood, its site from the parental couple to the good and bad breast. This feminization of psychoanalysis by Klein (1945) and others sidelined the significance of fathers and placed the nursing couple of mother and baby at centre stage.

Post-Kleinians have retained the Oedipus complex as a central fact of psychological life, but the internal couple that they have focused on does not rely on there being an actual mother and father for a child to develop the observing and self-reflective capacities that make involvement with and exclusion from others tolerable (Steiner, 1989). Achieving a "third position" (Britton, 1998) in relation to the parental couple, one that allows feelings of love and hate to co-exist, has become synonymous with maturity, a state of mind that is constantly having to be fought for and regained as adults move between paranoid–schizoid and depressive positions in their mental functioning. These ideas have had a substantial influence on thinking about adult couple relationships at the Tavistock Centre for Couple Relationships (see, for example, Fisher, 1999; Grier, 2005; Ruszczynski, 1993; Ruszczynski & Fisher, 1995), and this will be evident in some of the chapters in this book. Nevertheless, the fear remains that, with the emphasis on mothers and infants, on the social rather than instinctual motivation to form and sustain relationships, on hate rather than desire, and on the capacity to think as the hallmark of maturity, the sex may have gone out of psychoanalysis.

Attachment theory and relational psychoanalysis has not, until very recently, done much to alleviate this concern. Bowlby (1969, 1973, 1980) focused his attention on the attachment of infants to their care-givers (principally their mothers), and to associated care-giving, exploratory, and affiliative systems of behaviour. While he recognized the likely effects of infant attachment on childhood and adult relationships, he paid scant attention to sexual activity other than to assert that it was motivated by a behavioural system quite separate from, although likely to be related to, that of attachment. The integration of sexuality into the attachment canon has only recently become of interest, and is currently at the stage of a work in progress (Diamond, Blatt, & Lichtenberg, 2007; Fonagy, 2008; Holmes, 2007; Mikulincer & Goodman, 2006; Target, 2007). Recent developments focus attention on the inherent tension between the separate motivational and behavioural systems driving sex and attachment. Sexual interest is heightened by novelty and unfamiliarity, whereas attachment thrives on the predictable and familiar. The sex drive hormones (androgen and oestrogen) agitate and energize, while the neuropeptides associated with attachment (oxytocin and vasopressin) foster feelings of calm and security (Ammaniti, Nicolais, & Speranza, 2007). Their presence and changing order of ascendancy over time is integral to the process of forging loving relationships from romantic liaisons, and biology once more provides a metaphor for states of mind and patterns of relating. The optimal solution to the problem of incompatibility between sexuality and attachment, it is argued, is to form partnerships on the basis of *optimal similarity*:

> choosing as a mate someone who is not too similar to family members deals with the incest taboo and permits sexual feelings; and choosing someone who is not too different generates feelings of comfort and safety and facilitates the formation of an attachment bond. [Eagle, 2007, p.45]

So, we have a psychoanalytic debate that has two poles. At one end is the strict Freudian perspective that explains sexual behaviour through instinctual drive. At the other is relational psychoanalysis, whose best known exponent, Stephen Mitchell (2002), subordinates the role of biology to that of interpersonal processes in generating and shaping the expression of sexual feeling. Relational narratives link biology and interpersonal processes in perpetual cycles of mutual influence. At its most minimal, sex in this context is a form of sociability, a medium of contact, a route to intimacy. Here, what might be attributed to body and instinct is understood as being shaped by social interactions. Both Freudian and Relational perspectives recognize the significance of biology and environment in shaping sexuality; their differences are more in terms of whether psychological meaning derives from preformed forces, or whether it is created and shaped through relationships.

Whichever perspective is preferred, we are still left with the uncomfortable feeling that psychoanalysis has gone off sex. Fonagy (2006) notes the diminished interest in sex in psychoanalytic publications over time, and offers some explanations: the problematic nature of drive theory that underpinned Freud's narrative and a difficulty reconciling it with the approaches of object relations theory and developmental psychology; unconscious resistance or prudishness among the psychoanalytic community (and maybe a scorning of a subject that nowadays receives much more of a public airing than ever it did in Freud's day); the influence of Klein in focusing theoretical interest on the mother–infant dyad; and the high level of borderline pathology presenting to psychoanalytic practitioners, where sexual interpretations may be unhelpful. He concludes that "... sex has left psychoanalysis because psychoanalysis has been unable to provide a strong, intellectually satisfying account of [normal psychosexual experience]" (p. 6).

This is something of a problem for psychoanalytic psychotherapists working with couples. Given that a defining feature of most intimate couple relationships is sexual activity, or, at least, concern about an absence of such activity, it is hard to conceive of a psychotherapy for couples that is not, at the very least, alive to the sexual component of the relationship. So, this book is timely. It comes at a point when the Tavistock Centre for Couple Relationships (TCCR), to which all the contributors are affiliated either directly or through its professional association the Society for Couple Psychoanalytic Psychotherapy (SCPP), celebrates its sixtieth anniversary. Coincidentally, it also comes in the year SCPP marks twenty years since its inception. It represents a kind of taking stock, a mapping of where couple psychoanalytic psychotherapy has reached in understanding and treating sexual problems, and some indications of where it might go.

The book opens with a challenging exploration of why couple psychoanalytic psychotherapists sometimes fail to enquire about the sexual lives of those who consult them. This apparent lack of curiosity might be thought by some to constitute a shocking, if not shameful, fact of professional life. Pursuing this phenomenon, Brett Kahr charts in fascinating detail the tumultuous response that greeted Freud and the early psychoanalysts when they addressed sexual behaviour and unconscious sexual fantasy (the distinction between the two being something that can continue to perplex and confuse us today as it did our psychoanalytic forbears). He argues that this history may have played a part in inhibiting sexual curiosity among some psychoanalytically trained psychotherapists working with couples.

Although not part of the ground he covers, it is interesting to note that the public outcry that greeted the "outing" of sexuality by Freud and his early colleagues similarly greeted the sexological research of Alfred Kinsey, whose ground-breaking study of male sexual behaviour (later to be followed by the study of female sexual behaviour) also celebrated its sixtieth birthday in 2008 (Kinsey, Pomeroy, & Martin, 1948). Kinsey, and the researchers that followed in his footsteps, provided us with apparently objective data about the "facts of life" through macroscopic questionnaires about, and observations of, what people actually did together in (and out of) bed. But what of the subjective, more idiosyncratic "facts of life" that find expression—or fail to do so—in the psychoanalytic encounter?

Kahr focuses on the potential for psychoanalytic interest to access the internal world of couples through their individual and shared sexual behaviour and fantasies. Data from these sources might be said to constitute the "facts of life" that we, as individuals, construct from our microcosmic interpretations of experience. As erotic daydreams, fantasies can provide an insight into the world of internal object relations, since patterns of attachment are a primary influence upon the configuration of sexual fantasy as well as behaviour. Examining sexuality can generate anxiety specifically because it touches on questions of attachment. In Kahr's chapter we are presented with evidence not only of the price psychoanalysts have paid in the past for daring to be curious about sex, but also, and most importantly, with the contemporary challenge that we, as psychotherapists, face when we are invited to engage with the sexual lives of the couples who consult us. Our avoidance, when we shy away, as he claims we so often do, might be linked with a sense of threat, perhaps born of an anxious curiosity about, and fear of peering into, the parental bedroom and the social retribution that we fear will follow from our professional parents (to draw on the Oedipal metaphor).

From a psychoanalytic perspective, the level of felt threat we experience as psychotherapists can never be divorced from the subjective field in which we practise. If partners are anxious about their sexual relationship, their therapist will pick this up at some level. Perhaps it is for this reason that so many of the chapters in this book focus on the significance of the therapist's countertransference for accessing the unconscious state of mind of the patient, whether the patient is an individual or a couple. This assumption provides a unifying perspective within the psychoanalytic community, which can sometimes feel that it is torn between reconciling or rejecting different conceptual narratives of sexuality.

Warren Colman takes us straight into the tensions between different psychoanalytic narratives by asking what we mean by "sex". He considers the enormous leap forward that Freud took when he interpreted the stories of sexual seduction told by his patients not as historical facts, but as statements of psychic reality. The stage was then set for unconscious wishes to become the cornerstone of Freud's theory of sexuality. While some have said that he turned away from what might have been an uncomfortable historical reality, in much the same way that questions of child and adult sexual abuse continue today to be debated in terms of establishing fact or fantasy, Colman argues that the path was then prepared for sexuality to be considered as metaphor and symbol. From his perspective as a Jungian analyst, he offers critical assessments of the limitations of Freudian biology, Kleinian unconscious phantasy and Fairbairnian object relations theory in capturing the nature of sexuality. He resists the notion that there are "givens" in the sexual equation, on the basis that they take us away from the individual meanings that sexual fantasy and sexual behaviour contain for our patients and tempt us to assess them against templates of "reality" that we might then use to mark progress or development. Instead, he argues for a hovering of attention across the different potential domains with which sexuality might correspond, and for a technical approach that sometimes "interprets towards", and sometimes "interprets away from", sex in the endeavour to promote the integration of sexuality with other domains of life.

Francis Grier follows the expansive sweep of Colman's chapter with an exploration of the interpersonal dynamics of the consulting room. Drawing on the work of Bion and Glasser, he roots sexual experience firmly within the domain of the intersubjective, demonstrating, through rich clinical illustrations, how sexual behaviour can be related to both positive (developmental) and negative (defensive) aspects of affective experience. He examines how the changing nature of the emotional experience can link, and fail to link, the couple and their therapist during the therapeutic process, and offers examples of how the fluidity of this experience can be affected by the therapist. From his perspective, what is problematic in sexual behaviour is not whether or how couples have sex, but when sexuality is used defensively and damages the capacity of partners to be openly enquiring about the real nature of their experience together, as individuals and as a couple.

Susie Orbach adopts a different conceptual narrative in considering sexual behaviour as a product of attachment security, focusing not only on the security of the partners as individuals, but also on the relationship that they have constructed together as a couple. Using the poles of "merged" and "separated" attachment (that correspond with "insecure" and "secure" attachment in terms of attachment classifications) she examines in detail the case of a couple in which ambivalent care-seeking and care-giving behaviour adversely affected the sexual dimension of their relationship. The question of who takes the sexual initiative in relationships is explored in this context. While she alludes to some broader implications—for example, the discovery of sexual desire through being desired by one's partner supporting the mirroring deficit theory of sexual functioning, and the feminist critique of patriarchal sexuality with its "men on top"/heterosexual insistence (see, for example, Orbach, 1999)—she stays with the unique and particular in exploring connections between attachment and sexuality.

Maureen Boerma and I also draw on attachment narratives in exploring what drives sexual behaviour, and link these with object relations perspectives on the affects surrounding such intimate bodily encounters. Our focus is on the dynamics and disorders of desire, and we argue that desire is inherently disorderly because it engenders inescapable conflicts that lie at the core of our psychological and relational being. We see sexual desire as the affect that both triggers sexual behaviour and is sated through it, and as an emotional state that itself is driven by love and hate. Clinical vignettes illustrate our thesis, and draw attention to the potential of the therapist's countertransference in accessing and working with unprocessed emotional states. We contend that the dynamics of desire form an appropriate focus for psychoanalytic psychotherapy with couples, and distinguish this focus from that of other approaches concerned with changing the behaviour itself.

Susanna Abse picks up this clinical challenge with a moving and deftly observed account of therapy with a couple. Her starting point is the conundrum of why some couples report a positive change in their relationship at the conclusion of therapy while continuing to experience the same level of sexual difficulties that may have brought them into therapy in the first place. She follows the proposition that embodied symptoms may not be immediately amenable to the "talking cure" if it relates simply to what can be put into words. It is through acting out, and through the countertransference of the therapist, that access may be provided to what cannot be thought and known about. Her approach resonates strongly with the developmental view that understands the problem of integrating sexual feelings in adulthood to be linked with deficits in the maternal mirroring of infantile sexuality (Fonagy, 2008; Target, 2007). The clinical example she provides supplies good evidence for how the transformation of dread into desire in the countertransference, through tolerating not knowing what is going on and risking sexual curiosity, can pave the way for a similar transformation in the couple's sexual relationship.

The phenomenon of loss of desire is approached from a research perspective by Sandy Rix and Avi Shmueli in a unique study of the countertransference experiences of psycho-sexual therapists working with this condition. Their examination of available research reveals the ambiguity about whether loss of desire is a physiological condition that can be categorized within individuals, or an affective state that needs to be understood within a relationship context. On the one side are studies that classify loss of desire as a purely female psycho-medical disorder, on the other are the experiences of patients. How is this dissonance to be understood? The authors describe their attempt to explore the intersubjective, relational aspects of loss of desire through a small-scale research study undertaken at the Tavistock Centre for Couple Relationships as part of a Masters degree course. The study focused on the affective responses of experienced psycho-sexual therapists working with

patients seeking help for loss of sexual desire. Taking countertransference experiences as their primary data, they suggest that disorders of desire may reflect an impenetrable defence operating within
the couple relationship to protect the partners from perceived
threats to their identity. They speculate that the medicalization of
loss of sexual desire might itself be a defence against perceived
threats to potency and identity, a defence that couples and therapists might unconsciously collude in maintaining.

Countering this argument, Laura Green and Jane Seymour illustrate through a detailed case example how using the countertransference experience in psycho-sexual therapy can be harnessed
alongside behavioural techniques to overcome the problem of
hypoactive sexual desire. As the therapy unfolded in the case described, it became clear that abusive dynamics operating in each of
the partner's family of origin had left a residue of potential for
sado-masochistic relating between them as a couple. The authors
demonstrate clearly the anxiety of the couple in bringing together,
in their relationship and within themselves, the sexual identities
contained in their representations of each of their parents, and the
ways projective identification had been used defensively to protect
them against these anxieties. While this couple are a graphic example of Freud's observation that every sexual act can be regarded as
an event between four individuals (each partner bringing into the
conjugal bedroom an element of bisexuality arising from their identification with each of their parents), Green and Seymour show that
working at this level of interpretation can be assisted by behavioural programmes that reduce anxiety about sexual performance,
and that these programmes can also facilitate exploration of other
anxieties associated with intimacy in the couple.

All the contributors to the book subscribe to the view that sexuality can be used to meet different ends: psychic survival, a substitute for intimacy, a mask concealing hatred and hostility. David
Hewison develops these themes by exploring the nature of sado-
masochistic relationships, taking his cue from Jung's "fact of life"
that the opposite to love is not hate or indifference, but power.
Defining his terms, he argues that both sadism and masochism
involve sexuality, and he is critical of the de-sexualizing of sadomasochism in the Kleinian lexicon, where the term is applied more
generally to unconscious fantasies and behaviour driven by hate

and envy. The corrupting effects upon individuals caught up in an eroticized contract between power and subjugation are vividly illustrated by extracts from Sacher-Masoch's novel, *Venus in Furs*. In contrast, the relationship between Beth and Jan in Lars von Triers film, *Breaking the Waves*, is presented as a love story, despite the degradation and ultimate destruction that follows from the care and concern that the partners have for each other.

In similar vein, Mary Morgan and Judith Freeman illustrate the potential for confusing intimacy—including sexual intimacy—with intrusive projective identification in their fascinating analysis of the film *Sex, Lies and Videotape*. Exploring the sexual configurations between the four players in what, essentially, is an Oedipal story, they consider the scope for enacting internal dramas in the world of external relationships. Their position is that real intimacy is reliant upon partners having attained security as separate individuals, containing within themselves an internalized couple relationship that has creative associations. While the fear of intimacy may drive the psychological processes of splitting and projective identification that can result in intrusions upon others, they suggest that when that fear converts to feelings of hatred, anxious sexuality converts into perverse sexuality. Sameness and difference are then demarcated in defensively rigid ways that pointedly turn away from "truth" and "reality", with fantasy being substituted in their place. Morgan and Freedman's chapter raises interesting questions about the point at which projective processes, and the behaviour stemming from them, move the motivation for different kinds of sexual behaviour from fearfulness to perversity, and what the defining influences might be in marking that tipping point. Their chapter concludes with a consideration of what marks psychotherapy out from voyeurism, given that psychotherapy involves asking about and listening to stories about the sexual lives of others.

Joanna Rosenthall continues the exploration of what constitutes perverse forms of sexuality and relating through a detailed clinical example to illustrate its nature and psychogenesis. She notes that the psychoanalytic arena has been caught in the crossfire between social change, political debate and its own orthodoxy, some of which has been controversial because it has been seen as pathologizing sexual relationships between gay, lesbian, and bi-sexual partners. "Perversion" is a word that carries a general association of censure, and she is careful to locate her use of the term in a technical context, and to associate it with compulsive violations of personal boundaries that are often associated with the denial of sexual and generational differences in families. The consequent distortions of "truth" and "reality" can undermine individual integrity and threaten the survival of the self at a fundamental level. As in Morgan and Freedman's chapter, these realities echo the "facts of life" proposed by Money-Kyrle (1971), in which innate knowledge of the breast as a good object, and parental intercourse as creative, provide the foundations for healthy psychological development. The negation of the infant's experience at the breast, and the unpicking or reversal of generational differences within families, threaten the "truth", "reality", and authenticity of the child's experience. Her illustration supports the view of others who contend that "relational perversion" (Lieberman, St John, & Silverman, 2007) results from the interaction of two factors: exploitative parents and vulnerable children (vulnerable because of their affective dependence on the parents for security). In this context, she argues, perverse forms of relating can be understood as mechanisms for protecting against intense and fundamental existential anxieties raised by the prospect of intimacy.

In the last chapter of the book, Andrew Balfour considers the impact of ageing on sexuality, including the ultimate existential threat of death itself. The reality of time passing constituted a third "fact of life" for Money-Kyrle (1971), and the waning of sexual powers can be an uncomfortable reminder of mortality for men and women. Coming to terms with the loss of the vigorous sexuality of youth can be hard, and is something that is affected by the meaning of that loss for the partners in a relationship as well as by how previous losses have impacted on and been managed by them. Interweaving poetry and theatre with vivid clinical illustrations and theory Balfour considers the implications for a couple's shared defensive system of the changes made inevitable by ageing. He considers how Oedipal anxieties can resurface late in life, with a reconfigured dynamic such that now it is not the parental couple that is envied, but the pairings of the young. From a psychoanalytic perspective, problems do not, as he says, "grow old and wither", but can reappear in accentuated form as dependence on others increases and physical powers diminish. While this can result in a sense of oppression and despair, it also offers new opportunities for reworking and repair.

Threading through the chapters of this book is a strong sense of the interconnection between sexual behaviour and patterns of attachment in couple relationships. Each provides a window on the other, and, like a double helix, they snake an intertwined pathway together over the life course. Different psychoanalytic conceptual narratives might give one spiral prominence over the other, and they might differ in the images they use in telling this central story of life, but there is an emerging relatedness and coherence between the perspectives that they offer. This goes, too, for the contributors to this book. They have drawn on different mentors to provide a framework for understanding the sexual problems of the couples they see, and to inform the work they do. But whether Freud, Jung, Klein, or Bowlby has been the progenitor of their own particular therapeutic narrative, the spirit of enquiry and curiosity is evident in their approach. This has created space to explore the dimensions of sex, love, hate, and power in ways that allow the facts of life to emerge and be discovered as something unique and authentic to each couple. It has also created a platform from which new understandings may emerge to inform practice in the future.

References

Ammaniti, M., Nicolais, G., & Speranza, A. (2007). Attachment and sexuality during adolescence: interaction, integration or interference. In: D. Diamond, S. Blatt, & J. Lichtenberg (Eds.), *Attachment and Sexuality* (pp. 79–105). New York: Analytic Press.

Bowlby, J. (1969). *Attachment and Loss: Attachment*. London: Hogarth.

Bowlby, J. (1973). *Attachment and Loss: Separation*. London: Hogarth.

Bowlby, J. (1980). *Attachment and Loss: Loss, Sadness and Depression*. London: Hogarth.

Britton, R. (1998). Subjectivity, objectivity and triangular space. In: *Belief and Imagination: Explorations in Psychoanalysis* (pp. 41–58). London: Routledge,

Diamond, D., Blatt, S., & Lichtenberg, J. (Eds.) (2007). *Attachment and Sexuality*. New York: Analytic Press

Dicks, H. V. (1967). *Marital Tensions*. London: Routledge.

Eagle, M. (2007). Attachment and sexuality. In: D. Diamond, S. Blatt, & J. Lichtenberg (Eds.), *Attachment and Sexuality* (pp. 27–50). New York: Analytic Press.

Erikson, E. (1950). *Childhood and Society*. New York: Norton.

Fairbairn, W. (1952). *Psychoanalytic Studies of the Personality*. London: Tavistock.

Fisher, J. (1999). *The Uninvited Guest. Emerging from Narcissism towards Marriage*. London: Karnac.

Fonagy, P. (2006). Psychosexuality and psychoanalysis: an overview. In: P. Fonagy, R. Krause, & M. Leuzinger-Bohleber (Eds.), *Identity, Gender and Sexuality 150 Years after Freud*. Controversies in Psychoanalysis: 1. London: International Psychoanalytical Association.

Fonagy, P. (2008). A genuinely developmental theory of sexual enjoyment and its implications for psychoanalytic technique. *Journal of the American Psychoanalytic Association*, 56: 11–36.

Freud, S. (1905d). *Three Essays on the Theory of Sexuality. S.E.*, 7: 125–245. London: Hogarth.

Freud, S. (1924d). The dissolution of the Oedipus complex. *S.E.*, 19: 173–182. London: Hogarth.

Grier, F. (Ed.) (2005). *Oedipus and the Couple*. London: Karnac.

Harding, C. (Ed.) (2001). *Sexuality: Psychoanalytic Perspectives*. London: Routledge.

Holmes, J. (2007). Sex, couples and attachment: the role of hedonic intersubjectivity. *Attachment. New Directions in Psychotherapy and Relational Psychoanalysis*, 1(1): 18–29.

Kaplan, H. (1979). *Disorders of Sexual Desire and Other New Concepts and Techniques in Sex Therapy*. New York: Brunner-Mazel.

Kernberg, O. (1995). *Love Relations. Normality and Pathology*. New Haven, CT: Yale University Press.

Kinsey, A., Pomeroy, W., & Martin, C. (1948). *Sexual Behaviour in the Human Male*. Philadelphia, PA: Saunders.

Klein, M. (1945). The oedipus complex in the light of early anxieties. *International Journal of Psychoanalysis*, 26: 11–33.

Larkin, P. (1971). This Be the Verse. In: A. Thwaite (Ed.) *Philip Larkin. Collected Poems* (p. 180). London: Faber & Faber, 1988.

Lieberman, A., St John, M., & Silverman, R. (2007). "Passionate attachments" and parental exploitations of dependency in infancy and early childhood. In: D. Diamond, S. Blatt, & J. Lichtenberg (Eds.), *Attachment and Sexuality* (pp. 179–200). New York: Analytic Press.

Mikulincer, M., & Goodman, G. (Eds.) (2006). *The Dynamics of Romantic Love. Attachment, Caregiving, Sex*. New York: Guilford.

Mitchell, S. (2002). *Can Love Last? The Fate of Romance Over Time*. New York: Norton.

Money-Kyrle, R. (1971). The aims of psychoanalysis. *International Journal of Psychoanalysis, 52*: 103–106.

Orbach, S. (1999). *The Impossibility of Sex*. London: Penguin.

Pincus, L. (Ed.) (1960). *Marriage: Studies in Emotional Conflict and Growth*. London: Methuen.

Ruszczynski, S. (Ed.) (1993). *Psychotherapy with Couples: Theory and Practice at the Tavistock Institute of Marital Studies*. London: Karnac.

Ruszczynski, S., & Fisher, J. (Eds.) (1995). *Intrusiveness and Intimacy in the Couple*. London: Karnac.

Scharff, D. (1982). *The Sexual Relationship. An Object Relations View of Sex and the Family*. London: Routledge and Kegan Paul.

Scharff, D., & Savege Scharff, J. (1991). *Object Relations Couple Therapy*. Northvale, NJ: Jason Aronson.

Steiner, J. (Ed.) (1989). *The Oedipus Complex Today: Clinical Implications*. London: Karnac.

Stoller, R. (1979). *Sexual Excitement: Dynamics of Erotic Life*. New York: Pantheon.

Target, M. (2007). Is our sexuality our own? A developmental model of sexuality based on early affect mirroring. *British Journal of Psychotherapy, 23*(4): 517–530.

CHAPTER ONE

Psychoanalysis and sexpertise

Brett Kahr

PORTIA: Within the bond of marriage, tell me, Brutus,
Is it excepted I should know no secrets
That appertain to you? Am I your self
But as it were in sort or limitation?
To keep with you at meals, comfort your bed,
And talk to you sometimes? Dwell I but in the suburbs
Of your good pleasure? If it be no more,
Portia is Brutus' harlot, not his wife.

BRUTUS: You are my true and honourable wife,
As dear to me as are the ruddy drops
That visit my sad heart.

PORTIA: If this were true, then should I know this secret.
I grant I am a woman, but withal
A woman that Lord Brutus took to wife.
I grant I am a woman, but withal
A woman well reputed, Cato's daughter.
Think you I am no stronger than my sex,
Being so fathered and so husbanded?
Tell me your counsels; I will not disclose 'em.
I have made strong proof of my constancy,

Giving myself a voluntary wound
Here in the thigh. Can I bear that with patience,
And not my husband's secrets?

[Shakespeare, 1599. *The Tragedy of Julius Caesar*, 2, 1: 279–301]

R ather like the Freudian dream, the sexual life of the couple contains both manifest and latent ingredients. The manifest content of a couple's sexual life might include all those behaviours, activities, and conversations that the members of the pair share with one another. By contrast, the latent components of the couple's sexual life might include all those elements that remain either unspoken, such as extramarital affairs, masturbatory sexual fantasies, and coital sexual fantasies, or completely unconscious, such as the subterranean phantasy structures that propel partners towards tenderness, masochism, sadism, or some combination thereof. As Brutus's wife, Portia knew only too well that the temptation for a husband to hide aspects of his life from his wife (or vice versa) may be very great indeed. Indeed, Portia urges her husband to tell her his "counsels" and promises to bear the revelations of his secrets with patience, much as a good psychotherapist would.

This fragment of dialogue between Brutus and Portia reminds us not only of the delicate struggle that marital partners might experience when speaking with one another about their private life, but it may also resonate with the work of the couple psychoanalytic psychotherapist, who must proceed with tact and diplomacy in talking with troubled partners about their sexual histories. In my experience, some of our colleagues work very effectively with the sexual lives of couples, demonstrating a marked capacity for what we might call *sexpertise*, while others, by contrast, remain sheepish and far too timid in their ability to explore the erotics of couple life. Many of these individual differences among couple psychoanalytic psychotherapists may be explained as a function of our own sexual education, whether liberal or conservative, as well as our own experience of being psychoanalysed. Some of us will have had personal analyses that privileged the discussion of sexual biography, and even sought full details of it, whereas others will have had more delicate personal analyses that analysed sexuality only if they chose to introduce the subject in a direct fashion.

Our struggle between a posture of sexual frankness and one of sexual reticence can also be explained as a function of our complicated professional ancestral relationship to sexuality. I propose that only by exploring certain aspects of the history of psychoanalysis and its relationship to sexology might we begin to acquire a greater sense of the complicated legacy that we as contemporary practitioners have inherited.

A sexless night at the clinic

Some time ago, I attended a clinical case discussion, one evening, at a psychoanalytically orientated mental health clinic. Each of the fifteen or so psychotherapists in attendance had graduated from an intensive full-training programme in psychoanalytic marital psychotherapy or couple psychoanalytic psychotherapy. A small handful of trainee couple psychotherapists also participated in the seminar. Each member of the audience had extensive clinical experience of working psychoanalytically with couples in distress, and quite a few had practised as marital/couple psychotherapists for many decades.

Dr U, the colleague who presented the paper, spoke with intelligence and compassion, describing his struggles and achievements in his ongoing marital psychotherapeutic work with Mr and Mrs A. He provided us with extensive details of the presenting problem—a shared couple depression—as well as copious background information about the infancy and childhood of each member of the marital pair. He also offered us a good survey of the couple's present life, including their working capacities, their creative blocks and inhibitions, their skills as parents, and much more besides. In fact, our colleague Dr U generously shared so much data about Mr and Mrs A that he succeeded in conjuring a very lively image of the couple, bringing them greatly to life in a very vivid fashion.

Towards the end of the seminar, I realized that although we had examined virtually every aspect of this couple's private life in microscopic detail, no one had mentioned the word "sex" at all. In fact, although we had learned an infinite amount of data about their unconscious fantasies of rescuing and of being rescued, of their suicidal tendencies, and of their hostile feelings towards one another, we did not even know whether they had an active sex life, or, indeed, whether they slept in the same bedroom.

With great honesty, Dr U admitted quite openly that he did not know anything about the sexual life of Mr and Mrs A even though he had worked with them in weekly couple psychotherapy sessions for more than three years. This revelation caused a flurry of giggles among the members of the audience. I then asked my colleague—a man whom I like and respect greatly—why he had never asked the couple about either their sexual history or their current sexual practices. Dr U retorted, quite simply, "Well, it never came up in the material, and I don't like to ask about topics that the couple haven't brought up themselves."

Dr U's confession received a great deal of support from the other members of the seminar. Mrs V, a longstanding couple psychoanalytic psychotherapist, revealed, "I would agree with Dr U. I never ask sexual questions because it would feel too intrusive and too voyeuristic." And Dr W, another highly accomplished couple psychotherapist, confessed, "Well, maybe I have an inhibition about sex, but I never ask about it with couples. I just keep forgetting. Sometimes my supervisor has to remind me to talk about sex with couples." Dr W's revelation produced even more titters, laced with anxiety, as though all of these insightful, compassionate, and gifted couple psychotherapists had just discovered their Achilles' heels.

I intervened once again, explaining to my colleagues that I always ask about the sexual life in every single preliminary consultation with a couple. Of course, I will wait to see whether the couple introduces the subject at their own behest. If not, I will search for a pause in the narrative and ask, "I notice that neither of you has made any mention of your physical relationship." Over the years, I have found that this particular phrasing both authorizes the couple to begin to talk about sexuality, and also allows them to skirt around the issues if they should so choose. In my experience, I have found that couples seem deeply relieved that someone has expressed a professional interest in this aspect of their lives, and, furthermore, that the psychotherapist has the capacity to hear about this still often unmentionable aspect of human behaviour.

To my great relief, rather than raising eyebrows, my comment stimulated Dr X, a very senior, septuagenarian female colleague, to interject, "I agree with Brett. I always ask about the sexual life. With every couple." Dr X's intervention seemed to facilitate an air of great relief among colleagues in the seminar, as though everyone had begun to think, "Ah, well, if this respectable, elderly lady can talk about sex with such frankness, then it must be all right."

In the interests of promoting some technical discussion about how one speaks about sexuality in couple psychotherapy, I then suggested to Mrs Y, the Chairperson of the evening's seminar, that we ought to devote some forthcoming conferences to a more detailed examination of the role of sexuality in couple psychotherapy, a suggestion to which Mrs Y responded with alacrity.

At the end of the seminar, as we began to collect our coats and briefcases, preparing to depart the clinic, another colleague approached me. Dr Z, a much-admired, middle-aged woman, had just read my newly published book *Sex and the Psyche*, a study of the psychodynamics and traumatic origins of sexual fantasy, based on a five-year qualitative and quantitative research project (Kahr, 2007). The book contained not only a detailed report of the primary research findings, as well as several hundred pages of psychoanalytical theorizing and observations about the origins and functions of sexual fantasies, but also the complete, unexpurgated texts of more than 1,100 British adult sexual fantasies themselves. Dr Z congratulated me warmly on the completion of this large-scale research publication, and she praised some of the ideas contained therein. She did, however, take the trouble to tell me that although she had read the theory section in great detail, she insisted on saying that she had completely skipped over the actual fantasies themselves, explaining, "I'm too old and too married to spend time reading them," laughing as she uttered her disclaimer.

Dr Z could not have known that, since the appearance of *Sex and the Psyche*, numerous other colleagues (all older females, in fact) have pointedly informed me that they had read my book, but that they had omitted to read the fantasies. Perhaps these psychotherapeutic colleagues feared that if they had confessed to reading the fantasies I might have regarded them as sexually voyeuristic. Perhaps they regarded me as sexually voyeuristic for having undertaken the research in the first place. By contrast, ordinary members of the general public (whether doctors, lawyers, accountants, actors, or lorry drivers) have either written to me, or telephoned me, or approached me at conferences to tell me how much they had enjoyed reading the fantasies, and that they have found the frank publication of the many sexual fantasies contained in the book to be a great relief in helping them to understand their own sexual fantasies.

Although my account of an evening at this particular mental health clinic may seem little more than an anecdote, I have found myself wondering about the role of sexuality in the working life of the contemporary psychoanalytically orientated couple psychotherapist, and I regard my description of the sexual anxiety at this seminar as by no means unusual. I must confess that I felt somewhat shocked and disappointed that so many of my deeply cherished colleagues had admitted, almost proudly, that they would not discuss sexuality with a couple unless the couple had begun to talk about it first. During my own training, more than one of my teachers had counselled us against introducing the subject of sexuality as part of the clinical interview. And yet, all of my clinical experience with couples has revealed how many difficulties they have in speaking about sex with one another, let alone with the psychotherapist, leading me to believe that it would be unkind not to offer a gentle enquiry in order to facilitate verbalization.

I began to wonder not only why my colleagues refrained from engaging with sexual matters more directly, but also why the subject seemed to raise so many stifled chortles and chuckles throughout the evening. Furthermore, I also pondered why Dr Z had the need to tell me that she had elected not to read the sexual fantasies published in my book—a unique archive of primary data from the human sexual unconscious mind that might prove very instructive to workers in the psychological and sexological arena. I could not help but ask myself whether I had happened to stumble upon an unusually sexually naïve, unsophisticated, and stereotypically "British" group of colleagues, or whether, perhaps, I had too *much* of an interest in the sexual lives of other people. Of course, one might argue that the reluctance of the psychotherapist to address sexual matters with a couple might well be understood as a countertransferential reaction to the couple's own reluctance to talk about sexuality, and no doubt this occurs in various treatment situations; however, I suspect that not all inhibitions of useful and sensitive sexual communication in psychotherapy stem from the countertransference alone.

Having taught psychology and behavioural sciences to young medical students at a medical school in London for nine years, I have had many opportunities to observe the difficulties of the trainee physicians in developing a "sexual interviewing skin" that would allow them to talk to patients about sexual matters in a frank and non-sensationalist manner. The young twenty-year-old students struggled mightily in our yearly module on "Taking a Sexual History". At first, they sniggered whenever a male student had to present the case of a female whose breasts needed examining, or whose heart required auscultation. Then they smirked salaciously whenever someone had to discuss a genito-urinary case, which involved the examination of a penis. Fortunately, as the training unfolded, these students developed greater ease in coping with interviewing patients about ordinary bodily and sexual matters. Indeed, upon reflection, I have found my twenty-something medical students much more adept at discussing sexuality than many of my fifty-something and sixty-something colleagues in the psychotherapeutic profession. This difference may be understood quite simply as a generational phenomenon, wherein those students born post Beatles and post birth control enjoy a greater sexual comfort, but the differences between the medics and psychoanalytical practitioners may also reveal something about an historical inhibition in the psychoanalytical community more generally.

How much sex can a psychoanalyst tolerate?

The ostensible sexual discomfort of some of my colleagues from the field of couple psychoanalytic psychotherapy left me extremely perplexed. After all, those of us who work in the psychoanalytical profession will all have had many years of formal analysis, on the couch, at a frequency of four or five times weekly in most instances, and, unlike the patients who attend for once-weekly, short-term work, those of us who have graduated from ongoing, often "interminable" analyses will have had ample opportunities to explore our own sexual histories in considerable detail. Surely, this training "on the couch" ought to have helped each of us to acquire a "sexual interviewing skin" that would permit us to discuss delicate sexual matters with our clients or patients without any sense of titillation or invasiveness. And yet, in my experience, many well-trained psychoanalytical clinicians—whether psychoanalysts or psychoan-alytical psychotherapists—continue to shy away from the exploration of sexuality in a straightforward manner.

I have vivid memories of Professor Robert Stoller's Edward Glover Memorial Lecture, sponsored by the Portman Clinic, delivered at the Royal Free Hospital in London in 1983. As I described in *Sex and the Psyche*, Stoller showed the audience a drawing from a pornographic magazine used by heterosexual men who became aroused by sexual stories of being forced to wear women's clothing. As Stoller discussed the unconscious origins of the wish to be thus humiliated, the audience of predominantly senior clinicians from different mental health disciplines erupted in gales of laughter. Stoller had obviously encountered this reaction before, and in a compassionate way he stared us down and admonished us gently: "Perversion is always funny . . . as long as it's not yours."

Some years later, I attended a seminar on sexual perversions facilitated by a very distinguished psychoanalytical psychiatrist. The teacher presented a case of a sexually compulsive man who used to talk about his conquests in great detail. The psychiatrist told the seminar, "His account of his sex life used to make me sick. I had to fight back the nausea in the session." Now, it might be that the patient had attempted to project something unbearable into the therapist, or make the clinician experience some of the split-off disgust that the patient could not tolerate himself. But, in fact, this particular clinician seemed to feel revolted after so many of his interviews with a variety of sexually perverse patients that it prompted one of my colleagues to quip, "Perhaps Dr A ought to have a shower installed in his consulting room. One feels that he always wants to shower after having seen each of his patients . . . to wipe away the dirt."

My observations about the priggishness of some psychoanalytical workers may be surprising to those who believe that, of all mental health professionals, the *psychoanalytically* orientated have the greatest interest in sexuality. After all, according to popular conception, Sigmund Freud and his followers wrote about little else besides sexuality. To quote but one example of the popular idea that

Freud and the Freudians have suffered from an obsession with sex, consider the statement by Edward Dolnick (1998), an American science reporter, who observed that, "almost compulsively, Freud reduced the spectrum of possible human motivations to a single vivid hue, sex" (p. 34).

True, Freud did expound about sexuality at great length. In 1905, the founder of psychoanalysis published a small monograph entitled *Drei Abhandlung zur Sexualtheorie*, now better known in English as the famous *Three Essays*, which constituted one of the very first publications to discuss human sexuality in such a frank and forthright manner (Freud, 1905a). Furthermore, Freud wrote his book entirely in vernacular German, whereas, by contrast, many of his medical forebears would have rendered all of the sexual references in Latin, a ploy used notably by Professor Richard von Krafft-Ebing, author of the infinitely more graphic textbook of 1886, *Psychopathia Sexualis: Eine klinisch-forensische Studie*. Although Freud's straightforward, undisguised writing style endeared him to successive generations of psychoanalytical practitioners, it undoubtedly exposed him to tremendous suspicion and vitriol as well.

In November and December of that same year, Freud (1905b) published his two-part case study of a young hysterical patient, Fräulein Ida Bauer, disguised by the name of "Dora", in the *Monatsschrift für Psychiatrie und Neurologie*, under the title "Bruchstück einer Hysterie-Analyse" ["Fragment of an analysis of a case of hysteria"]. The "Dora" case may well constitute Freud's most sexually explicit clinical analysis, containing references, *inter alia*, to a plethora of sexually orientated topics, ranging from the erotogenic zones, homosexual love among women, masturbation, the female genitalia, pubic hair, copulation, and phantasies of defloration, to the satisfaction of sadistic tendencies, bed-wetting, sexual orgasm, and to what Freud (*ibid.*) referred to as the "infantile germs of perversion" (p. 113).

Unsurprisingly, Freud's explicitly sexual vocabulary caused tidal waves of controversy throughout the German-speaking community of clinical psychopathologists and beyond. Indeed, on 27 May, 1906, Professor Gustav Aschaffenburg, the distinguished German psychiatrist from Heidelberg, lambasted Freud at the Congress of South-West German Neurologists and Psychiatrists in

Baden-Baden, dismissing psychoanalytical work as objectionable and immoral. Freud's new Swiss disciple, Dr Carl Gustav Jung (1906), then a staff member at the Burghölzli asylum, mounted a vigorous defence of psychoanalysis, and attempted to assuage Professor Aschaffenburg in the course of "a lively correspondence" (p. 4), but to little avail. Early twentieth century psychiatric investigators struggled with the overt sexuality of Freud's theories. Even Jung's mentor, Professor Eugen Bleuler, an early Freudian enthusiast, could accept only "70% of the libido theory", in large measure because he objected to Freud's use of the very word "libido" (Jung, 1907, p. 32). Bleuler, a descendant of Swiss Protestant farmers and a teetotaller, would have found some of the more overtly sexual references in Freud's writings rather unpalatable.

Others held even more overtly aggressive opinions about Sigmund Freud's psychoanalysis. In 1908, a young Italian medical student at the Universität zu Wien, one Edoardo Weiss, began to express an interest in Freud's increasingly debated work, and he soon arranged to meet the noted Viennese neurologist and psychoanalyst. But Weiss's mentor, the eminent Professor Otto Marburg, warned the young physician-in-training to approach Freud cautiously, describing the founder of psychoanalysis as none other than a "Casanova" (Weiss, 1970, p. 2).

In the very same year, Dr Ernest Jones, Freud's principle epigone in London, had to resign from his neurological post for having made enquiries into the sexual lives of his patients. After Jones had assessed a ten-year-old girl with a hysterical paralysis of her left arm, the young person began to complain. As Jones (1959) recalled years later, in his posthumously published autobiography *Free Associations: Memories of a Psycho-Analyst*:

> Shortly after I saw the girl, she boasted to other children in the ward that the doctor had been talking to her about sexual topics, and this got to the ears of one of their parents. The incensed father complained to the hospital committee, who at once interviewed me. The atmosphere was charged with suspicious antagonism, and I well remember one elderly clergyman who was very worked up. I was told later that he got a hospital rule passed to the effect that no sexual topic was ever to be broached with children. [pp. 150–151]

Jones, in desperation, had to flee to Canada, and it was several years later that he returned to England.

Even after Jones' arrival in Toronto, he had to be increasingly circumspect about the extent to which he could discuss sexual matters in his new professional home. Writing to Freud from New York City during a brief trip below the Canadian border, Jones (1909) observed that,

> A man who writes always on the same thing is apt to be regarded here as a crank, because to the superficial American every subject is easily exhausted except for cranks, and if the subject is sexual he is simply tabooed as a sexual neurasthenic. Hence I shall dilute my sex articles with articles on other subjects alternately. [p. 15]

Other colleagues cautioned Ernest Jones—now Sigmund Freud's principal North American disciple—about the dangers of too much explicitness. The sympathetic Bostonian, Dr Morton Prince, Editor of *The Journal of Abnormal Psychology* (which published many early psychoanalytical articles) counselled Jones that his subscribers included " a large lay circulation of both sexes, and there is great danger of our losing our circulation if we shock unsympathetic readers" (Prince, 1909, quoted in Maddox, 2006, p. 73). Morton Prince (*ibid.*, p. 74) further advised Ernest Jones that "People resent theories which are distasteful even if true, and take it out on the author". Indeed, news of Morton Prince's cautiousness had reached Freud from numerous sources, prompting Freud (1909) to explain to Jones that Prince

> declined papers sent him on his demand on the account of their containing too much of sexual matter—you say he is not prudish, but he answered Abraham that he could not accept the term "homosexual" because he has so many lay readers (or ladies may be). [p. 19]

In spite of the numerous cautions from colleagues, Jones and his early psychoanalytical confrères found it impossible to refrain from writing about the sexual experiences of their patients and about the sexual underbelly of neurotic symptomatology, both in the consulting room, and even at home. Jones' son, the novelist Mervyn Jones (1987), reminisced that from time to time his father would become indiscreet, and drop the names of his aristocratic patients, noting that on one occasion, Dr Jones had to replace the corduroy covering of his analytical couch, because "a lordly patient had an orgasm when he reclined on it—'something to do with a stable-groom', my father explained" (p. 11). Even the children of psychoanalysts had a sense that their parents practised an unusually sexually-charged profession.

Ernest Jones' uncompromising sexual frankness even cost him a faculty appointment at Harvard University. On 23 March, 1910, the distinguished Harvard psychologist Professor Hugo Münsterberg wrote to the equally pre-eminent Harvard neurologist Professor James Jackson Putnam that Jones possessed impeccable medico-psychological credentials, and that, "Among the younger men I hardly know anyone who seems to fill the bill so well as Dr. Jones." However, Münsterberg demurred, and explained to Putnam,

> The only objection which troubles me is his inclination to put more emphasis on sexual factors than would be desirable in a course which is not intended for medical students and which is open to undergraduates. It might too easily degenerate into a sensational course by the loafers on account of its piquancy. [p. 206]

As the second decade of the twentieth century began, Freud's works became infinitely more widely known, and also more widely despised. On 29 March, 1910, the noted German psychiatrist, Professor Wilhelm Weygant, addressed the Medical Society of Hamburg, and threatened to call the vice squad to crush the sexually salacious psychoanalysts. According to the account published on 4 April, 1910, in the *Hamburger Ärzte-Correspondenzblatt*, Weygant claimed that,

> Freud's interpretations were on a level with the trashiest dream books. His methods were dangerous since they simply bred sexual ideas in his patients. His method of treatment was on a par with the massage of the genital organs. [Jones, 1955, p. 130]

Contemporaneously, during an after-dinner speech at a meeting of the American Neurological Association, Professor Joseph Collins, a former President of the organization, publicly attacked his neurological colleague Professor James Jackson Putnam for having presented a psychoanalytical paper that Collins caricatured as full of "pornographic stories about pure virgins" (quoted in Jones, 1910, p. 55), noting that the American Neurological Association must take a stand not only against "Freudism", but also Christian Science, supernaturalism, transcendentalism, and all other such "bosh".

On 12 February, 1911, Freud's pioneering Hungarian colleague, Dr Sándor Ferenczi, delivered a talk on "Suggestion and psychoanalysis" to the Physicians' Association in Budapest. After he spoke, a medical colleague who practised hydrotherapy (the treatment of neurotic illness through the use of therapeutic baths and douches), "rose in opposition and read aloud a long prepared lecture", attacking Ferenczi, Freud, and psychoanalysis, decrying the Viennese doctrine as little more than "*Schweinereien*" (which might best be translated as "filthy, pig-like, sexual hanky-panky"), and as a method "which creates illness and destroys culture". After the hydrotherapist spoke, a dermatology colleague stood up and lambasted psychoanalysis as "a dangerous poison", and warned that, "Analysis is pornography; so analysts belong in jail" (Ferenczi, 1911, p. 256).

Of course, the members of the psychiatric fraternity did not have a monopoly on the condemnation of sexuality; in fact, their attitudes merely reflected those of their fellow citizens. To speak of sexuality in an open fashion at the height of the Edwardian era would have provoked a great deal of outrage. After all, women in Europe covered their bodies in multiple layers of undergarments, and the men wore stiff collars and other tight-fitting clothing. To cite but one example, which provides some sense of the anti-sexual context of the early 1900s, let us consider the opening night of John Millington Synge's now-classic drama *The Playboy of the Western World*, which débuted at the Abbey Theatre in Dublin on 26 January, 1907. At one point, one of the characters spoke of "a drift of females standing in their shifts"; and this mere mention of undergarments caused so much outrage that members of the audience began to shout death threats toward the author, and to storm the stage, stopped only by the quick-witted "call-boy" who swore that he would decapitate any patron crossing the footlights. When Cole Porter penned his famous 1934 lyric "In olden days, a glimpse of stocking / Was looked on as something shocking" (the opening lines to the chorus of his song "Anything Goes"), he may well have had the so-called "Playboy Riots" in mind. At any rate, if a brief reference to underwear caused so much scandal and interrupted the performance of Synge's play, imagine the hatred directed towards Freud and his early followers for their sustained discussions of sexual matters that dared to look beneath the undergarments.

As the 1910s and 1920s unfolded, psychoanalysts throughout the Western world encountered accusations of impropriety and corruption in many different countries ranging from France (Roudinesco, 1982) to Australia (Damousi, 2005). And even in Russia, the pioneers of Freudianism had to endure great resistance and abuse. In 1921, Vera Schmidt, one of the founders of Russian psychoanalysis, opened the pioneering school, the "Detski Dom" Psychoanalytic Orphanage–Laboratory on Malaya Nikitskaya Street in Moscow, located on the second floor of a sumptuous art nouveau building once owned by the wealthy merchant Stepan Ryabushinsky. Schmidt's school, supported by the Russian psychoanalytical movement, and in particular by Ivan Ermakov and Moshe Wulff—two of Freud's key disciples—practised non-abusive paedagogy, and promoted love for children rather than punishment. Its pupils included none other than Vasily Iosifovich Dzhugashvili, the young son of Joseph Stalin (Angelini, 2008). In spite of the school's success, it had to close in 1924 in the wake of gossip and accusations of pornography and sexual experiments, as well as attempts to stimulate the children's sexuality prematurely (Etkind, 1993; Miller, 1998).

As we have seen, large numbers of the early pioneers of psychoanalysis had to combat disapproval, criticism, even ostracism and humiliation, as a result of their sympathy for Freud's sexually explicit psychology. Ernest Jones (1955) spoke of the prevailing "*odium sexicum*" (p. 121) in the first half of the twentieth century, which made discussion of sexual matters, even by psychoanalysts, rather tricky.

To compound matters further, one must appreciate that Freud and his followers not only had to survive the suspicions of their anti-sexual contemporaries but also their own *internalized odium sexicum*. Although Freud approached sexuality head-on, in a historically refreshing manner, he also suffered from the same inhibitions and restrictions that would have characterized most bourgeois

Viennese intellectuals of the late nineteenth century. For instance, in the case history of "Dora" (Fräulein Ida Bauer), Freud boasts to his readers about his readiness to speak about genital parts in a straightforward, non-euphemistic manner, unlike many previous clinical psychopathologists. As Freud (1905b, p. 48) indicated, "I call bodily organs and processes by their technical names, and I tell these to the patient if they—the names, I mean—happen to be unknown to her." Indeed, Freud then trumpets that he would always *call a spade a spade*; but, tellingly, when Freud does use this expression in the "Dora" analysis, he does not do so in his native German, but rather he lapses, uncharacteristically, into French, and writes, "*J'appelle un chat un chat*" (which means, literally, "I call a cat a cat"—the French equivalent of "I call a spade a spade"), thus unconsciously underscoring his own difficulties in speaking in a completely uncensored manner about sexual matters.

We certainly know that in his private life Freud upheld certain anti-sexual conventions, counselling at least one of his three sons— middle son Oliver—about the dangers of masturbation (Roazen, 1969b). Furthermore, Freud sent all of his sons to see another physician to explain the "facts of life" to them (Roazen, 1969a). Other early analysts protected their children from seemingly unnecessary and potentially harmful sexual experiences. Professor James Jackson Putnam had the seat of his daughter Marion's bicycle specially adjusted to reduce the possibility of the child obtaining any masturbatory pleasure (Roazen, 1966).

Although I do not have the luxury of documenting the longstanding historical reluctance of psychoanalysts to engage with sexuality, in spite of our reputation for being sexually obsessed, I shall present three further simple examples to stress the point:

1. In 1915, Freud's loyal disciple Dr Eduard Hitschmann (1915) published a psychoanalytical study of the love life of composer Franz Schubert in the *Internationale Zeitschrift für Psychoanalyse*. As the contemporary psychoanalytical musicologist Maynard Solomon (2007) has observed, Hitschmann completely avoided writing about Schubert's putative homosexuality, even though he had access to a great deal of biographical data concerning, *inter alia*, Schubert's relationship with the misogynistic Graecophile poet Johann Mayrhofer, a well-known nineteenth-century

homosexual. Solomon understandably chastises Hitschmann for neglecting to note that Schubert and Mayrhofer shared a room together for several years, even though Schubert scholars had known this information for quite some time.

2.   During the 1950s, the well-known Indian-born British psychoanalyst Masud Khan wrote two papers about homosexuality, which he submitted for publication to the *International Journal of Psycho-Analysis*. Dr Willi Hoffer, the incumbent editor of the publication, rejected both of Khan's papers, in spite of the latter's widely acknowledged gifts as a skilled writer. According to the late Professor Joseph Sandler, who would himself become Editor of this journal, Hoffer hated homosexuality, and he rejected papers on this topic as a matter of course (Hopkins, 2006).

3.   In 1963, the American psychoanalyst Philip Wagner (1963) reported that a psychoanalytical training institute had forbidden its candidates to attend a scientific meeting at which a colleague presented a paper on "Pornography and psychotherapy".

The struggle to achieve sexpertise

Thus far we have observed that psychoanalysts have had to withstand great hatred from their enemies for daring to speak about sexuality in a forthright and professional manner; and, at the same time, they have had to struggle with their own inhibitions in terms of discussing sexual matters, especially the traditionally "other" aspects of sexuality, such as homosexuality and pornography. Perhaps this observation should not surprise us at all. Fewer aspects of human behaviour produce more anxiety than sexuality. After all, sexual behaviour and sexual fantasy can produce our greatest bodily and psychological pleasures, but sexual behaviour and its fantasmatic antecedents can also result in abuse, rape, even torture and lust-murder. And the anxiety around sexuality—an overarching aspect of human experience which can create life or cause death—will be reflected not only in the general population, but among experts and professionals as well. Frank discussion about sexual matters generates very primitive, archaic fears about our own conception. As we know, each of us entered the world as a product of a sexual union between our parents, and each of us must bear the narcissistic injury of knowing that our parents never consulted us before procreating. We carry within ourselves the awareness that when our parents "made" us, their thoughts may have been elsewhere. Furthermore, our relationship to sexuality becomes in many ways the symbol of our crude attempts to resolve that Titanic Freudian conflict between our most visceral, psychophysiological desires and the multiple taboos to which we become subscribed throughout the course of maturation and acculturation, generating shame, guilt, and fear in the process.

While preparing to write a magazine article about psychoanalysis, the American journalist Janet Malcolm interviewed a number of distinguished members of the New York Psychoanalytic Society. In the course of her research, Malcolm spoke to a Middle European émigré who had ultimately come to settle on Manhattan's Fifth Avenue, one Dr Greta Koenig (a pseudonym designed to protect the analyst's confidentiality). Janet Malcolm (1981) recalled her meeting with Greta Koenig thus:

> We sat around a coffee table laden with pastries, little rolls, cheeses, fruit, chocolates, and bottles of liqueur, and as my hostess pressed delicacies on me she talked of female orgasm. She sliced *Dobos Torte* onto translucent old flowered porcelain and remarked thoughtfully that a clitoral orgasm may be accompanied by feelings in the vagina and thus, properly speaking, can be called a vaginal orgasm. I felt a strong urge to laugh. As if reading my thoughts, Greta Koenig smiled and said, "It used to be very difficult for me to talk about such things. I used to have to force myself to talk about them to patients. But the analyst must talk about the genitals. There is no way around it, and now there is nothing I can't talk about." [pp. 82–83]

In many ways, Dr Greta Koenig's relationship with sexuality typifies the position of many psychoanalytical workers: each possesses both an historical discomfort and a contemporaneous need for comfort in speaking frankly about sexuality.

Our relative ease or dis-ease as couple psychoanalytic psychotherapists in relation to sexual discussion can be situated within an historical context. Shortly before her death, Anna Freud reminisced about the differences between sexual talk among analysts in the 1920s and 1930s, as compared with those in the 1970s and 1980s, in connection with the phenomenon of resistance Miss Freud noted:

> If a patient says to the analyst, as many patients now do, "Of course I can't tell you anything about my sex life, that's much too embarrassing," many analysts would accept it now and say to themselves, "perhaps next year." Whereas in the past one would have said, "All right, but don't expect me to help you until you tell me about it, because we will not be doing the analysis until you do." [quoted in Sandler & Freud, 1985, p. 9]

Obviously, psychoanalytical clinicians do have a great capacity to talk about sexual matters, perhaps greater than that of many other professionals. But, none the less, in my experience I continue to encounter colleagues and students who shy away from talking or thinking about the more complicated aspects of sexuality with their patients, clients, or analysands. Perhaps, as a couple psychoanalytic psychotherapist, I have had to confront sexuality and its vicissitudes in the most direct of fashions, as it has extruded itself into the consulting room, without much prompting, in the form of couples who present with impotence or vaginismus, ejaculatio praecox, ejaculatio retardata, dyspareunia, gender confusion, shame and guilt about sexual fantasies, addiction to pornography (internet and otherwise), extramarital affairs, loss of libido, and a whole host of other sexual complexes that can sometimes be hidden from view in one-to-one psychotherapeutic work but that remain harder to conceal in the context of couple work.

No doubt, many sexually sophisticated colleagues will claim that I have erected a straw man or straw woman, misconstruing that psychoanalysts and psychotherapists suffer from sexual prudery. I congratulate these sexually sophisticated colleagues on their ability to handle the multitudinous sexual matters that emerge in analytical sessions with professionalism, tact, and sensitivity. However, having published a large-scale study of the sexual lives of over 19,000 adult Britons (Kahr, 2007), and over 3,000 adult Americans (Kahr, 2008), I know only too well how many individuals have never managed to share their sexual histories in full with their psychologists, psychiatrists, psychotherapists, or psychoanalysts.

Some of the early psychoanalysts enjoyed a delightfully rough-and-ready approach to the treatment of sexual matters, in spite of the constraints that I have previously described. For example, in 1925, the young Viennese physician Dr Richard Sterba undertook the psychoanalytical treatment of a twenty-year-old male patient who suffered impotence following a minor venereal infection. Sterba soon discovered that the patient had developed a secondary symptom: compulsive brushing of his hair, which, the patient feared, kept standing up on end, causing him great embarrassment. In the course of the analysis, Sterba (1982) made an interpretation that had an "immediate, almost magical effect" (p. 38) by suggesting to the patient that he had displaced his penile erection on to his hair. Thereafter, the young man became cured of his compulsive hair brushing.

Although many contemporary psychoanalytical practitioners would undoubtedly understand the logic of Richard Sterba's intervention, we would perhaps proceed more diplomatically, more delicately, and more slowly, at least in the early stages of treatment. None the less, many colleagues would perhaps shy away from such typically "Freudian" approaches to sexuality, and might not explore the history of the symptom as fully as necessary. Certainly, the colleague whom I described at the outset of this chapter, "Dr U", had failed fully in his attempt to take a sexual history or to engage with the sexual life of the couple in treatment. So, anti-sexual colleagues do continue to exist alongside those who enjoy a much greater capacity for what I have come to think of as *sexpertise*.

In my clinical experience with patients, and in my anthropological experience as a participant–observer in the psychotherapeutic and psychoanalytical communities, I have come to regard sexpertise as the ability to possess a sexual skin, which can accomplish all of the following tasks:

- undertake a full sexual history;
- process sexual data without shame or undue anxiety;
- retain a posture of concern, while remaining truly neutral about a patient's sexual behaviours and fantasies;
- explore the unconscious, symbolic meaning or meanings of a patient's sexual behaviours and fantasies;
- facilitate discussion of sexual material with patients without being intrusive or excited.

One might suggest that any well-trained, well-analysed mental health professional does possess these capacities, or should possess them. But although many do, it seems that others lack a sense of grace and comfort in sexual matters, and it may be that our training institutions and membership institutions can provide additional coursework or continuing professional development opportunities for mental health professionals to become more sexologically sophisticated.

In 1936, the great American popular songwriter Cole Porter contributed a beautiful ballad "Down in the Depths", to his musical show *Red, Hot and Blue,* which premiered at the Colonial Theatre in Boston, Massachusetts, sung by the inimitable Ethel Merman, prior to its Broadway début at New York's Alvin Theatre. At this point in American history, psychoanalysis had already become quite an institution among the cognoscenti of Manhattan, and Porter paid tribute to psychoanalytic chic by including a revised lyric for the refrain, in which the love-traumatized Miss Merman laments, "Why, even my analyst's wife / Has a perfectly good love life". When considering Porter's words, "*Even* my analyst's wife", his well-crafted phrase suggests only too powerfully the fear that analysts might not be as sexually proficient (either at home or at the office) as they might wish to be. This lyrical choice seems to have raised few eyebrows at all; indeed, it seems to have struck a realistic chord.

Perhaps we may discover in the final analysis that psychoanalytical workers have neither greater nor lesser skills as lovers than general members of the public, but, in the professional context, we ought at least to possess a greater sense of sexpertise, a quality that may not yet be quite as well developed in our community as it might ultimately be.

References

Angelini, A. (2008). History of the unconscious in Soviet Russia: from its origins to the fall of the Soviet Union. G. Iannaco & A. Wood (Trans.). *International Journal of Psychoanalysis, 89*: 369–388.

Damousi, J. (2005). *Freud in the Antipodes: A Cultural History of Psychoanalysis in Australia.* Sydney, New South Wales, Australia: University of New South Wales Press.

Dolnick, E. (1998). *Madness on the Couch: Blaming the Victim in the Heyday of Psychoanalysis*. New York: Simon and Schuster.

Etkind, A. (1993). *Eros of the Impossible: The History of Psychoanalysis in Russia*. N. Rubins & M. Rubins (Trans.). Boulder, CO: Westview Press, 1997.

Ferenczi, S. (1911). Letter to Sigmund Freud. 16th February, 1911. In: E. Brabant, E. Falzeder, P. Giampieri-Deutsch, & A. Haynal (Eds.), P. T. Hoffer (Trans.), *The Correspondence of Sigmund Freud and Sándor Ferenczi: Volume 1, 1908–1914* (pp. 255–256). Cambridge, MA: Belknap Press of Harvard University Press, 1993

Freud, S. (1905a). *Drei Abhandlungen zur Sexualtheorie*. Vienna: Franz Deuticke.

Freud, S. (1905b). Fragment of an analysis of a case of hysteria. *S.E., 7*: 7–122. London: Hogarth.

Freud, S. (1909). Letter to Ernest Jones. 22nd February. In: R. A. Paskauskas (Ed.), F. Voss (Trans.), *The Complete Correspondence of Sigmund Freud and Ernest Jones: 1908–1939* (pp. 18–19). Cambridge, MA: Belknap Press of Harvard University Press, 1993.

Hitschmann, E. (1915). Franz Schuberts Schmerz und Liebe. *Internationale Zeitschrift für Psychoanalyse, 3*: 287–292.

Hopkins, L. (2006). *False Self: The Life of Masud Khan*. New York: Other Press.

Jones, E. (1909). Letter to Sigmund Freud. 7th February. In: R. A. Paskauskas (Ed.), F. Voss (Trans.), *The Complete Correspondence of Sigmund Freud and Ernest Jones: 1908–1939* (pp. 13–16). Cambridge, MA: Belknap Press of Harvard University Press, 1993.

Jones, E. (1910). Letter to Sigmund Freud. 4th May. In: R. A. Paskauskas (Ed.)., F. Voss (Trans.), *The Complete Correspondence of Sigmund Freud and Ernest Jones: 1908–1939* (pp. 54–57). Cambridge, MA: Belknap Press of Harvard University Press, 1993.

Jones, E. (1955). *Sigmund Freud: Life and Work. Volume Two. Years of Maturity. 1901–1919*. London: Hogarth.

Jones, E. (1959). *Free Associations: Memories of a Psycho-Analyst*. London: Hogarth Press.

Jones, M. (1987). *Chances: An Autobiography*. London: Verso.

Jung, C. G. (1906). Letter to Sigmund Freud. 5th October. In: W. McGuire (Ed.), R. Manheim & R. F. C. Hull (Trans.), *The Freud/Jung Letters: The Correspondence Between Sigmund Freud and C. G. Jung* (pp. 4–5). Princeton, NJ: Princeton University Press, 1974.

Jung, C. G. (1907). Letter to Sigmund Freud. 11th April. In: W. McGuire (Ed.), R. Manheim & R. F. C. Hull (Trans.), *The Freud/Jung Letters: The Correspondence Between Sigmund Freud and C. G. Jung* (pp. 30–32). Princeton, NJ: Princeton University Press, 1974.

Kahr, B. (2007). *Sex and the Psyche*. London: Allen Lane/Penguin Books.

Kahr, B. (2008). *Who's Been Sleeping in Your Head?: The Secret World of Sexual Fantasies*. New York: Basic Books/Perseus Books Group.

Malcolm, J. (1981). *Psychoanalysis: The Impossible Profession*. New York: Alfred A. Knopf.

Miller, M. A. (1998). *Freud and the Bolsheviks: Psychoanalysis in Imperial Russia and the Soviet Union*. New Haven, CT: Yale University Press.

Münsterberg, H. (1910). Letter to James Jackson Putnam. 23rd March. Cited in: N. G. Hale, Jr. (Ed.), *James Jackson Putnam and Psychoanalysis: Letters between Putnam and Sigmund Freud, Ernest Jones, William James, Sandor Ferenczi, and Morton Prince, 1877–1917* (p. 206). Cambridge, MA: Harvard University Press, 1971.

Prince, M. (1909). Letter to Ernest Jones. 30th March. Archives of the British Psychoanalytical Society, British Psychoanalytical Society, Byron House, London. CPA/823/01. Quoted in Brenda Maddox (2006). *Freud's Wizard: The Enigma of Ernest Jones*, pp. 73–74. London: John Murray (Publishers).

Roazen, P. (1966). Interview with Marion Putnam. 22nd September. Cited in Paul Roazen (1969). *Brother Animal: The Story of Freud and Tausk*. New York: Alfred A. Knopf.

Roazen, P. (1969a). Interview with Esti Freud. Undated. Cited in Paul Roazen. *Brother Animal: The Story of Freud and Tausk*. New York: Alfred A. Knopf.

Roazen, P. (1969b). Interview with Oliver Freud. Undated. Cited in Paul Roazen. *Brother Animal: The Story of Freud and Tausk*. New York: Alfred A. Knopf.

Roudinesco, E. (1982). *La Bataille de cent ans: Histoire de la psychanalyse en France. Volume I*. Paris: Éditions Ramsay.

Sandler, J., & Freud, A. (1985). *The Analysis of Defense: The Ego and the Mechanisms of Defense Revisited*. New York: International Universities Press.

Solomon, M. (2007). Taboo and biographical innovation: Mozart, Beethoven, Schubert. *American Imago*, 64: 7–21.

Sterba, R. F. (1982). *Reminiscences of a Viennese Psychoanalyst*. Detroit, MI: Wayne State University Press.

Wagner, P. S. (1963). The second analysis. *International Journal of Psycho-Analysis, 44*: 481–489.

Weiss, E. (1970). My recollections of Sigmund Freud. In: *Sigmund Freud as a Consultant: Recollections of a Pioneer in Psychoanalysis* (pp. 1–22). New York: Intercontinental Medical Book Corporation.

CHAPTER TWO

What do we mean by "sex"?

Warren Colman

Introduction

The way that we understand sexuality will obviously affect the way we interpret sexual issues brought to the consulting room. In this chapter, I describe the way that, in practice, if not always in theory, psychoanalytic practitioners now think about sexuality in metaphorical and symbolic terms. The development of object relations theory has led to a shift away from thinking of sex in terms of instinctual aim towards an increasing emphasis on the qualities of relatedness to the object (Parsons, 2000). This shift enables us to think about sex in terms of relating and relating in terms of sex. I suggest that, rather than thinking of some kind of biological "bedrock" to which either sex or relating can be reduced, we need to think in terms of metaphorical and symbolic representation as a kind of irreducible currency of meaning. In my view, the aim of analytical psychotherapy is to create a climate in which meaning can be elaborated through the use of metaphorical language, thus enabling patients to bring their sexuality into relation with other aspects of their lives. This two-way approach is able to explore interpersonal relating in terms of metaphors of sex, while simultaneously exploring the way actual sex reveals relational dynamics in metaphorical terms. This way of thinking fosters an interpretive stance I call "interpreting towards" and "interpreting away from" sex.

This way of seeing is particularly apparent—and useful—in working with couples. Here is a typical example.

> The sexual relationship between Mr and Mrs A had all but ceased. Mrs A could not bring herself to have sex with her husband when he was so hostile and unsupportive towards her in every way, while Mr A's resentment of his wife's refusal came out in contemptuous and dismissive criticism of her—a classic vicious circle. In one session they described an argument where Mrs A, feeling overwhelmed with the work of managing home and family, criticized what she regarded as her husband's half-hearted and inept attempts to help. Mr A became furious and stomped off. I interpreted this incident as a form of failed intercourse where Mrs A invites her husband to give her something but then criticizes the way it is given. Mr A then feels unable to tolerate any criticism of his potency and withdraws. My aim in using a sexual metaphor was to show the couple how their usual way of relating is the reverse of what happens when they fail to have sex. Here it is Mrs A who initiates intercourse (asking for help), but when it is not quite the way she likes it Mr A cannot tolerate the criticism and *he* is then the one who withdraws and refuses to continue.

In this example I was interpreting *towards* sex, but the same understanding can be applied to the couple's actual attempts to have sex by interpreting *away* from sex to their typical relational interaction of "frustrated intercourse". From either direction, the sexual problem can be reframed as a shared defence against being disappointed and criticized in an intimate relationship

This kind of interactional approach, derived from object relations theory, involves a radical departure from Freud's original instinct-based theory of psychoanalysis. For Freud, and all those who maintain a drive theory model of psychoanalysis, sexuality is the bedrock of psychic life, and thus the thrust of interpretation is always towards sexual issues. By contrast, relational analysts, from Fairbairn to the intersubjectivists, typically interpret away from sexuality towards relational issues. For somewhat different reasons, Jungians also tend to interpret away from the biological aspects of sexuality towards the psychic and spiritual end of the archetypal spectrum. However, there is a third approach, which is particularly interesting and complex. Kleinian theory is rooted in an underlying metapsychological structure of drive theory, but gives primacy to the transformation of instinct into unconscious phantasy. Although unconscious phantasies are held to be psychic derivatives of the bodily instincts, Kleinian theory in practice has developed an extremely rich language that describes psychic states in terms of sexuality and the body. Nevertheless, the Kleinian language of unconscious phantasy tends towards a reification of its own meta-phors, so that unconscious phantasy is itself taken to be the bedrock of psychic life, rather than a metaphorical way of describing it. In my view, there is no ultimate bedrock of definitive actual phan-tasies "in" the unconscious. While *conscious* fantasies may be taken concretely, *unconscious* phantasies are, in my opinion, always a metaphorical interpretation of purported psychological events in which even their supposed concreteness has an "as if" quality (Colman, 2005).

Freud, Jung, and the Relationalists: interpreting towards and away from sexuality

Freud's libido theory was intended to be a bridge between psyche and soma. As a convinced materialist, Freud hoped to discover the physical basis for psychic life and looked for this in terms of some kind of energy that "drove" the psychic system. He believed that he found this energy in an extended conception of the sexual instinct, which he termed *libido*. In the absence of hard, physical evidence, Freud was prepared to utilize psychological speculation, but he always believed that this would eventually be grounded in biology.

The theory of psychoanalysis began when Freud reinterpreted his patients' stories of sexual seduction as *fantasies* that expressed their own unconscious sexual wishes. Freud's great leap of under-standing here was to recognize the significance of *psychic reality*: when fantasies are unconscious they are indistinguishable from actual events, and so their impact on the mind is the same as if seduction had taken place in reality. Despite criticism that Freud downplayed actual sexual abuse, this insight remains extremely significant today: it is often very difficult to tell whether patients' accounts of sexual abuse refer to actual events or unconscious fantasies. Freud did not regard these unconscious fantasies as symbolic, but rather saw the symbolic phenomena that emerged into conscious life through dreams and (conscious) fantasies as being symbolic of sexual wishes expressed in bodily terms. For Freud, symbols were a kind of code that referred back to the literal reality of the physical body, especially the genitals (Jones, 1916).

The clinical relevance of this debate can be seen in the different ways we might think about something like castration. Freud sees phenomena such as fear of authority, a man's feeling of powerlessness, or a woman's feeling of being wounded, as derivative of castration anxiety. The fundamental fear is a bodily one, so that one might say, for example, that fear of authority is a symbolic derivative of castration. But, at least in part due to the influence of Freud's ideas, we now tend to see things the other way around; when we talk about a weak, frightened man as "being castrated" we are using the image of castration as symbolic *of* that state of mind. The image of castration has become a symbolic signifier of meaning, whereas initially it was that which was signified *by* those meanings.

The question of symbolism was one of the key areas of dispute between Freud and Jung. Jung objected to the way that Freud regarded symbols as having a literal, definable meaning. He argued that a symbol was the best possible expression of an unknown psychic content and, therefore, not reducible or translatable to that which it symbolized. He believed that incest fantasies, for example, did not refer to literal sexual wishes but symbolized an unconscious striving for psychological transformation, a process of being reborn through a return to the "womb" of the unconscious.

Jung's approach has one immediate advantage. Freud's theory of censorship in dreams enables him to reduce a whole host of manifest images to their putative latent origins in forbidden and repressed sexual wishes. But how would Freud interpret explicit sexual dreams? What, for example, could he make of a woman who dreamt, as one of my patients did, of having sex with her father? This shows how we need to think of symbolic meanings as pointing in both directions: sex is not only symbolized in dreams, as Freud argued, but, as Jung claimed, is also symbolic in itself.

In the case of my patient's dream, which occurred near the end of her analysis, I saw it as symbolic of a process of reconciliation with her late father that had been achieved through the transference with me. An important element of her difficulties had been a split between sexual excitement and being cared for. In her dream these two elements came together. Perhaps the most moving element in the dream was the leave-taking that took place after the sex. In this way, the coming end of the analysis was represented by a saying farewell to her father. And yet, of course, the reverse was also true—she was reworking the loss of her father through the ending of the analysis. Essentially, I saw it as what Jung called a *coniunctio*—a coming together of the opposites. While the *coniunctio* is often represented in sexual form, it is nevertheless a symbolic image that always points beyond itself.

One potential criticism of this approach would be that interpreting away from sexuality runs the risk of ignoring it altogether by artificially "spiritualizing" what is actually bodily and sexual. However, Jung often spoke of images as being *both* sexual *and* spiritual, and pointed out that "nothing is more repulsive than a furtively prurient spirituality; it is just as unsavoury as gross sensuality" (Jung, 1954 [1925], par. 336). For Jung, sex and spirit formed a typical pair of opposites that needed to be held together in a *coniunctio*.

A similar criticism might be made of relational schools of psychoanalysis which attempt to dispense with instinct theory altogether. Sexual issues are seen in purely relational terms, as if sex is no more than a function of object relating. The clearest example of this approach is Fairbairn, who argued that the primary drive is not pleasure seeking but object seeking. Sexuality is then seen merely as a means to the primary aim of seeking a good object relationship. In a similar vein, Jessica Benjamin, an American intersubjectivist, has written of the pleasure in sexual union as the satisfaction of the desire for recognition, apparently making little or no distinction between sexual activity and other situations where the need for recognition may be met—in analysis, for example (Benjamin, 1990, p. 126). Even when a link is drawn between the physical intimacies of infancy and adult sexuality, there is a tendency to lose sight of the particular qualities of genital excitement and fantasy that are definitive of adult sexuality *per se* (Budd, 2001). Interpreting away from sexuality to elaborate the relational configurations implicit in sexual activity and fantasy should not be confused with the defensive avoidance of sex, including the tendency to retreat to the safer ground of the mother–infant relationship (Searles, 1959, p. 290).

Klein: the language of unconscious phantasy

Klein's development of the idea of unconscious phantasy makes it far more than an unconscious form of wish-fulfilment. Klein effectively introduced an entirely new idea of a sort of liminal area between mind and body, where body is in the process of *becoming* mind. For Klein, the whole of psychic life is continually underpinned by unconscious phantasies, especially those concerning the relation to the mother's body, the father's penis, and the parental intercourse. Unconscious phantasy is regarded as "the psychical representation of instinct" (Isaacs, 1952), so that the interplay of internal objects represents the interplay of libidinal and destructive instincts within the personality. However, Klein's use of unconscious phantasy goes beyond instinctual drive and includes elements that necessitate a concept of innate knowledge. The infant is held to have innate knowledge not only of the breast, but also of the penis, the vagina, and the parental intercourse.

Furthermore, the internal objects of which unconscious phantasies are composed do not merely refer back to actual physical organs but are symbolic of a whole range of psychic phenomena. It is impossible to understand what Klein means by the breast, for example, without seeing it as a symbolic image for the source of goodness, nourishment, life, and love. As Kleinian thinking has developed, there has been an increasing tendency to use the language of unconscious phantasy in this symbolic way. The body is used as a *metaphor* for psychic processes that are then taken to be concretely rooted in biological reality, because the biological body is used to represent them. That is to say, the bodily metaphor is used to give a spurious materialist legitimacy to psychological speculation. In effect, unconscious phantasy has become the "bedrock" of psychic life, rather than the instincts that supposedly generate it.

One significant example of this concerns the capacity for linking. Bion (1959) introduced the concept of attacks on linking to describe the way the psychotic part of the personality attacks the meaning of thoughts and feelings by destroying the links between them. This process is described in metaphorical terms as an attack on the link between the parents in intercourse. The linking theme was taken up in Britton's influential paper "The missing link: parental sexuality in the Oedipus complex" (Britton, 1989). Britton does not seem to regard parental intercourse as a metaphor, though: in his view, the capacity for linking is dependent on the child's internal relation to the parental couple. That is, the negotiation of the Oedipal triangle is not merely a way of describing the development of mental objectivity that Britton calls "the third position"—it is *the* way, and the only way, in which this capacity can develop. This view reverses Jung's conception of the *coniunctio*, where the couple in intercourse is merely a *symbol* of an abstract process and therefore not dependent on any particular representation of it in phantasy (Colman, 2007).

Reified meaning in "the parental intercourse"

I now want to consider the impact of this kind of reification on how sexuality itself is understood. If the sexual body is conflated with the symbolic meanings it is used to represent, then sexuality is understood to be a literal and concrete expression of those symbolic meanings. That is, a particular set of meanings is "read in" to the sexual body and the fact that this has been done is "read out" again, so that the symbol appears to be a concrete fact of psychological and sexual experience.

This is particularly apparent in the case of the parental intercourse or "primal scene", which has come to be regarded as a template against which sexual activity (in behaviour or fantasy) can be judged. The acceptance of reality *per se* is equated with the acceptance of the "facts of life"—i.e., that the child is excluded from the parental intercourse, which alone is capable of producing babies. It is claimed, for example, that the phantasy of producing a baby is unconsciously present whenever people have sex and, if it is not, then psychic "reality" is being denied (cf. Grier, 2001, pp. 475, 487). This argument is used both ways round: the obliteration or denial of various aspects of reality—a common difficulty among narcissistic patients—is interpreted as a denial of the reality of the parental intercourse (Britton, 1992, p. 40). More worrying, though, is the interpretation of forms of sexuality that apparently deviate from the acceptance of the exclusive baby-producing nature of the parental intercourse as a denial of reality. This may be applied to a whole range of sexual phenomena, such as celibacy, masturbation, pornography, infidelity, sado-masochistic sex, and, most controversial of all, homosexuality. Nowadays, most analysts are at pains to deny that the theory of the parental intercourse is prejudicial to homosexuals. They may point out that it is only a metaphor, for example, or they may insist that the "facts of life" apply no matter what one's sexual preferences (Carvalho, 2003). Nevertheless, any interpretation of sexual activity in terms of a "perversion" of the facts of life risks imposing a particular framework of meaning on patients' experiences as if it were a statement about the nature of reality. However illuminating these interpretations might be, there is nothing inevitable about them, and certainly nothing that is biologically given.

The more we take our sexual metaphors as statements about the nature of reality, the less attention we are likely to pay to our patients' own meanings. Instead, these meanings are likely to be reinterpreted in terms of the analyst's symbolic language, without an acknowledgement that this is a language of meaning and not a statement about the nature of reality. The sexual body is then overwritten by the symbolic language of unconscious phantasy in a way that obliterates this having happened. We think that we are talking about sex when we are really talking about the particular symbolic meaning we have ascribed to sex.

Metaphor as meaning

It is not that I think that there is some other way in which we might *really* talk about sex. The central point of this chapter is the suggestion that we are always talking metaphorically and symbolically whenever we are talking about psychic experience, and that we cannot experience sexuality any other way but psychically. We might be able to describe the physiological processes of sex in great detail, but this says nothing about the experience of feeling turned on—or turned off (another metaphor, of course). In order to understand sexuality, Freud had to turn to the psyche, to the language of metaphor and fantasy, and it is, I suggest, the same for us all. From the sublime to the ridiculous, we all use metaphor as a way of making sense of sex and sex as a metaphorical way of making meaning.

Consider, for example, the diversity of sexual slang together with the non-sexual meanings it also conveys. If I call someone a "cocky fucker" I am more likely to be referring to his arrogant over-confidence than his sexual prowess: the sexual reference is thus being used as a metaphor, whether or not it actually applies in the sexual domain. But what about the young man who is feeling so sexually frustrated that he wants to "fuck everything up"? Here, it might well be helpful to point to the sexual root of his self-destructive urges. This kind of "facing both ways" frees us from the literalism of reification while providing us with a language of great symbolic richness and vigour to offer our patients. In psycho-analytic therapy, metaphorical interpretations provide a way of helping our patients think about their sexual experience as part of their emotional and imaginal lives, and their emotional and imaginal lives as part of their sexual experience.

In order to demonstrate this, I shall give examples taken from the individual psychotherapy of two male patients, illustrating the use of metaphor and symbol in the interpretation of sexual material. Some of these interpret "away from" sexuality, some towards it, and some move in both directions. The important point is the linking of one domain of experience with another, especially the way that metaphor can be used as a "bridge" which links relational issues with sexual–bodily ones and *vice versa*.

Making a stink: Brian

My first example concerns an extremely compliant patient with chronic irritable bowel syndrome. Brian's life was dominated by crippling anxiety that his bowels would "misbehave" (as he put it) and he would offend people with the smell of his farts. This anxiety had made him almost phobic about any social activity and completely unable to engage in sexual relationships with women.

One day he was talking about his fear of having to confront a female subordinate at work who had "ballsed things up" in a big way. Exploring his fear further, he talked about his sense of guilt and shame—as if in confronting his colleague he would somehow be "exposed" himself. When I pressed him as to what being exposed meant, he said that he was afraid he would be found boring and smelly. I then said "You are afraid that if you stand up to her and show her your hard penis, it will turn out to be nothing but a smelly turd." This interpretation had a profound effect on him. He saw it as "absolutely right" and chiming in exactly with his fear of being seen to be disgusting and causing offence. It was, he said, an image that was very powerful, utterly distasteful, and completely accurate.

My interpretation could be seen in rather Meltzerian terms as having something to do with "zonal confusion" and the "faecal penis" (Meltzer, 1966) and it is true that I probably could not have made such an interpretation without being aware of these ways of thinking. Primarily though, it was, as he said, a metaphorical image that brought together the sexual feelings represented by his penis with his long-standing preoccupation with his bowels, both of which were linked by inner feelings of self-disgust. The interpretation was also connected with his relationship to his dominating mother and his subsequent attitude towards women, involving shame, fear, and guilt compounded by unconscious hostility.

None of the different spheres that are linked together by the interpretation can be reduced to the other. The aim of the interpretation is not to suggest that his difficulties are "really" sexual or "really" relational any more than they are "really" to do with his physical disorder. The aim is rather to bring each into relation with the other, to weave together an elaborated network of meaning within which he is able to think about the various aspects of himself in a more integrated way than was previously possible.

This way of thinking leads to a rather different view of unconscious phantasy. Instead of regarding something like the faecal penis as a pre-existing concrete phantasy that governs the patient's sexual life, we might rather think of it as something akin to a mythological narrative, which is "dreamed up" in the interaction between patient and analyst. This would place the analyst's associations to images from psychoanalytic theory in the realm of "the analytic third" (Ogden, 1994). The sharing of the analyst's association in the form of an interpretation is akin to a mythological amplification that brings the phantasy into being as an emergent form of meaning. The patient's experience is restructured by the co-constructed interpretative narrative rather than being seen as prestructured by a concrete phantasy that it is the analyst's job to "discover".

I am well aware that some readers might disagree with my explanation of the helpful effect of this interpretation. They might take the view that it was the elucidation of the patient's concrete unconscious phantasy of having a shitty penis that was mutative, freeing him from an unconscious belief experienced as a literal certainty. However, I would argue that while there may well be some such belief about how unwelcome his sexual arousal might be to a woman, it would not be in the form of a concrete phantasy, but would rather belong in the realm of "implicit relational knowing", derived from early interaction and patterns of attachment with his mother (Boston Change Process Study Group, 2007). The interpretation enables the patient to bring such implicit states into reflective awareness, but to read this back into a pre-existing unconscious phantasy is to mistake the image for that which it imagines.

Cutting the Gordian Knot: Simon

Like Brian, Simon's problems were connected with difficulty in expressing his aggression. However, Simon initially presented these difficulties in the sexualized form of an obsessive preoccupation that he was gay. There was very little evidence for this—despite some homosexual fantasies, his sexual and romantic interest was always in women. Nevertheless, the preoccupation persisted, and much time in the therapy was spent interminably going over his obsessive rumination as to whether he was or was not gay. Simon was convinced that any relationship with a woman would result either in him being swallowed up or in her being damaged when she discovered his homosexuality. As a result, he had spent his twenties in a lonely wilderness, and sought therapy only in his early thirties.

In the early stages of a once weekly therapy that eventually lasted seven years, I interpreted mainly away from sexuality, attempting to draw out the meaning of his sexual fantasies and preoccupations in relational terms, especially the link with his feared aggression, his difficulty in separating from his parents (especially his mother), and generally becoming a man.

One session in particular enabled him to realize the link between his homosexual fantasies and his thwarted aggressive feelings towards his anxiously controlling mother. In this session, he described a pleasant sexual fantasy he was having about a girl on the train that was interrupted, out of the blue, by a fantasy of a penis in his mouth which he described as an "intrusion". I commented on the way the homosexual fantasy *destroyed* the heterosexual one, and linked this with his angry and destructive feelings. He admitted that he did sometimes feel angry, but was afraid that if he expressed it other people would be "pissed off" with him. For example, a female friend had asked him to come round and fix her bed, which had collapsed after a bolt had sheared off. He came round with a suitable bolt only to find that some other friends had already fixed it. He was "pissed off" that he had wasted his time and effort, but could not say so.

There were obviously a number of ways I could have taken up this richly symbolic piece of material. For example, I might have seen it as some kind of Oedipal phantasy in which father's "bolt" repairs the collapsed mother, leaving him the excluded child. I might also have linked this to the transference in which he feels hopelessly small and ineffective in relation to my superior "bolt". What I actually said was: "You felt it was an affront to your potency." Here, I was deliberately using a word which interpreted towards his sexuality while simultaneously indicating the relational issues encapsulated in his sexual preoccupations. The issue of potency drew together the inhibition of his anger and his sexuality with his sense of lacking a strong masculine gender identity—he is "upstaged" by the others and affronted that the friend had not even told him that the job had been done.

He went on to think about his fear of damaging his parents if he were angry with them. Just as his mother had been unable to break away from her mother, he felt afraid to break away from his. This led him to make an important connection: that, for him, being gay was like "throwing rocks at his mother": a way of attacking her without doing so openly. Homosexuality represented a rebellion against the world of mother, a way of being a "bad boy", whereas heterosexuality was a way of being nice to mother, being a "good boy". This seemed to explain the "intrusive" homosexual fantasies: at the point at which he imagines an aggressive penetration of a woman (still unconsciously equated in his mind with mother), his aggression is diverted into a homosexual fantasy.

Following this session, the defensive function of Simon's homosexual fantasy as a way of warding off aggressive feelings became much clearer. In this sense, these fantasies were not really "sexual" at all (hence the lack of erotic desire towards men), but a form of disguised aggression. Subsequently, we were able to reach a further understanding of the significance of this particular "penis in the mouth" fantasy. Here, again, this pointed to the way a relational configuration was finding expression in terms of sexual fantasy. Simon imagined that, for a woman, being penetrated meant being submissive, and felt intolerably guilty that he would therefore be dominating a woman by penetrating her. Thus, in his homosexual fantasies, he was reversing this wish as a kind of punishment—by putting *himself* in the submissive (masochistic) position of being penetrated by a man. Unravelling this eventually led him to be able to recognize his real sexual wishes towards women. His sense of himself, which he expressed in metaphorical terms as not being "cocky" and "lacking balls", was not so much a feeling that he was castrated but a guilty and fearful defence against what he might do if he did have a cock and balls, especially his wish for oral sex, which he saw as "wrong sex", not like the "nice sex" he imagined his parents having. His wish for a woman to "go down" on him, which he felt would be a way of dominating and forcing himself on her, expressed a way in which he could actually unite his sexual and aggressive wishes, along with a more passive infantile longing to be done to rather than to do. In the enactment of such a fantasy "instinctual satisfaction" is brought together with a complex series of object related fantasies that the sexual act expresses through a kind of embodied symbolism.

While it is true that the symbolic *meaning* of such sexual fantasies might remain unconscious, it is important to remember that the fantasy itself is conscious. So, rather than suggesting that the conscious fantasy is simply the equivalent of a pre-existing unconscious one, I would suggest that, as with Brian, the conscious fantasy is "dreamed up" as a kind of "image" that brings together and finds expression for a range of complex implicit meanings. In the enactment of these fantasies the body can be used in a symbolic way, with the emotional meanings strongly endorsed by the physical sexual excitement and satisfaction.

After a couple of years or so, Simon's fear of his potentially sadistic aggression towards women was sufficiently modified for him to enter into a relationship with a woman a few years older than himself. Although she seemed to be the dominant partner in the relationship whose control he attempted passively to resist, in the sexual relation-ship this was reversed. He was surprised and delighted to discover that she liked him to "fuck her rough", but began to feel disturbed when the sexual play extended not only to his forbidden desire for oral sex, but also to the extent of her inviting him to ejaculate in her face. Although he was excited by all this, he felt terribly guilty about abusing her.

I, too, wondered what this was all about until I began to get some understanding of the couple fit where each relied on the other not being what they seemed. His partner could enact her masochistic–submissive fantasies with a man who was clearly *not* going to dominate her, while for Simon there was the possibility of enacting his fantasies with a woman he could not destroy. The difficult question was whether he could manage to be genuinely strong and assertive in the relation-ship and whether, if he was, she would be willing to relinquish her own attempts to control him.

In the final phase of the therapy, Simon's homosexual anxieties entirely faded away as he became more aware of the hidden destructiveness of his passive–aggressive attitude to all aspects of his life. Only then was he able to appreciate the similarity between his lack of self-assertion at work, his struggle to become more psychologically separate from his mother and his girlfriend, and his ambivalent wish to terminate his therapy with me.

He also became able to make conscious use of symbolic images as a means of reflecting on his inner conflicts. On one occasion he referred to feeling tied up in knots, as if his mind was full of spaghetti. I reminded him of the image of the Gordian Knot that I had mentioned early on in the therapy, related to the impossibility of sorting out the tangle of his obsessional rumination. He had been struck by this at the time, and now, several years later, took up the idea with some enthusiasm, realizing that there was no point trying to untie the obses-sive knot—he just had to cut through it. "And, of course," I added, "you do know that this is an umbilical cord, don't you?" Although this must have been implicit in my original use of the image, my comment had for both of us a quality of being a new realization. Simon said that he knew I must have been going on about this for years, but only now had he finally understood what I meant. This realization helped him to feel more separate and less fearful of being controlled by his mother and his girlfriend. In turn, this enabled him to risk more commitment to his girlfriend and feel sufficiently assured in his masculine indepen-dence to terminate his therapy with me and embark on the path of adult life.

This symbolic interpretation brought us full-circle: whereas Simon had initially expressed his conflicts unconsciously through bodily fantasies, now he was able to reach a conscious understanding through the use of a bodily image as a fully elaborated symbol that might well be described as archetypal. In the same way that Klein used the breast or the penis as a symbol of something much more than the physical organ, so the image of the umbilical cord uses a bodily image to describe something much more than the physical situation. It grounds the symbol in the body (interpreting towards sexuality) while simultaneously referencing a multitude of analogous relational situations (interpreting away from sexuality). As with Brian, I would regard the emergence of this interpretation as a process of co-construction, aided by the rich store of symbolic images available to the analyst through his immersion in psychoanalytic discourse.

Pattern-making, links, and multiple meanings

I would not want to suggest that there is anything out of the ordinary about the clinical work I have described. It is more that I want to encourage an open and flexible way of thinking about what is going on in this kind of work. Neither biological instinct, unconscious phantasy, nor object relating can, in themselves, provide a sufficient basis for understanding sexuality. This is because what is being understood is a multi-faceted, complex way of being that the patient has developed and is living out. Our task is to imaginatively enter into the patient's way of thinking, especially through the metaphors he or she uses, and to elaborate this in terms of our own metaphorical and symbolic meanings. These meanings are continually "on the move", so that what is being defined exists only in the shape or pattern they describe between them. For Brian, there was a pattern that had to do with self-disgust in which "shit" has multiple meanings around which most of his life had been organized. And for Simon, there was a pattern that clustered around a conflict between domination and submission in relation to penetrating and being penetrated. These are examples of what Jung called *complexes*. Complexes are formed through the way each individual constructs meaning in the course of their individual life. Although there are numerous regularities that might justify the attribution of being archetypal, there is no single template to which these patterns can be reduced. The Oedipus complex is only one among many possible complexes, and to use it as the "bedrock", or core of all psychic development, requires us to shoe-horn enormous diversity into a single template.

Cross-modal perception

Rather than looking for a "one size fits all" pattern that underlies clinical diversity, it may be helpful to shift perspective to the meta-level of making meaning through the various patterns we might find. For there is now considerable experimental evidence to suggest that what is innate is not any particular pattern or organizing structure, but the pattern-making capacity itself; that is, the capacity to link two or more things together in a meaningful way. Stern (1985) describes the earliest form of this capacity in young infants as "cross-modal perception". For example, a blindfolded baby is given two dummies, one smooth and one with knobs on. She is "asked" which one she prefers by recording the rate of sucking on each. If she is then shown the two dummies, she will preferentially gaze and show interest in the previously preferred one. This is just one of hundreds of experiments showing that a pattern detected in one sense modality can be recognized in another: in this instance, what is felt in the mouth can be recognized by the eyes (Metzoff, 1981, quoted in Zinkin, 1991, p. 105). Stern comments:

> Infants appear to experience a world of perceptual unity, in which they can perceive amodal qualities from any form of human expressive behaviour, represent these qualities abstractly, and then transpose them to other modalities. [Stern, 1985, p. 51]

This seems to me to be at the root of how metaphor works, and how we build up a sense of meaning. Whatever can be represented and recognized in another modality is felt to have meaning; whatever cannot is felt to be meaningless. The meaning is not in one mode or another, but in the pattern that exists between them. We delight in expressing meaning in this cross-modal way, since it gives a sense of depth to the intricate patterns we perceive within and around us. Music shows this feature particularly well: how is it that abstract sound patterns can conjure up emotional states, represent the natural world, or indeed, express sexual excitement? (Neil Sedaka has described how he composed the "bridge" to his first hit song, "Oh, Carol" to express a feeling of lifting, then swooping down as if on the cusp of an orgasm. A more dramatic example of a musical "orgasm" can be heard in the powerful finale of "Voodoo Chile" by Jimi Hendrix [1968].)

The implications of all this is that "linking" is a primary activity of the mind that is only secondarily represented by symbolic images such as "the link between the parents" in the image of the parental intercourse. This way of thinking, in which bodily symbols are utilized for their expressive potential, acknowledges their emotional significance but suggests that this is being utilized for the purposes of effective symbolic representation rather than thinking of the image as the source of all that the symbol represents. This also gives us greater flexibility in thinking about our patient's material without attempting to find in it the pre-existing templates of psychoanalytic theory.

Biological determinism vs. *plastic sexuality*

There are also implications for how we understand sexual diversity. Young (2001) has described the way psychoanalytic ideas of sexuality have been "relocated" from biology to history. Once sexuality is decoupled from any fixed biological imperatives it takes its place "inside the symbolic order"; that is, it is dependent on the vagaries and contingencies of cultural meanings and, potentially, is infinitely variable. So, where Freud saw culture as fundamentally a sublimated expression of sexuality, modern cultural theories have taken the opposite view, arguing that culture and history inscribe their own meanings upon sexuality and the body. Freud's biological determinism has been eroded and transformed into what the sociologist Giddens calls "plastic sexuality", the idea that no one form of sexuality is more "normal" than another (Giddens, 1992).

Young is uncomfortable with this view because of his allegiance to the modern Kleinian conception of Oedipal development. He concludes that, "the problem posed by the Oedipal triangle cannot be evaded if one is to become a person capable of profound thoughts and concern for others" (Young, 2001, p. 31). Yet, this also means that something called "perversion" remains neurotic for orthodox Kleinians, since it appears to represent just such an evasion of the Oedipal triangle (*ibid.*, p. 32). I think the position I have outlined provides a solution to Young's dilemma. If we recognize that the Oedipal triangle is merely *symbolic* of the processes by which objectivity, concern, and respect for others are generated, we no longer need to tie these capacities to particular sexual practices.

It seems to me that the reality of sexuality is that it *is* highly plastic and has always been so, and that this is a feature of the enormous flexibility that humans have in relation to their instinctual base; so much so that it is virtually impossible to say just where and what that instinctual base is. The only thing that has changed is that people are generally less condemning and more open about their sexual practices than before. It is interesting, for example, that Simon could recognize the psychological nature of his problems precisely because, intellectually and morally, he regarded both homosexuality and oral sex as *normal*.

All sexuality is a form of "enactment"—the issue is the difference between enactments that are concrete and shut down meaning and those that allow for different meanings and have the quality of playfulness that is characteristic of creative, living metaphors. Where meaning is fixed and concrete, and there is a lack of capacity to think metaphorically and symbolically, sexuality is also likely to be fixed and rigid. This may create fixed inhibitions, as with Brian and Simon, or it may create very fixed and compulsive patterns of sexual behaviour.

This view does not mean that the body is merely an endlessly malleable signifier on which we might write whatever metaphorical meanings we choose. To say that the meaning of sexuality is inevitably historical and cultural is not to say that sexuality itself is nothing but cultural and historical. Sexuality *is* a biological force, an instinctual imperative, yet it can only be *accessed* via the cultural meanings with which it is imbued. We create meaning through processes analogous to, and perhaps derived from, cross-modal linking. These include instinctual responses as one mode among many. The sexual body is an inherent force in psychic life, but it is inextricable from the meanings by which we elaborate it and it enlivens us. The biological aspect of sexuality is itself part of the "shape" or pattern of its meaning. This view accords with Jung's idea of a transcendent function in the psyche that constantly works at producing symbols that unite the opposites and so promote individuation. Meaning is not reducible to any one thing, but is rather an emergent property of the coming together of two (or more) things. While this may be represented by "the baby produced by parental intercourse", this is only because the parental intercourse has the same shape and is another example of the same pattern. What, if anything, this pattern fundamentally represents, is unfathomable.

References

Benjamin, J. (1990). *The Bonds of Love. Psychoanalysis, Feminism and the Problem of Domination.* London: Virago.

Bion, W. R. (1959). Attacks on linking. In: *Second Thoughts.* London: Heinemann, 1967.

Boston Change Process Study Group. (2007). The foundational level of psychodynamic meaning: implicit process in relation to conflict, defense and the dynamic unconscious. *International Journal of Psychoanalysis, 88*(4): 843–860.

Britton, R. (1989). The missing link: parental sexuality in the Oedipus complex. In: J. Steiner (Ed.), *The Oedipus Complex Today: Clinical Implications* (pp. 83–101). London: Karnac.

Britton, R. (1992). The Oedipus situation and the depressive position. In: R. Anderson (Ed.), *Clinical Lectures on Klein and Bion* (pp. 34–45). London: Routledge.

Budd, S. (2001). No sex please—we're British. In: C. Harding (Ed.), *Sexuality: Psychoanalytic Perspectives* (pp. 52–68). Hove: Brunner-Routledge.

Carvalho, R. (2003). Analytical psychology and homosexual orientation. A comment on Denman. In: R. Withers (Ed.), *Controversies in Analytical Psychology* (pp. 171–178). London: Routledge.

Colman, W. (2005). Sexual metaphor and the language of unconscious fantasy. *Journal of Analytical Psychology, 50*(5): 641–660.

Colman, W. (2007). Symbolic conceptions: the idea of the third. *Journal of Analytical Psychology, 52*(5): 565–583.

Giddens, A. (1992). *The Transformations of Intimacy: Sexuality, Love and Eroticism in Modern Societies.* Cambridge: Polity Press.

Grier, F. (2001). No sex couples, catastrophic change and the primal scene. *British Journal of Psychotherapy, 17*(4): 474–488.

Hendrix, J. (1968). *Electric Ladyland*. Track Records. Re-mastered CD: MCA Records, 1997.

Isaacs, S. (1952). The nature and function of phantasy. In: M. Klein, P. Heiman, S. Isaacs, & J. Riviere (Eds.), *Developments in Psychoanalysis*. London: Hogarth.

Jones, E. (1916). The theory of symbolism. In: *Papers on Psychoanalysis*. London: Balliere, Tindall & Cox, 1938.

Jung, C. G. (1954) [1925]. Marriage as a psychological relationship. *C.W., 17*: 324–345, R. F. C. Hull (Trans.). London: Routledge and Kegan Paul.

Meltzer, D. (1966). The relation of anal masturbation to projective identification. *International Journal of Psycho-Analysis, 47*: 335–342. Also in: E. Bott Spillius (Ed.), *Melanie Klein Today: Developments in Theory and Practice*, Volume 1 (pp. 102–116). London: Routledge, 1988.

Ogden, T. (1994). The analytic third: working with intersubjective clinical facts. In: *Subjects of Analysis*. London: Karnac.

Parsons, M. (2000). Sexuality and perversion a hundred years on: discovering what Freud discovered. *International Journal of Psycho-Analysis, 81*: 37–49.

Searles, H. (1959). Oedipal love in the counter-transference. In: *Collected Papers on Schizophrenia and Related Subjects*. London: Maresfield Library, 1986.

Stern, D. (1985). *The Interpersonal World of the Infant*. New York: Basic Books.

Young, R. M. (2001). Locating and relocating psychoanalytic ideas of sexuality. In: C. Harding (Ed.), *Sexuality. Psychoanalytic Perspectives* (pp. 18–34). Hove: Brunner-Routledge.

Zinkin, L. (1991). The Klein connection in the London School: the search for origins. *Journal of Analytical Psychology, 36*(1): 37–61.

CHAPTER THREE

Lively and deathly intercourse

Francis Grier

The question I am proposing to address in this chapter is one that often perplexes couple psychotherapists: what is going on when a couple tells us that their therapy is definitely helping, that they are feeling better and relating better, but the only problem is they are not having sex? What do we make of that? How should we respond?

"Not having sex" might not itself be put forward as a problem. A couple might pretend that it is not that important to them, and that other things matter more, or that it is a sacrifice worth making for everything else. But, even in such cases, it is unlikely that the therapist will regard their situation as unproblematic. Not that it is my contention that couples should forever be busily having sex and that there is something definitely amiss if they are not. That would be to apply a very crude measurement of the health of the relationship, one that sophisticated couples would immediately see through and look down on, and that would soon become very persecuting both to the couple and to the therapist. After all, there is general agreement that a sign of maturity is the capacity to tolerate frustration and to refrain from precipitate action. Being prepared not to have sex and to tolerate the accompanying frustration can be a mark of genuine maturity. In any couple's life together, fate will demand this of each of them at different times.

So, one of the couple therapist's tasks is to make a judgement as to whether the current situation does or does not signal something problematic. In this area of considering the place of sex in the couple's relationship, therapists are constantly being pushed and pulled unconsciously, both by their own unresolved unconscious conflicts and by their being affected by the couple's projections. None of us is ever quite sorted out in the area of sex, and it is perhaps both a torment and a comfort to realize that we never shall be, that an ultimate resolution is impossible, and that never fully solving this dilemma is part of what makes us human and alive rather than god-like and dead. It follows that this central area of our work with couples is an area we can never quite adequately deal with. This obviously makes for real difficulties: we can react by being over-confident, reaching towards an omnipotent defence, denying our fallibility and our own anxious unresolved conflicts, or we can respond by becoming too humble, defensively giving up the challenge, taking on the self-comforting role of comforting our patients through emphasizing our mutual impotence, but actually letting them down by not risking giving them enough. It is really quite hard to know one's limitations, to be in touch with one's anxieties, and also to know and value one's substantial experience and risk putting this to use in the service of the couples one is treating.

These introductory points mark how I wish to tackle the subject of sex: by thinking not only about the intercourse between the partners comprising the couple but also, and centrally, considering the interpersonal dynamics of the therapy room, making comparisons with the couple's stated sexual situation and reflecting on the quality of the psychological intercourse between couple and therapist.

In a previous paper (Grier, 2005), I set out some thoughts about the same presenting problem, exploring material from the perspective of three theories: the Oedipus complex, the primal scene, and catastrophic change. Here, I propose to extend this exploration further, using Bion's (1958) theory of linking, Joseph's (1989) use of that theory, and Glasser's (1979) theory of the core complex. Bion's theory gives us a solid but intricate theoretical framework; Joseph's subtle and flexible application and development of it helps Bion's abstract theory to come alive, making it of immense clinical value;

Glasser's theory helps us to understand why some links set off intense anxieties, in their turn giving rise to steely defences.

Bion's theory of linking is of central relevance to couple work because it is all about subjects and objects linking up with each other, or not, and about the quality of these links. These are fundamental couple issues. In his lexicon, L stands for a loving link, H for a hating link, and K for a link of knowledge. The K link is as fundamental as the other two: it is Bion's development of what Freud (1916–1917) and Klein (1930) referred to as an "epistemological instinct", and it expresses his insight that it is as fundamental for the mind to seek Truth and Knowledge, if it is to be healthy and grow, as it is for the body to seek food. And the knowledge in question is emotional knowledge, knowledge gleaned from L and H.

I find it a useful axiom to consider that if a couple's relationship is to be healthy, to be vital and growing, it needs to be functioning on all three of these cylinders. The partners need not only to love and hate each other, but they must also consciously know that they are loving and hating. They must be thinking about themselves and each other in the light of these emotional experiences, with thoughts rising spontaneously and organically. For example, what is it about their partner that evokes love or hate, why did *this* set of circumstances trigger off a loving or hating response and not *that* train of events, why *this* week and not *last* week . . . and so on. These lively questionings are symptomatic of a healthy, searching-for-truth, K link. Partners that can bear to ask fundamental questions of themselves and of each other, who can link up and join forces in thinking about what the answers might be, have a good K link and are likely to be in good shape psychologically. They are also unlikely to be our patients and unlikely to have a serious sexual problem. We, as therapists, might hope for such outcomes as the result of our couple therapies.

The therapist often symbolizes the K function through reflecting on the experiences of the couple and getting to know them and him/herself in relation to them. Interpretation is the tool whereby the therapist hands his or her thoughts to the couple. If their thirst for knowledge is activated, the couple will take in not only the content of the interpretation, but also the therapist's interested and curious attitude, and the process and emotional quality of his or her thinking. It is gratifying when the couple start to make this role their own, and interest the therapist in their insightful reflections about an experience they have recently undergone, perhaps in the previous few minutes of a session, or one that has gone before, and one that involves the therapist. Then it is not hearsay, the experience is current. As the therapist, one is involved oneself, and one can really test the quality of the couple's thoughts and compare them with one's own, and *vice versa*.

It is challenging that Bion designated H (hate) as a *healthy* link, and to learn that what he regarded as hostile to emotional health was not hate but the active *unlinking* that occurs in the negative functions he called −L, −H and −K. What he emphasizes here is the *anti-link*. Often a masquerade is involved. −L and −K can appear masquerading as love and knowledge: the couple, for example, who present *as if* they love each other, but one senses how terribly cut off from each other they are, and how false their loving talk is; or the couple who talk *as if* they have understood something, *as if* they know each other, but one senses how false this appearance is.

It is said that George Bernard Shaw opined, "If you hit your child, be sure that you hit him in anger." I think the words attributed to Shaw describe a positive H link, which, precisely because the anger is hot and vital, is something that might be borne by both child and parent through its emotional honesty, particularly if it is followed up not by defensive denial, but by reflection that is driven by K. If that happens, each party knows the other better, knows the relationship better, and might come to know themselves better. This is different from the situation in which a child gets punished, not in hot anger, but in an emotional atmosphere in which any warmth or heat is denied, subtracting from that which links parent and child. Here, cold, unlinked, depersonalized hatred prevails instead. A famous example would be Brontë's heroine, Jane Eyre, who, when she was shut up in solitary confinement in the Red Room as a young child was told by Bessie (the nurse), "What we tell you is for your own good . . .", Miss Abbot (the maid) adding "Besides, God will punish her: He might strike her dead . . . if you don't repent, something bad might be permitted to come down the chimney and fetch you away" (Brontë, 1847). This emotional quality can be discerned in couples where the partners hate each other, not hotly, but in a cold, dissociated way.

Bion's theoretical framework makes it possible to examine the quality of couple relationships, and couple–therapist relationships, using these six categories. Fundamentally, there are two, rather than six, categories: positive and negative links (either the links are vital, vibrant, with some "heat" [+]; or they are sluggish, inimical to vitality, and cold [−]). It is not as simple as to say that the minus links should not be there, but only the plus links. Bion's overall frame of reference is one that encompasses the death instinct as well as the life instinct, so his perspective is that both sides will always, in the nature of things, be there. However, what often seems to make a sizeable clinical difference is for the therapist to get *interested* in the emotional links (K), whether the links are − or +, and to describe and interpret them to the couple. I would assert that this, in fact, is our most potent therapeutic tool.

This view is widely held in the field of individual psychoanalysis. Joseph (1989) has described the putting into practice of following the moment-to-moment movement of a session. The focus is always on the emotion driving the movement, whether it derives from love, hate, and a desire for knowledge, or from a drive to replace love with an artifice, hate with a cold desire to punish sadistically, and knowledge with a manipulative and cynical masquerade of understanding.

One of the L, H, or K categories often presents particular difficulties for a particular couple: perhaps it causes too much pain, or provokes too much guilt, or resentment, or jealousy, or envy, or sadism, or excitement. As a result, the couple outlaws this link, inescapably inserting its negative in its place. At the very least, this puts the couple system at risk, out of a healthy balance. If this process continues with intensity, or over a long period of time, or both, the other positive links inevitably also get undermined and contaminated.

It is perhaps to be expected that the H link will often cause the most obvious problems. Hating can evoke guilt and punishment, and it is so often experienced as unpleasant to hate or be hated that it leads to the experience being rationalized away. Hatred tends to evoke hatred in return, which is also unpleasant. There are, of course, innumerable varieties of hatred, such as the cold superego hatred that often lies behind righteous indignation (exemplified in the vignette from *Jane Eyre* quoted above), in which the identification with the superego and the "legalized" hatred of another person may gratify one's sadism as well as defending oneself from being the target of one's own cruel superego by projecting that role on to someone else. On the other hand, if one really loves one's object, it is always, at some level, hugely troubling to feel intense hatred for that same object (Klein, 1935). So, we tend not to be surprised when couples present their inability to hate each other, something they will often have a partial insight into, perhaps describing themselves as "having difficulty with anger". But, when hate cannot be allowed, −H invariably takes its place. Indeed, couples with insight often then know that something malign, cold, punishing, and impersonal has entered into the core of their relationship, spoiling it from within.

I saw such a couple, who had massive problems with H but who demonstrated in fairly equal quantities K and −K. Considering how much they outlawed H, their −K comes as no surprise. But they were impressively clinging on to K, showing a sincere desire really to know and understand, to ask each other and me awkward questions, which seemed very much on the side of linking and life. I could believe them easily when they said they knew they still loved each other, but were worried that they were pulling apart, getting remote from each other, feeling anxious that their genuine love for each other was under threat.

In one session, the wife was imploring the husband to spend more time with her, begging him to put time aside for her as he did with the children and his work, pinning him down with passionate intensity. She spoke about how humiliated she felt having to ask like this. The temperature rose steeply: it was painful to watch and be close to this scene. She was able to say how angry she was with him for not giving her what she felt she needed. She said she normally felt inhibited from showing her anger, because she feared he might just walk away.

In response, her husband listened carefully and patiently, giving her an encouraging smile every now and then, saying "Mmm . . ." empathically at various moments. When she had finished he said he had really heard her, thought she had a point, and he would see what he could do.

I was not surprised when the wife backed off, clearly disappointed and defeated. I probed the husband, asking him what his actual experience had been while his wife had been tearfully addressing, not to say haranguing, him. He was able to reply, with an anxious glance at his wife, that he had felt completely out of his depth, quite unable to respond to her. He did not know how to. Then he said it felt just like being with his mother, who had regularly "lost it" with her husband and the children. Nobody knew how to handle her, but his father had managed by just switching off, not trying to shut her up, learning that nothing he could offer would be acceptable, and letting his wife's entreaties and imprecations flow off him like water off a duck's back. He said he supposed he had learnt to be like his father.

The wife rallied, and said that her experience had been like being with her mother, who never responded personally in the way she needed her to when she was angry or distressed, but always with a quasi-professional therapist's attitude.

Things then quietened down. It was quite tempting to leave it there, but I sensed that there were other powerful elements that had remained unexpressed. I thought that, on her part, the wife had been not merely angry, but in a rage with her husband. She had pinned him down, knowing that he could not escape, that he would be humiliated, particularly in front of me as witness, and shown up as emotionally incapable. I thought she had whipped things up as much as possible, and got herself quite excited. I did not think this side of her wanted the matter to be resolved, but was invested in repeating this punishing attack over and over again, even if, perhaps especially if, it involved her own humiliation. I also thought her husband had been treating her with cruelty and contempt, and that what might have started as a schizoid defence against being overpowered by extreme emotion had developed a life of its own in which he now derived sadistic pleasure from knowing that the more impassive and coolly unaffected he was, the more his wife would whip herself up in a frenzied but futile attack, making a humiliating spectacle of herself.

What should I do with these observations and intuitions about this likeable couple? I did not know how to tone them down; in fact, I thought that if I did they would lose their veracity, and yet I did not know if the couple could stand hearing them, or, conversely, whether they might get excited by hearing them. I was quite sure that I was intentionally involved by each party in their interaction with the other. Each had me there as a witness to the awfulness of the other. But there was something additional, something tending to the perverse. I thought that I was being tricked in a similar way by each of them. Under the guise of being appealed to for sympathy by the wife, I think she thought that I, too, would derive sadistic pleasure in identifying with her. I think this was meant to excite me and undermine my capacities for concern and analytic thought. Similarly, I think the husband, underneath his desire that I should witness how badly his wife nagged him, was appealing to me, man to man, to enjoy the spectacle of how degrading he was being to the woman, relating to her with an insouciance and a cynical caricature of the attention she actually craved, which was bound to drive her to demean herself even more. I think I was expected to derive anxious, guilty pleasure from this, and in the process lose my analytic balance. I also thought his impassive stance towards his wife was a provocative identification with me and a caricature of my own analytic attitude—provocative, that is, both to me and his wife.

Initially, I did not have the courage to voice these observations and intuitions. Instead, I expressed my concern and compassion for each of them. It was amazing how quickly an emotionally false situation developed, with us all voicing rather predictable expressions of concern. The couple started to claim that they supposed they might feel better as a result of at least having this out in the therapy, and tried to convince each other and me that this would be the case in flat voices and shallow tones that conveyed just the opposite. I think we were all caught up and colluding in a "minus" situation: none of the real H (or −H) links was being expressed or interpreted. As a result, the L and K links were becoming more and more false, more and more −L and −K.

So I then did say that I thought they might be feeling that the present, apparently friendly atmosphere was in fact artificial and misleading, and that I might be unable—perhaps because too anxious—to interpret what had just been played out, in which case I would be in the same boat as them and of no use to them. The couple looked anxious, but interested. I started to make some interpretations along the lines I have laid out above, stressing not only their mutual hatred but also their attempt to disguise it, as well as how each involved me in their attack on the other. There was a rather tense silence, and then the husband said, "Well, that's cleared the air then! I had no idea I had it in me to be doing such things." She said, "And I always thought I was such a nice girl! But I can believe it of *you*." At which they both laughed, but then engaged seriously with the interpretations. They left the session much more warmly than usual, and I remember wondering whether they might go away and make love. When they returned the next week they told me that they had done just that, for the first time in months.

This is an example of how a couple can begin to own their hatred through becoming interested in how they are disowning and splitting off this crucial dimension of their relationship. To their intense surprise and relief, the result was not catastrophe, but a freeing of their capacity to love and get to know each other, which led spontaneously to their recovering sexual links in the marriage. Knowledge about H was engaged with, and this increased their desire for intellectual, emotional, and sexual intercourse.

However, the example is not meant to be representative with regard to how quickly one might expect a couple to respond. This particular couple was clearly just ready for the interpretation of their collusive destructiveness. When the therapist looked as though he was not up to making it, they experienced disappointment and depression, but, when he eventually did his job, they could quickly own what he was showing them. They had also managed to create an atmosphere where there was more or less the right amount of difficulty for the therapist. Strachey (1934) describes in a famous paper how difficult emotionally it is for an analyst to make a mutative interpretation, and how easy it is to shy away from it, or to dilute it. I think his description also implies that, for an interpretation to be effective, there often needs to be a tension in the analyst's mind, which he has to dare to risk confronting in order to make the interpretation. This reflects the tension and the risks the couple have to face if they are similarly to try to engage with their true feelings and actions towards each other. If a therapist makes confrontational interpretations too easily, it suggests he is in an unlinked, −K state of mind, and possibly acting from −H, a split-off and disowned hatred towards the couple, perhaps in projection from his own internal parental couple. This, then, will be the figure the therapist invites the couple to introject: an internal object that would clearly make their problems worse.

However, the norm is for one's first interpretations of a couple's unconscious destructive side to meet with rejection. In time, the partners might begin apparently to accept such interpretations, but only in an intellectualized, quasi-rational mode. In other words, one might commonly enough reach a −K agreement. The therapist has to bear being alone with his real, as opposed to intellectualized, insight for some time—maybe months, sometimes years. And it is unlikely, even with a couple ripe for insight such as in my example, that a once-off interpretation will right things for ever. Joseph (1989) has shown clearly the constancy of the regressive pull towards re-establishing defences in the service of restoring psychic equilibrium in response to movements towards development.

This is a further clinical challenge. It is so natural for therapists to be on the side of health, wanting a cure for the couple, that it can be very difficult, after a positive development such as the one I have described, for the therapist to step back and become again a research scientist, as it were, whose primary concern and interest is to observe and analyse the couple, whatever they do, without especially favouring movement in one direction rather than another. In other words, when the inevitable regressive reaction occurs, and with it the tendency to re-establish the couple's defensive system, one emotional task for the therapist is to be alive to feelings of disappointment and defeat, while becoming interested in just how, at this particular time, and with this particular couple, valuable work can be undone. I have found that, if and when I am able to cultivate this kind of attitude (in which I am just as interested to analyse how my good work is to be undone and defeated as in how it is to be accepted positively), couples gradually begin to be fascinated themselves by this oscillation and not just to be depressed by it, to tolerate better their regressions, and more quickly become ready to risk moving developmentally again.

All this can be reflected in the couple's reported sexual activity. With the couple in my example, who were preponderantly non-perverse and whose basic attitude was one of hope and co-operation, sex unsurprisingly tended to occur when they were in a developmental phase, and was inhibited when they regressed and moved towards defensive or perverse solutions. For such couples, sex is very much bound up with being able to love freely, to hate openly, and actively to inhabit the process of getting to know each other. The opposite can happen with couples who are much more conflicted about loving. They can feel that when development threatens they become more, not less, anxious. Such couples can often present as feeling most free to have sex when things are at their least loving between them.

Rather schematically, I have suggested that the couple I had been examining had a basic problem with H. But they had also what one might rather crudely think of as a basic stash of L and a lively leaning towards K, so that, once their H was interpreted, it could begin to be integrated with their L and K relatively smoothly. But what of couples whose basic problem is not with H, which they may be quite confident about feeling and expressing, but with L? And what does it mean to have a basic conflict around L? Let me approach this question through an illustration.

A supervisee of mine had an individual patient who never missed sessions, arrived on time, and who regularly appeared glad to see her. Although middle-aged, he usually bounced into her room like a teenager, confident of being in a good place, with someone who would listen to him, put everything down, and attend just to him. But then an anomaly occurred. He would tell his therapist he had nothing to say and ask why he needed to come. He often said that he thought he had nothing wrong with him, no serious problems, but then went on, nevertheless, to bring a current problem.

From then on, whatever his therapist did was wrong. If she made a transference interpretation she would be severely criticized for thinking that what her patient said had to do with her; this, in his view, only demonstrated her narrow-minded self-centredness. Or, if she made other kinds of interpretation, he would disagree violently, conveying, almost on principle, that his therapist was wrong and that he should be the supreme arbiter of what was correct or incorrect understanding. His therapist was not permitted to have an insight regarding her patient that he did not have himself. The idea that she might think she could have such an insight, and that she might think she could also make judgements herself about the quality and correctness of her interpretations, furthered the patient's view that his therapist was arrogant and narrow-minded, insisting on being the powerful one and on oppressing him. If an interpretation was accepted, the therapist was informed that it was only correct because it was so generalized and vague as to be right for anyone at any time, but its generality made it meaningless so it was effectively rebutted, too. While being open to receiving supervision from one's patients is one thing, this went far further than that. The aim was not actually to put the therapist right, collaboratively, in the service of the analysis, but to tread the therapist down and make her so uncertain about the quality of her own thoughts that she should cease to be able to function effectively and back right off. At the same time, these constant criticisms seemed on the verge of being flirtatious and teasing, although they would often tip into really serious hostility.

The relationship the patient set up in the transference with his therapist demonstrates one variety of the sort of defensive couple relationship a person very troubled by the L link might seek out. It was not that this man did not have an L link; his non-verbal behaviour at the start of sessions showed very clearly the strength and positive quality of his attachment. Yet, what he shoved in his therapist's face all the time was a mightily strong H component, which, other than verbally, utterly denied the L. His K was quite false: in fact, he seemed largely in the grip of −K. His reasoning, and his view of himself and his therapist, proved tenacious, though in his therapist's judgement these were no more than rationalizations. The therapist came to suspect that they were not meant to be *reasonable* statements, but provocative assertions designed to defend the patient from the perils of a loving link by attacking and destabilizing his object. He was not really in control of this defence, so he often left the sessions seduced by himself, as it were, into really believing the truth of his own tirade of hate, losing touch with the fact that it was defensive and artificial. In supervision, we sensed that these harangues were not quite emotionally truthful, consisting not only of denial, but also of an erotic teasing designed both to give expression to sexual feelings as well as to deny them. However, his attempts at destabilizing his object were often effective enough to get under the therapist's skin, so that, understandably, she would often lose contact with her own "K", her thoughtful self, and simply feel exasperated with him, full of doubts about the worth of her analytic self.

I considered that this patient suffered from what Glasser (1979) called the *core complex*. I think he was terrified of a close, intimate relationship with his primary object, fearing that if he were to let his hunger and need push him too close, the object might swallow him up, or that his desire would drive him to push so hard to get into the object that he would end up actually inside it, suffocated, his identity threatened by annihilation in the fusion. Moreover, I think he feared that if he were to allow himself nakedly to show his intense need and desire for the object, the object, instead of responding with love, would turn away and reject him, or, worse still, would misleadingly turn towards him, responding to his desire for a total relationship only with sex and not with love. I think he particularly feared this form of rejection, which had its roots in what he felt had been his experience of a depressed mother who had managed to look after him physically while her mind was elsewhere, which felt to him like rejection. This, I think, is what L and its associated anxieties meant to this man.

It appeared that he then mounted a defence of exploiting his hatred, his H link, for this tantalizing and rejecting object, effectively identifying with it and trying to reverse the relationship so that his object would be driven into the exposed and vulnerable role. When he exaggerated his hatred for this rejecting object, it no longer remained emotionally true: his style of relating began to transform into something like *playing* at H, exploiting H to mock and humiliate the object. He had transformed his genuine H, which still left him needy and vulnerable, into −H, which was felt to afford him an invulnerable shield (like the impassivity of the husband in my previous example). He also tried to get a −L link going with his object: from time to time he tried to get his therapist to be nice to him, but he was too emotionally honest to be able to deceive himself convincingly about this. The area that caused him almost phobic anxiety was not H, but L, so that he could hardly tolerate bringing the K link to bear on his L difficulties. Only for an instant, sometimes in sessions, could he bear to think about the intensity of his hunger to be loved, analytically, by his therapist, and for her to accept his love, and how he exploited his hatred in order to deny and hide from himself the intensity of his love and his need.

This patient had no regular sexual partner, a fact that deeply frustrated him. But from time to time things became almost unbearably intense in the therapy: his non-verbal attachment intensified, his accompanying verbal vilifications became seriously venomous, and his anxiety escalated. He would then go off and have sex with a particular woman "friend" whom he knew would treat him cruelly, in that she would appear to show him in their love-making that she felt very strongly and tenderly towards him, but would act afterwards as though nothing meaningful had occurred, repudiating any link that he might believe had arisen between them. This reflected his analytic experience, just as his analytic experience reflected his external and sexual life.

Perversity entered the picture when he began to look forward to these sporadic sexual encounters, deriving a conscious, masochistic gratification from his own hurt and a (denied) sadistic thrill from taunting his therapist with his exploits. I think his therapist was punished, and was meant to feel as impotent, anxious, and guilty as possible about what he was doing. She was also pushed away from her analytic role and towards becoming either a persecuting superego or a moral adviser. The whole gamut of −L, −H and −K were now operating together, the death-instinct links defeating the life-instinct links of L, H, and K. This, moreover, was a clear example of something *actively* deadly. It was not a case of a lack of life-instinct links. Instead, something sado-masochistically perverse was attacking the life-giving links and seducing the personality with the promise of something exciting, pleasurably dangerous and destructive, both to its object and to itself. Something that might have started as a defence was beginning to develop an exciting life of its own, and was threatening to become the dominant principle of the personality.

Being in therapy was clearly experienced intensely sexually by this patient. His acting out discharged some of his sexual tension, but it also intentionally, if unconsciously, prevented him from seeking out a true substitute object for the therapist, a woman he could really risk loving with the intensity of the feelings he had for his therapist. In a sense his perverse solution kept the Oedipal situation intact, in that he kept returning to the analytic mother with all his frustrated feelings and desires. The analytic parent was also, I think, meant to appreciate how "faithful" her "son" actually remained, especially to "her". The patient went through a period that, to him, felt endless, in which he feared he would never find a mate, particularly, I think, because he feared unconsciously that through using and developing the defensive and destructive mechanisms described he had spoilt his capacity to love, and, even more fundamentally, his own loveableness. After a sustained period of working through these serious and chronic difficulties, the patient began to acquire genuine insight into his defensive and destructive behaviours. He could then begin to risk placing much greater trust in his therapist. The therapist and I were pleased and relieved when, in due course, the patient felt able to search out and link up with a quite different kind of partner, whom he now seemed enabled to trust and love and, on occasion, to hate in a much less defensive and more straightforward manner.

To end, I will re-emphasize how the deadly links, the minus links, are more than just an absence of positive, vital links. A dream, of a different patient, showed this very pithily. She was a profoundly unlinked-up person, who had systematically deprived herself of almost anything that might bring her joy or fulfilment. She had misused her talents (which she undoubtedly possessed), was very lonely, was judged by herself and others to be a failure in life, and was disliked and shunned by most people who got to know her. Nevertheless, she usually acted and spoke as if she were emotionally very rich, looking down compassionately on the rest of us. In the analysis she began to take on board what she had been realizing intellectually for some time: that, in contrast to this pathetic illusion, her actual position was a parlous one, and, if she were to have any hope of turning her life around and moving towards real happiness before her time ran out, she had better recognize how very little happiness or achievement she actually had, and how her superior view of herself was a grandiosely inflated illusion to which she was addicted.

This is her dream.

> She was in a small town where there was a good take-away restaurant. It gave her a warm feeling that there was this lovely take-away where you could get really good meals and they made you feel fine. But the odd thing was that a couple had been attacking it, throwing stones at its front and smashing windows. She could not think why they would want to do that, but she wanted to find out. Later there was to be a meeting with a man who was going to tell her something about who had been smashing up the take-away, and why.

I thought the dream expressed beautifully how "taking away", the minus link, is not just felt to be an absence of a positive link, which one might think would leave one hungry and deprived. The perverse side of human nature represents it as offering good food. It is felt to be substantial in its own right, not a nothing. It was not only I who had been throwing stones at this edifice. In the analysis, she had begun to join me, forming a couple, no longer colluding in the view that this was a lovely structure to be cherished, but unmasking it as a dangerously destructive and deceitful masquerade that actually delivered very bad food and provided a rotten foundation to her illusion of being so rich and superior.

The dream illustrates how this subtracting of the vital connection, even if initially defensive and motivated by anxiety, can build up a life of its own, playing into the hands of something actively deadly and perverse. It was a part of her deadened internal situation, dominated by −L, −H, and −K, that my patient had had virtually no sexual feelings or contact over several years, that she had not been able to experience this as a loss or deprivation, and that her previous sexual history had been exclusively perverse. The dream also illustrated my patient's sense of there being a couple joining forces to try to dismantle the idealized, destructive system. I think this couple represents, at a deep level, a loving, parental couple who want the best for their child, hate seeing her feed herself with deceitful, trashy food, and are prepared to go into battle on her behalf. They are also a sexual couple, who come together in love for their child, rather than in a perverse, narcissistic, and barren intercourse. They represent the emergence in my patient of L (the couple's love for her), H (their hatred of the perverse "take-away"), and K (their insight into the true nature of the "take-away").

The mobilization of this fundamentally good and loving (and hating and insightful) internal couple is of elemental relevance for our work with couples and individuals. If and when such an internal couple emerges, one of the areas partners can then feel freer and bolder to approach is the sexual dimension of their relationship. No sex, withdrawing sex, or perverse sex gradually ceases to be the superior strategy and best defence. A realistic sense of deprivation, loss, and hunger grows in its place, and the partners who comprise the couple can begin to approach each other with a more genuine sense of their incompleteness, need, and desire. It is not that the −L, −H, and −K links disappear; they are part of our nature and here to stay. But the more we can bear to know, face, and think about them, using K, the more L, H, and K links can come into the ascendant. This can only be good news for all aspects of the couple, the sexual dimension very much included, and for partners who wish to have as full an intercourse with each other as possible.

References

Bion, W. (1958). Attacks on linking. *International Journal of Psycho-Analysis, 40*: 308–315.

Brontë, C. (1847). *Jane Eyre*. London: Smith, Elder.

Freud, S. (1916–1917). The development of the libido and the sexual organizations. *Introductory Lectures on Psycho-Analysis, S.E., 15–16*: 320–338) London: Hogarth.

Glasser, M. (1979). Some aspects of the role of aggression in the perversions. In: I. Rosen, (Ed.) *Sexual Deviation* (2nd edn) (pp. 278–305). Oxford: Oxford University Press (2nd edn).

Grier, F. (2005). No sex couples, catastrophic change, and the primal scene. In: F. Grier (Ed.), *Oedipus and the Couple* (pp. 201–220). London: Karnac.

Joseph, B. (1989). *Psychic Equilibrium and Psychic Change*. London: Routledge.

Klein, M. (1930). The importance of symbol-formation in the development of the ego. In: *Love, Guilt and Reparation*. London: Hogarth, 1975.

Klein, M. (1935). A contribution to the psychogenesis of manic-depressive states. In: *Love, Guilt and Reparation*. London: Hogarth, 1975.

Strachey, J. (1934). The nature of the therapeutic action of psychoanalysis. *International Journal of Psycho-Analysis, 15*: 127–159.

CHAPTER FOUR

Separated attachments and sexual aliveness

Susie Orbach

W e meet couples in difficulty. These were not always couples in difficulty, but couples who were once sexually vibrant, engaged, enthusiastic, partners who were eager to be closer and closer and to find themselves through their attachment to one another.

The exquisite tuning that allowed the individuals in a couple to sense each other's strengths is matched by an equally exquisite sensitivity to the other's attachment patterns. In getting to know one another, each person finds out about past loved ones, the nature of their previous relationships, and what went wrong and what went right. Quite unselfconsciously they are each acquiring the emotional information that will, in part, enable them to solidify their choice of life partner. They listen carefully to hear what was problematic about the previous partner as they build knowledge about attachment patterns, defences, how disappointment or betrayal are or have been dealt with, as well, of course, as discovering the nature of the attachment bonds in each of the individual familial relationships.

Love is much about finding psychological fits: fits that work and enhance each individual, and fits—particularly the fits we encounter as couple psychotherapists—that enact and confirm some of the most unwanted sense of selves that make relationships sites of disappointment. People seek loving partnerships, but the click of connection can reside in the unconscious patterns of relating experienced in one's first attachments now echoed in the couple relationship. To put this starkly, for those couples we encounter whose relationship has turned violent, we often discover an equation of love and attachment linked with an ambience of violence in the early parent–child relationship. Violence, we come to understand for those individuals, can feel as though it belongs, as though it is almost an essential feature of the attachment. The relationship might even be experienced as lacking intensity without it. Similarly, children who grow up in apparently sexless marriages can feel there is something "right" at the feeling level of that emotional tableau. They do not, in the marrow of who they experience themselves to be, easily imagine themselves to be in a sustaining sexual relationship. They might be in one, but this can challenge the internal image of relationship that permeates their sense of self, and it takes a long time for new experience to become as emotionally compelling as the states of being that have been absorbed from early life.

For me, attachment is a descriptive, pictorial category, and only schematically a diagnostic one. What I mean by this is that in my mind I have a geometrical picture of the distance or lack of distance between couples, and a three dimensional dynamic picture of their attachment patterns. This kind of geometric attachment picture enters into my thinking in couple work when I am trying to understand the space between the individuals in the couple, their capacity to share, their individual and joint ability to desire, the disposition of the dependency needs between the two people and the intensity of, or absence of the search for, recognition from the other, and the attachment features of the relationship the couple jointly creates.

There are three different attachment schemas at work: that of each individual and that of the entity—the couple relationship, the marriage, the partnership—they have made. This last feature, which can be psychically idealized, disdained, or made use of in a helpful way, is something I take up later in this chapter. For the present, I use less the conventional attachment categories of secure, avoidant, dismissive, preoccupied, or disorganized than the words that emerge for me when working with couples. These words are specific to particular couples but, nevertheless, in broad terms, fit into the main attachment categories.

Formulating attachment out of our work at The Women's Therapy Centre in London, Luise Eichenbaum and I came up with two overarching clinical categories. They are the reference points that guide the poles that illuminate couple relationships for me: poles that go from merged to separated attachments (Figure 1). I put merged attachments running along one surface of a trapezoid, which can include a range from sticky at one end to avoidant or dismissive at the other. At the smaller base of the trapezoid is the optimal outcome we call separated attachments. Separated attachments equate with the clinical assumption about where a couple might need to get to in order for intimacy to be sustainable.

A separated attachment would be equivalent to the couple having a secure base between them. The couple relationship creates a third category, the relationship, which itself may function as an external and yet, at the same time, a lived attachment by which they are both underpinned.

These poles, from merged to separated attachment, hold equally for the same sex couples as the heterosexual couples I have worked

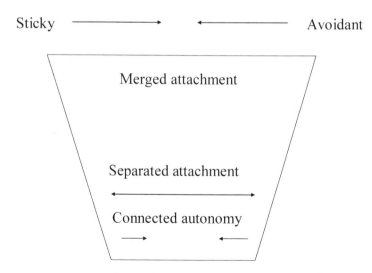

Figure 1.   Styles of attachment.

with. With heterosexual couples, the differing biological sex of the individuals may confer (although I am not necessarily sure it does) a brief, temporary advantage in that each can use the other's sexual difference in the very short term to institute a degree of differentiation. When merger occurs, the differentiation is then of a "false" or defensive nature—such as in avoidant or dismissive attachment— that is not especially protective at all.

Within the category of separated attachments, there is recognition of the space required by differing individual couples. Importantly, there is no is absolute sense of what a separated attachment is for each individual and for the couple. There is only a sense *of what a separated attachment would look like for this particular couple*. What would make it possible for them to create and maintain sufficient distinction from one another in order to be close, in order for there to be an actual other as opposed to a predominantly fantasized internal other (an object relation) that is being related to? The challenge of couple therapy for me is enabling a couple to actually create a platform of good enough closeness together from which each can feel secure enough to express their distinct identities while appreciating and sustaining an experience of the difference as well as the similarities of the other.

Jonathan and Kusum

Let us look at Jonathan and Kusum. Jonathan is Catholic, upper middle class, educated at Ampleforth, Cambridge, and Harvard. He is from a large family, and many aspects of him would lead me to believe that he was securely attached. He is quite laid back, has the confidence of class, and is an artist who, compared to his siblings, who work in the city, makes little money. Kusum is first generation Iranian/Indian English. Her middle-class Indian parents moved here when she was five. They have several small businesses. She is a successful agent for Indian artists. She is intense and dramatic. They have two teenage daughters and a twelve-year-old son. I would describe her as insecurely attached.

Although Jonathan made the initial phone call for therapy, when they entered the room Kusum delivered Jonathan to me to be dealt with. She was extremely unhappy. She had had enough of Jonathan. I was designated as the one to fix him or she was going to leave. What needed fixing? He did not make enough money *for her*. He did not pay enough attention to her. And he could not meet her sexually.

I found Jonathan personable and open. In the countertransference, I noticed a part of me was increasingly unsympathetic to Kusum. He seemed to be a punchbag for her, and it took me a while to comprehend the manner of his neglect of her, the projections of one on to the other, and to put on the table how or whether Kusum might be disappointing him. The asymmetry in the complaints was not unfamiliar from couples work, nor was the rage and blame that permeated the initial sessions. Kusum complained about how weighed down she was, how much work she had, and how very sad she was. The expectation that got in the way of their relating, or forced their relating in this unproductive and hurtful pattern, was that Jonathan should fix, make up for, sort out, or compensate her for her burdens. In the first instance Jonathan seemed to accede to this, as though it was indeed his responsibility to make it better for her. But, while he tried, he could not quite get it right for her. Kusum would then feel a kind of contempt for his "insufficient" efforts, which would diminish both of them and increase their unhappiness.

Jonathan felt sad to be upsetting Kusum and sad that she was so unhappy. His kindness and caring could further inflame Kusum, who carried many of the domestic uncertainties about the finances for the couple. For her part, she envied his ability to be so laid back and unworried. In the countertransference, I felt protective towards Jonathan; I saw this as my identification with his retreating in response to her asking too much.

Formulating my countertransference as a response to her "asking too much" intrigued me. It had the tinge of that sexist mantra of a woman being and wanting too much. But a gender-conscious psychoanalytic approach allows one to engage with curiosity the sense that was aroused in me of Kusum's "asking too much". Why might I be feeling that? What was that feeling for? What might it illuminate about Kusum's own conflicts around her needs and desires?

Asking myself these questions decontaminated me from the negative reaction I unwittingly experienced. Could my countertransference indicate its opposite: Kusum not being able to ask in a way that could be heard? Could the "asking too much" arise out of an insecure childhood attachment that had left Kusum feeling uneasy about her needs? Was it that she was not asking too much, but that she felt unworthy to want, and that the countertransference response I was having was about her confusion over her needs and her desires, hence the difficult delivery of her complaints?

Kusum was showing the impact of an insecure attachment, her shrillness and insistence masking feelings of confused unentitlement (Eichenbaum & Orbach, 1982). The relationship and Jonathan became for her both a site of hope and a site of disappointment. Into it went the intensity of her longings and the ghastliness of her dissatisfactions. Her distress operated like a massive current overworking the circuit breakers in the relational fuse box.

The understanding of her confused unentitlement enabled me to go someway forward, and to be able to rebalance the therapy relationship to feel compassion for Kusum's struggle to legitimate her desires. She felt so unsure of her desires, and she was herself unable to use what came back to her. It was not even that she made them so intense that she courted dismissal or rejection. Jonathan appeared willing to meet them. It was more that her desires, once out, and even being addressed, would boomerang around the room. Jonathan could actually really hit the spot for her, but she could not assimilate his caring.

Identifying Kusum's difficulties with receiving as a consequence of her being insecurely attached made sense of her compulsion to attack Jonathan. The attack was a form of adhesive involvement. Her emotional battering was an act of desperation, an attempt to be noticed and valued because she could not value herself. At the core of her self experience was a struggle about how much she could matter *to herself* and thus feel on sure enough ground about trusting what emanated from her and receiving what was given back.

She had "chosen" Jonathan because he seemed so at ease, so securely placed in British society, so able to take for granted his place in the world and his very being. She wanted their alliance to give this to her. When she was unable to access his solidity and legitimacy for her own self, her despair led her to blister and rage all over him and the therapy room.

In the course of the therapy, Jonathan was able to expand his emotional repertoire. This happened in two main ways, which had an enormous significance for her and for him. In the first instance, he was able to express his own ambition. This was new for him. Yes, he was laid back, but he longed to join his peers who had become established and who were now named artists and sculptors. He was no less interested in making it and being financially secure than was Kusum, but his background did not consider ambition in the arts or money as being necessary. The secure nature of both his familial attachments and his attachment emerging from his class and school positioning mitigated the anxiety one might otherwise have expected. It did not mean, however, that he had no ambition. Appearing not to have ambition put all the striving in Kusum's court, which she experienced as depleting and isolating, particularly as she had gender-related conflicts about her own desires and ambition.

Where his anxiety did emerge, and what interfered with their intimacy from his side, was his guilt about not making things better for Kusum. They played out a guilty–recriminating dynamic between them, with Jonathan paralysed by not knowing what kind of response to give to Kusum's declarations of fatigue and burden. His position of guilt stemmed from an identification with his parental story, in which his father had "disappointed" his mother by not reaching the highest echelons of the diplomatic corps. This, combined with a sense of not knowing what might "help" Kusum, led him to fiddle with his pen in the sessions and go into silent withdrawal. Reacting to Jonathan's withdrawal, Kusum escalated into rage and blame. She felt driven mad by what for her was his abandonment. Frantic at the gulf between them, she would experience an intense desire for sex and closeness. Kusum would approach him. Jonathan would then feel hopeless and misunderstood, and retreat.

Although Jonathan was for the most part securely attached, he could move into a merged position, and at these times become avoidant. Then he would feel as hopeless as Kusum and be as unable as she was to access anything that might be helpful to her. From there he slid into aspects of a merged attachment in which she no longer became separate but became, as it were, a twin part of him, expressing for him those dissatisfactions, albeit in another domain, that were his own. When he felt helpless around her difficulties in receiving, he withdrew into ruminating about his own longings. And here a common phenomenon that occurs between couples emerged: he would access *her* rages for his own purposes: to reflect on his own unmet (and somewhat Oedipally conflicted) ambitions. The energy in her rages galvanized him in an area he had not easily been able to feel directly on his own behalf. He "borrowed" the energy of her affect to propel his personal struggle around work. When we could talk about this phenomenon in the therapy, they could see the shared function of her rages, and they endeavoured to find other ways to support each other in pursuing their separate and joint desires.

Managing to see her rages as something useful for both of them could not have happened unless Jonathan was able to make an adequate response to Kusum's emotional distress. He had to access the part of himself that was secure enough to ask her to tell him more about how *her burdens* were for *her*. He did not need to be instrumental or fix them, or even understand them. He needed only to be curious about them, as he might have been at the beginning of their relationship when they were getting to know each another. When he retreated into himself, it became a dismissal of her. What was actually required was that he be present *with* her.

This is where the therapy came in. It provided a platform of support that enabled Jonathan to ask Kusum about her distress and then to listen to it and empathize with it. This put both of them into a position where they felt adequate and interested in one another. Jonathan was then able to bring his need for her support with his professional struggles to her. She could help him with that. Their psychic positioning was redrawn. Kusum, seen and recognized, felt immediately calmed. Jonathan felt he was getting to know Kusum all over again and he was able to experience how powerful it was for both of them for her to talk and be heard. He also felt sexually drawn to her in an invigorated way, but he was reticent about it.

Over previous years their sexual life had all but disappeared. Children and overwork were their explanations to themselves. In the beginning, the erotic was a crucial aspect of their relationship, by which they created a bond, the connected two-ness in which their attachment needs, their desire for recognition, and their individual sense of being valued, loved, and secure occurred. This phase of their relationship created a merged attachment, as it does for most couples. Being able to take the love that emerges out of the merger, providing, as it does, a new positive embrace where an early attachment may have been problematic, provides for valuable and long sought psychic repair. The difficulty Kusum and Jonathan encountered was how to climb out of that state of psychic merger, which at the beginning was experienced as so blissful, wondrous, and completing, into a relationship in which they could use their attachment as a basis for supporting their individual senses of self (Orbach, 1999, Eichenbaum & Orbach, 1983). How could they be both connected and separate?

Paradoxically, in our initial "falling in love", being separate and connected is not a problem. It is simply how it is. One feels alive in the connection together while one's distinctness is emphasized. But, as time and life intervene, and intimacies deepen in ways other than sexual, the erotic aspect of a relationship is transformed. The slippage between a merged attachment and an on-the-way-to-being-separate attachment can be very difficult. It can produce over-connection or distance, rather than the space offered by a separated attachment. This has an impact on the sexual relationship.

So it was for Jonathan and Kusum. They slipped between being over-connected and being distant. For various reasons to do with Kusum's own development, she felt that Jonathan needed to take the lead sexually. If Jonathan did not initiate, she felt it as abandonment, as though he needed to be over present with his desire *in order to make her desire possible*. Her wish for him to initiate was another expression of her sense of unentitlement, stemming from her insecure attachments. She wanted to feel desired by Jonathan so that she could feel desire within herself. (This is something feminism has been addressing for many years: how a woman might feel desirable from the inside and not because she is desired from the outside.) But then she could not access her own sexual vitality, except out of the place of rage.

Kusum's wish for Jonathan to be the desiring other clashed with the legacy from his Catholic background, which left him reluctant to "impose" himself on others. His desire was present, but he had his own version of not bringing it forth for fear of being inappropriate. His upbringing, contact with the celibate monks at the monastery he attended, and the confusing cultural messages that Kusum had absorbed about femininity and the erotic, contributed to his sexual hesitancy.

Attachment theory offers a pictorial view of individuals and their capacity to "attach" and relate to one another. I use the geometry of the couple as a diagnostic tool, and observe how attachment categories and the attachment that pertains to the couple change during the course of therapy. In the beginning of a couple therapy, we are inclined to assess the individual attachment profile of the individuals in the couple. We ask ourselves: where do these two people stand in relationship to one another in the articulation of their needs and desires? Who complains? Who is able to receive?

Who retreats? Who is dismissive? Who shows their insecurity? Where are the points of mutuality? And so on. The way a couple sit together, the emotional valences, ambience, and utterances in the therapy room, combined with what is ascertained in the counter-transference, provide the first diagnostic clues.

During the course of the couple therapy, there are shifts in the way we look at the attachment profile. We no longer assess the couple as two individuals with their unique attachment history. It is the attachment that is co-created by the couple that is now of interest. The co-created attachment can provide either a secure or an insecure base for their relationship. The relationship itself becomes a third kind of attachment, taking on the capacity to become a platform as well as a container from and within which the individuals relate.

Interestingly, even if individual attachment patterns veer towards insecure, anxious, clingy, or sticky, the relationship itself can provide a robustness that mitigates some of that insecurity, and can provide a dynamic secure base from which each individual can venture out. By coming to couple therapy, partners consciously grant a respect and status to the couple relationship. This shifts matters psychically. The relationship that the couple has created becomes a potential good relational object, a third (Aron, 2006; Benjamin, 2004) from which the partners can view their inter-actions, and which feeds back into each of them and the relation-ship itself.

For some, the granting of status to the relationship, and making it potentially good, can produce dramatic changes. The individual partners move towards seeing the couple relationship as generative and creative. For Kusum and Jonathan, it meant seeing Kusum's concerns *as concerns they as a couple could address*. It meant seeing Jonathan's conflicts about his ambition as *something the couple rela-tionship could handle*.

Reformulating difficulties in this way does not take away from the partners their individual responsibility. Strikingly, it becomes imperative that the individual must take a particular kind of responsibility: one that allows the partners to act knowing that they are supported by the relationship they have jointly created, rather than making an isolated and isolating demand on each other. This dual position of respecting self and risking expressing directly what is felt to be wanted, rather than communicating through carping, put-downs or withdrawals, combines with a perception of the couple relationship as sufficiently resilient to provide a benign germinating platform for life in the couple. This opens up a more democratic view of a relationship, containing psychic parity and joint responsibility.

From this perspective, the issues that pertained to sexuality between Jonathan and Kusum (who initiated what and how it might express their intimacy) become a relationship issue rather than a contest between two people. What strengths can each bring to bear on this? What vulnerabilities exist for each of them? What untangling needs to happen so that they can accept that the relationship is there for them as a couple? And does that understanding enable them to move from a relationship of insecurity to one of promise and sexual aliveness?

Using the lens of attachment, we could see that the lack of sex had another function. It was a regulator, a needed protection in the struggle not to be merged. To have sex in an unproblematic and vibrant way, as they had in the early years of their relationship, might have brought them *too close*, as though there was no space between them. Kusum's complaints and Jonathan's reluctances acted as spacers, creating enough distance, albeit in a negative way, for them to get on. Of course, the price was high, leaving each of them rather stranded, but getting too close sexually in the state that they were in might have disturbed the equilibrium they had established.

In order to reinstitute a sexual relationship that was alive for both of them, the fundamental *dissonances in their attachment patterns needed to be recognized*. The nature of the complaints about Kusum wanting Jonathan to initiate were less significant than addressing the need to create equilibrium in the flux between merger, with its insecure and avoidant attachments, and their attempt to create a secure enough separated attachment where respect and excitement were both present (Clulow, 2001; Mitchell, 2002; Orbach, 1999). By asking the relationship to carry this sense of a secure base, there was more possibility for the risks, excitements, and pleasures associated with intimacy to breathe rather than collapse.

We might think that in couple work we need to adjust the attachment patterns of each individual. Would that we could! We might despair if we see both parties as insecurely attached. However, the couple relationship can be manipulated in a creative way to provide a proxy separated attachment for both individuals to use as they work through the difficulties that arise between them. The couple relationship is the key feature that needs to be used to enable conflicts, disappointments, and desires to be engaged. Sexual intimacy is dependent not so much on each individual sorting themselves out as individuals as it is on creating a platform of security from which the couple can nourish itself.

References

Aron, L. (2006). Analytic impulses and the third: clinical implications of intersubjectivity theory. *Inernational Journal of Psychoanalysis, 87*: 349–368.

Benjamin, J. (2004). Beyond doer and done to: an intersubjective view of thirdness. *Psychoanalytic Quarterly, 73*: 5–46.

Clulow, C. (2001). *Adult Attachment and Couple Psychotherapy: The "Secure Base" in Practice and Research*. London: Brunner-Routledge.

Eichenbaum, L., & Orbach, S. (1982). *Outside In, Inside Out: A Feminist and Psychoanalytic Approach to Women's Psychology*. London: Penguin Books.

Mitchell, S. (2002). *Can Love Last?* New York: W. W. Norton.

Orbach, S. (1999). *The Impossibility of Sex*. London: Allen Lane.

CHAPTER FIVE

Dynamics and disorders of sexual desire

Christopher Clulow and Maureen Boerma

Desire, sexuality, and disorder

The proposition that we shall be exploring in this chapter is that the expression and satiation of sexual desire contains, and is driven by, two emotional states that are in tension with each other: love and hate. By love we mean not only the affectionate, sometimes passionate, regard we have for another person as he or she actually is, but also more narcissistic patterns of object relating in which others become extensions of ourselves, and vice versa, through identification with them. We include in our definition attachment and care-giving behaviours that seek to connect with others, either through depending on them or being depended on by them, as well as enmeshed and borderline patterns of relating associated with preoccupied and disorganized attachment. By hate, we mean not only the aggression needed to differentiate ourselves from others through self-assertion, even anger, in the service of remaining engaged with them, but also the fear that drives us to control or distance ourselves from others, and ourselves from ourselves, through projection. We include in our definition of hate both the endeavour to remain connected with others by protesting

when threatened with separation or loss, and the emotional disconnection from ourselves and others associated with dismissing and
fearful patterns of insecure adult attachment.

Our argument is that the emotional states of love and hate are
activated in different measure by the allure and threat of merger in
relation to others, and they can act to inhibit as well as to encourage the expression of sexual feelings. Either state can assume ascendancy, love driving the desire to merge and hate the desire to
separate (although, paradoxically, love can facilitate separation and
hate result in merger). It is our contention that the dynamics of
desire form an appropriate focus for psychoanalytic psychotherapy
with couples, and we distinguish this focus from that of other
approaches concerned with changing sexual behaviour.

Our starting point is that sexual desire is inherently disorderly
because it contains within it the seeds of conflict. Consider the
following archetypal story.

> A man and woman find themselves alone together in a garden. The
> woman is tempted to eat the fruit in the garden that has been forbid-
> den to them. She offers the fruit to the man and he succumbs to her
> temptation. When they devour it, they move from a state of innocence
> to an awareness of their nakedness. The resulting feeling of shame
> leads them to attempt to hide themselves from public gaze by conceal-
> ing what is felt to be private to them and between them. The couple's
> transgression is, however, discovered, and they are banished from the
> garden because they have usurped the authority of the owner. So, they
> are punished: the price of succumbing to desire is domestic servitude
> for her and a life of hard labour for him.

This Old Testament story of the mythical original couple, told in
the Book of Genesis, is rich in symbolism that can be read in many
different ways. For our purposes, the sexual symbolism is foremost.
Sexual desire manifests itself in the form of a serpent, the uncoiling
penis, and the prospect of coitus. The allure of the forbidden fruit
is that it comes from the tree of knowledge, knowledge that not
only relates to an experience of the mind but also of the body:
"knowing" someone, in the biblical sense, is to have sex with them.
This kind of knowledge is forbidden by a parental figure (not a
parental couple), who sees it as threatening his (note the gender)
authority and position. The secret that the couple stand to unlock is

that of eternal life: reproduction through the conception of their own child, an act that triggers generational change and displaces the established order. "Eternal life" also follows from the capacity of the partners to know themselves and each other, providing the basis for secure attachments that can carry over from one generation to the next. The couple move towards sexual knowledge through defying parental authority and succumbing to desire, with the consequence that they are banished from the fantasy idyll of childhood to the drudgery of a marriage based on gender differentiated roles, an arrangement that kills off desire and might, in turn, prohibit the sexuality of the next generation through a mixture of envy and fear. Variations of this story will have been heard in many couple and family psychotherapy consulting rooms.

The tension between the libidinal dictates of the heart and the anti-libidinal constraints of conformity has a timeless capacity to engage and preoccupy us. A theme in many great Victorian novels pits the world of private passions against the forces of social order and control, throwing heroes and heroines into a turmoil of conflict as they choose between sense and sensibility (to lift the title of one of Jane Austen's best known and still popular novels). Even in our contemporary, sexually liberated culture, the performing arts associate the height of sexual desire not with the comfort and sanction of the marital bed, but with a craving for the unattainable, or what can only be attained at the cost of social disapproval. Even socially sanctioned happy endings have to be fought for, the course of true love never being allowed to run smooth; the emotional punch comes from finding a resolution to seemingly impossible conflict. Historically, religion and the law have been the regulators of sexual passion, punishing its unauthorized expression with exclusion and worse. The history of religion is marked by the repression of sexuality, leaving in its trail a legacy of guilt and shame. In this context, the institution of marriage acts, in the words of the 1666 Book of Common Prayer, as "a remedy against sin"; as St Paul put it in his letter to the Ephesians, "better to marry than to burn".

Despite the endeavours of social control, and some might say perversely because of them, our sense of longing can be heightened rather than reduced by the object of our desire being forbidden or unavailable. Secrecy fans the flames of illicit desire and passion, which can sometimes be increased by the risk of discovery and the different kinds of casting out that can follow. While sexual "knowledge", either in the form of information or experience, is less hard to come by these days than in former times, the affective component of desire can remain an enigma.

Conflicts intrinsic to sexual desire can result in fantasies of personal as well as social disorder, and both ways round become associated with the difficulty of throwing off or engaging with a disapproving parental object. The English psyche has often been represented as prototypically repressed when it comes to questions of sexuality and desire. The old male guard of the patriarchal order perhaps preferred to view women as sexually uninterested, rather than themselves as incapable of arousing a response. The split between idealized mother and sexualized whore may have been amplified, at least in the upper echelons of English society, by physical care being separated from maternal role, with wet nurses and nannies providing for physical and emotional needs in ways that "real" mothers did not. What was available physically and emotionally was undervalued and sometimes denigrated, whereas the unavailable and disapproving could trigger desire.

William Boyd's *An Ice Cream War* (Boyd, 1983) depicts—albeit as a sideshow to the main storyline about the ineptitudes of British colonialism—the consequences of sexual ignorance and repression for a newly-married upper-class couple just before the outbreak of the First World War. Gabriel Cobb is the admired elder son in a military family, good-looking, athletic, the world seemingly at his fingertips. His marriage to Charis is all of a piece until they are faced with the prospect of sex on their honeymoon. Gabriel defers consummating the marriage until it becomes unavoidable, but when he goes through the motions he is impotent, with no erection to make penetration possible. Charis is ignorant of what to expect and does not know whether anything has happened or not. On their second night, Gabriel, scolded by Charis for having drunk too much, bangs his leg after getting out of bed to turn off the light. Instinctively, she rubs his knee better, saying "Mummy'll be cross". Aroused, Gabriel nuzzles into her breast. Charis spreads herself underneath him, unthinkingly stroking the back of his head and murmuring "who's a naughty boy". The erotic charge ensures the marriage is consummated on this occasion, although the call to war and the possibility of death remains the less frightening prospect for Gabriel in the future, and an escape route from further intimate encounters with Charis.

How might we articulate the dynamics of desire in any meaningful way that travels beyond the idiosyncratic experiences of any one individual or couple in their particular historical and cultural context? If we are serious about disorder being intrinsic to desire, is this something that should be attempted at all? There is usually nothing neat and tidy about sexual longing, so why should we assume that it could be contained within a theory? Perhaps the attempt to distinguish between the dynamics and disorders of desire is itself defensive, rather like the apocryphal group of psychotherapists who, upon passing beyond the portals of this life, come across a signpost pointing one way to "The Garden of Eden" and the other to "The Lecture on the Garden of Eden", and opt for the latter. Adam Phillips's (2005) wry comment that "sane sex" is a contradiction in terms, since "all our stories about the madness of love are stories of impossible conflict" (p. 128), is sufficient to make us wary of the whole project. But it may also provide us with a key.

Dynamics of desire

Freud's model of infantile sexuality and psychic structures has at its core the "impossible" conflict between the channelling of sexual impulse (id) and the forces of social control (superego), a conflict that shapes the mediating structure of the ego. For him, adulthood and maturity were associated with relinquishing the primary and forbidden object of desire (the parent of the opposite sex) through resolving the Oedipus complex. Freud's model was essentially phallocentric, in that the psycho-sexual development of boys was his primary focus and the lens through which he understood developmental processes as a whole. For him, sexual desire was an instinctual force seeking expression through sexual behaviour and tempered by a patriarchal social order that discouraged usurping parental sexuality through the child's fantasy that this would result in castration. He proposed that it took a threat of this magnitude to contain the child's unconscious murderous feelings towards the same sex parent, who is seen as thwarting the wish to possess exclusively the parent of the opposite sex. This perspective led him to view the split between love and desire in men as having resulted from the genitalization of infantile sexuality, placing attachment to mother in conflict with sexual rivalry with father (Freud, 1912d). If this conflict was not resolved through relinquishing mother as a sexual object in favour of identifying with father, the need to protect loved objects from incestuous wishes resulted in a state of "psychical impotence" for boys/men, with the consequence that "where they love they do not desire and where they desire they cannot love" (*ibid.*, p. 183). This disorder of desire was thus associated with having failed to clear the developmental hurdle of resolving a complex that was deemed by Freud to be universal and exemplified through his reading of Sophocles' tragedy *Oedipus Rex*.

Attachment theory has in common with Freudian psychoanalytic theory some acknowledgement of the place of biology in the dynamics of desire, but gives emphasis to the significance of relationships in shaping and channelling its expression. Attachment, care-giving, and sexuality are considered from an attachment perspective to be interlinked systems of behaviour, activated by external stimuli (or perceived stimuli) and terminated by a response that assuages the driving emotion, which, in the case of sexual behaviour, is desire (Mikulincer & Goodman, 2006). In contrast to Freud, contemporary attachment theorists understand the split between love and desire not in terms of universal incestuous wishes, but as the failure to integrate attachment and sexual systems of behaviour that, at least from a male perspective, can be at odds with each other. So Eagle (2007) asserts that:

> One needs one's spouse or romantic partner, as one's attachment figure, to be familiar, predictable, and available. Yet there is a good deal of evidence that predictability, familiarity and availability frequently dampen the intensity of sexual interest and excitement. Thus, I am suggesting that, apart from any consideration of incest wishes, the antagonism between the attachment and sexual systems goes some way toward accounting for the split between love and desire, which, I propose, is essentially a split between attachment and sexuality. [p. 34]

He goes on to show, as do other attachment theorists (see, for example, Diamond, Blatt, & Lichtenberg, 2007) how the development of attachment in infancy, and especially the degree of felt security or lack of it, can provide a paradigm of relatedness that shapes the expression of sexuality in later life.

So, rather than viewing sex and attachment as behavioural systems that are independent of each other, it is more in tune with relational psychoanalysis to see the sexual arena as the site for enacting attachment dramas in which "emotional connection and intimacy is sought, established, lost and regained" (Mitchell, 1988, p. 107). A working group from the Centre for Attachment based Psychoanalytic Psychotherapy (CAPP) argues that the inter-weaving of sexuality and hostility has arisen because of an under-developed understanding of the relationship between sexuality and attachment (Laschinger, Purnell, Schwartz, White, & Wingfield, 2004). They differentiate between a sexuality of hope (where there is confidence to realize and develop attachment in adulthood through sexual relationships, incorporating feelings of love as well as desire) and a sexuality of despair (where the absence of such confidence, eroded by past and present attachment failures predis-poses towards autoerotic and sado-masochistic sexuality).

Reflecting on the "sexuality of hope", Messler-Davies (2005) writes that

> It is the affect state I will call "pleasurable anticipation" that holds the intensifying arousal and excitement, making it tolerable, even enjoyable, only because it also holds in mind a belief in ultimate sexual satisfaction and release. [p. 65]

She links this with what might be thought of as a kind of erotic dance between mother and baby, where it is in

> these very early cycles of arousal and soothing that a child's capa-city to believe in and rely upon the ultimate satisfaction of intense need states begins to coalesce. Her later ability to hold and actually extract pleasure from frustration and/or arousal, while at the same time anticipating its resolution, begins to form a physiologically based substrate to the capacity for later erotic pleasure. [p. 66]

It is in this dance that sexual identity is formed, a perspective that sees gender and sexuality as social rather than biological constructs.

It is, of course, true that the early stages of a love relationship incorporate behaviour that is reminiscent of infant attachment. The importance of eye contact, of the special gaze between lovers, of exclusive physical contact and stimulation, echo relationship patterns between mothers and babies. The process of discovering and enjoying the other's body marks the specialness of the relationship, the privileged access that each partner accords to the other, and a symbolic as well as physical intimacy. The wish to be in tune, to be responsive to every movement and gesture, to engage in baby talk and to find any separation intolerable suggests a wonderfully regressed state of mind, providing "uppers" and "downers" that most drugs would find hard to match (and, of course, there is an endomorphinal, pheronomal "buzz" to being in love). Indeed, the regions of the brain activated by maternal love are the same as those activated by romantic love, and use the same neurological pathways as those activated by addiction (Fonagy & Bateman, 2006). The state of being "in love" is a kind of intoxication, desire a variant of addiction, and in this heightened state interpersonal boundaries buckle under the pressure from lovers to melt into and merge with each other. Falling in love, if not the psychosis that Freud would have it to be, certainly approximates a borderline condition.

A key difference between "lovers" in infancy and adulthood is that it is only with the latter that sexual feelings can be fully incorporated and engaged. Inappropriate engagement of an infant's sexual feelings, or the intrusion of the adult's sexuality into the infant's experience (as in cases of child sexual abuse), can be very damaging to sexual development and account for disorders of desire in later life. In the more ordinary course of development the opposite is likely to occur: infant sexuality will be disregarded.

An important proposition recently advanced from a developmental perspective is that parents generally turn away from evidence of sexual excitement in their infants, or, alternatively, may eroticize their non-sexual experiences, resulting in a deficit or distortion in the mirroring of that part of the infant's mind. When there is a mirroring "deficit", sexual excitement may become associated in the infant's mind with a sense of absence. The quest to relocate one's own sexuality in the absent other might then drive sexual behaviour in adult life. The discovery and containment of one's own sexual feelings in another adult person then becomes the means by which sexuality is integrated into the self (Fonagy, 2008;

Target, 2007). This is a very particular slant on the Garden of Eden story, but it contains the central element of parental disregard for, if not disapproval of, sexuality. Evoking a sexual response in others in adult life is the process through which sexual feelings can become integrated within the self, because it is through seeing and experiencing the sexual excitement of another that sexual excitement can be fully located within the self. Otherwise, with eyes closed, so to speak, there is nothing for it but to pursue the absent, sexualized other.

Fonagy (2008) argues that while male sexual enjoyment might require the full externalization of the self into the other, where it can be controlled in unconscious fantasy, for women, sexual arousal is more likely to be associated with introjective identification with the partner and to become inward turning as excitement mounts. In this form, the gender constellation constitutes a complementary system, but there are likely to be other constellations operating between sexual partners. In whatever constellation it becomes manifest, the intersubjective aspect of the experience is seen as being crucial to sexual fulfilment. From this perspective, the declining urgency of sexual feeling in stable partnerships over time is accounted for by the integration of sexuality within the partners; no longer is there the same need to rediscover sexual desire within the self through evoking sexual excitement in others.

The intersubjective foundations of "good sex" are "hedonistic", to use Holmes' phrase (2007), and allow both partners to engage their individual erotic imagination in the context of what happens between them. Holmes draws on Winnicott's (1971) image of the secure child being free to play alone in the presence of the mother, confident that the mother is there and that she will not intrude on the child's play. The capacity to be alone in the presence of another is one of the foundations of enjoyable sex, but what is also needed is the mutuality that comes from being able to know about and merge with the subjective state of one's partner. Good sex, in Holmes' view, involves engaging the erotic imagination of both partners and "'thinking with the body' in tandem" (p. 145). He notes that from an attachment perspective enjoyable sex follows from and manifests imaginative freedom. This is in contrast to a post-Kleinian view that sees imaginative freedom as resulting from the pre-internalized phantasy of a creative parental couple.

Heard and Lake (1997), acknowledging that the sexual system is nascent from infancy onwards, propose that it has three functions in adult life: a reproductive function (taking forward the species and contributing to the development of adults through making them parents); a mechanism for raising and maintaining the vitality of couple relationships (through the building and discharge of heightened affective experiences that sex provides); and an auto-erotic defensive function (offering distraction from separation anxiety, loneliness, and internal conflict through mechanistic sex or masturbation).

The first of these propositions is supported by those who claim that the function of sexual behaviour, which emanates from desire, is to create the conditions in which intimacy and attachment might develop in the adult couple. This is considered important from an evolutionary perspective, not only for conception to occur, but also to provide a stable adult relationship that has the best chance of protecting children and optimizing their developmental prospects. Desire and sexual behaviour is considered from this perspective to be most important at the outset of romantic relationships, serving to keep partners together physically long enough for them to become emotionally attached. Once attachment is established, desire may wane and sexual activity become less frequent and important (Cassidy, 2001).

But is that the case? The second of Heard and Lake's functions proposes that sexuality and desire contribute to maintaining vitality between adult partners in long-term couple relationships. Sex between partners who are attached to each other has the capacity to release opiods (oxytocin) that may have a calming effect and reinforce their attachment to each other. There is evidence from research with non-human mammals that this is indeed the case, so the proposition has been extended to humans.

> When a parent comforts a crying infant, the parent becomes associated ... with the alleviation of distress. Similarly, through repeated comforting exchanges, including the release of tension brought about by sexual climax, a lover comes to be associated with stress reduction and calming. Relationships that develop into attachment bonds appear to be those in which heightened physiological arousal is repeatedly attenuated by the same person and in a context of close bodily contact. As such, attachment may involve

the conditioning of an individual's opiod system to the stimulus of a specific other. [Hazan & Zeifman, 1999, p. 350]

This, of course, is the real threat behind an affair: not the breach of sexual exclusivity so much as the possibility of a developing emotional involvement (perhaps the reason why those who sell sexual services avoid the kissing, cuddling, and eye contact of those who are in love?).

Their third proposition invites us to consider what we mean by disorders of desire. Infant attachment research draws a distinction between secure and insecure patterns of attachment (Ainsworth, Blehar, Waters, & Wall, 1978). Secure attachment is marked by the confidence of the infant in approaching his care-giver when feeling frightened or upset, and of being comforted by the response the care-giver provides. When these optimal conditions are not present, infants rely on two main "second best" strategies for managing threats and the need for intimacy: avoidance (evident in the down-playing of emotions and creating the impression that others are not needed in managing the crises of life) and anxiety (evident in the heightening of emotions and an ambivalent clinging to others who are thought to be only available on an unreliable basis). It is not hard to contrast the *sexuality of hope* associated with secure attach-ment to the *sexuality of despair* associated with insecure attachment and evident in the emotionally uninvolved sexual behaviour of a "dismissing" encounter, or the heightened sexual activity of a "preoccupied" encounter driven by fear of abandonment. There is also behaviour that signals disorganized attachment, when the infant has no way of managing the conflict caused by an attachment figure who is turned to as a protection against threat but who also constitutes the threat from which protection is sought. Such con-flicts can result in controlling patterns of behaviour in childhood and later life (Lyons-Ruth & Jacobvitz, 1999).

The key adaptation in moving from attachment in infancy to couple attachment in adulthood concerns mutuality: the capacity to move flexibly and appropriately between care-giving and care-seeking roles in the relationship (Crowell & Waters, 2005). Sex-ual behaviour is an additional system that needs incorporating within the attachment and care-giving models: sex may be used in the service of care seeking and care giving; it can be a means of promoting and maintaining pair bonds, and it may promote and underpin the companionability, turn-taking, and interest sharing that are the external manifestations of secure adult relationships (Diamond, Blatt, & Lichtenberg, 2007).

Recent research suggests that one of the distinguishing features between secure and insecure attachment is the degree to which sexuality might be recruited in the service of meeting attachment needs. This work has built on the distinction between affects that "hyperactivate" or "deactivate" the attachment system (Cassidy & Kobak, 1988), the former being associated with insecure preoccupied, and the latter with insecure dismissing, patterns of attachment. Positive models of self and others are associated with secure attachment, where sexual desire and engagement do not pose a threat, and can be enjoyed without the significance of the encounter being over-determined in attachment terms. Negative models of self and others are associated with insecure attachment and the hyperactivating and deactivating affective processes that we have referred to. Summarizing the evidence accrued so far, Mikulincer and Shaver (2007) conclude

> that the main sexual motive of anxious and avoidant people is not to enjoy sex per se, but rather to use sex as a means to meet attachment-related goals. For avoidant people, minimizing intimacy and gaining social status and power seem to be the main motives; for anxiously attached people the main motives are to allay fear of rejection and abandonment while maximising proximity, reassurance and love. [p. 64]

The flexibility of relationship patterns associated with secure attachment in adult couple relationships, and maintaining a boundary between the set goals of different behavioural systems, denotes an internal security in the partners' inner worlds of object relating. Kernberg (1995) suggests that

> in passionate love, orgasm integrates the simultaneous crossing of the boundary of the self into awareness of biological functioning beyond the control of the self, and the crossing of boundaries in a sophisticated identification with the loved object while maintaining the sense of separate identity. The shared experience of orgasm includes, in addition to temporary identification with the sexual

partner, transcendence from the experience of the self to that of the fantasized union of the oedipal parents, as well as transcendence from the repetition of the oedipal relation to the abandonment of it in a new object relation that reconfirms one's separate identity and autonomy. [p. 41]

Couples capable of such passionate love are, in his view, able to be psychically separate. They have sufficient trust that merger will not annihilate their individual identities. For the man, the ecstasy associated with fusion, and the early state of elation in the mother–baby relationship, can co-exist with the aggression needed to penetrate his partner, aggression that may be tinged with fear and mistrust at venturing into a site that contains dangers associated with unconscious fantasies about a maternal interior full of primitive projected rage and hatred. For the woman, the prospect of bodily fusion and aggression in intercourse does not unduly threaten her security, or evoke feelings of being intruded upon or invaded in ways that threaten her sense of integrity. This capability, Kernberg suggests, implies for both partners "the acceptance of the danger, not only of losing one's identity but of the liberation of aggression against these internal and external objects and their retaliation" (*ibid.*).

So, the couple expelled from the Garden of Eden might be the man and woman who can pursue their desire for pleasure and eat the fruit from the tree of knowledge, free to stimulate their "longing for closeness, fusion, and intermingling that implies both forcefully crossing a barrier and becoming one with the chosen object" (*ibid.*, p. 22). They can know about and accept their transgression of parental prohibitions, let go of an idealized childhood, be prepared to violate boundaries and gain/retain a sense of their separate identities through asserting a coupledom of their own. In post-Kleinian terms, they have negotiated the Oedipal developmental challenge in ways that have enabled them to establish what Britton (1989) describes as "third position" functioning, the capacity to be emotionally involved with others without compromising their ability to observe their own experience and that of others. This capacity has been worked into the concept of "mentalizing" by attachment theorists (Fonagy, Gergely, Jurist, & Target, 2002), when describing the capacity to have thoughts about feelings and to feel in ways that remain connected with thoughts in relation to specific experiences.

Whether this capacity is viewed as a transitional state—the ability to abandon oneself to a passionate encounter in order to create an intimate connection, and perhaps to cross the threshold into commitment—or whether it is regarded as a developmental achievement, is something that is open to debate. As has been suggested, it may be that a borderline state of mind is part of the process of falling and being in love, and we would be loath to cast that as a disorder. On the other hand, maintaining sexual desire and intimacy in an ongoing relationship, the active process of loving another person through thick and thin, may call for something different.

Disorders of desire

Disorders of desire might be considered in relation to insecure patterns of attachment, where mentalizing, or the capacity to adopt a "third position", is likely to be limited or absent. For example, one might expect avoidant attachment to be associated with low emotional intensity relationships such as one-night stands, the use of prostitutes, or the auto-eroticism associated with visiting pornographic websites. Alternatively, sex might be used by the anxiously attached to heighten emotional intensity, to forge and maintain relationships with others, perhaps through promiscuous behaviour. Patterns of abusive behaviour in childhood might also be unconsciously re-enacted in the sexual arena of adult life, resulting in coercive and intrusive sex. Framing the disorders of desire in such relational contexts draws us back to the affects of love and hate, and to what has been described as the "core conflict" for couples (Glasser, 1979): balancing the need for intimacy with maintaining and developing the integrity of an autonomous self.

In contrast to partners who are securely attached and capable of intimate involvement with each other, couples who fear sexual desire in a loving relationship allow themselves to experience no exciting letting go in a passionate sexual encounter between them. While ostensibly desiring ecstatic merger, they instead perpetuate a fusion in their relationship that kills off desire. They remain trapped in a Garden of Eden dominated by parental prohibition. Maybe what they really fear is giving way to an intercourse that threatens to unleash uncontainable repressed feelings, whether associated with the penetrating penis or the female interior. Insufficiently secure in their own identities, including their gender, they avoid the merger that threatens as well as excites them.

Couples of this kind may describe their relationship as close to idyllic in everything but sex, which they might describe as never having been satisfactory. Such couples may formulate a very specific sexual problem in their approach for help, perhaps disheartened by the difficulty in obtaining an erection or in achieving orgasm. The invitation to therapists might be to separate sex from other dimensions of the relationship and form it into some kind of disembodied object that can provide a common external focus of attention for couple and therapists alike (Clulow, 1984). The story that we can weave around such couples is that they are like "babes in the wood", maintaining their equilibrium by a "you and me against the world" stance, and perceiving all threats to their equilibrium as emanating from the "dark wood" surrounding them. In these circumstances it is not uncommon for therapists to experience an initial positive transference from the couple in which hopes are entertained about their ability to do something about the problem, which is soon followed by feelings of disappointment and anger. Attempts to link feelings expressed towards the therapists with unexpressed emotions in the partnership are resisted. Destructive impulses might be projected into the therapists, who may be branded as "marriage wreckers", and who may be walked out on if links are made to the partnership. Difference is located in the couple–therapist relationship, and the fear of psychic separation located in the inability to tolerate the separate mind(s) of the therapist(s) in the intercourse of therapy.

In its acute form, Britton (1998) postulates that the meeting of two separate minds might be associated with a catastrophic intercourse in which an idealized understanding object is engulfed by a denigrated misunderstanding one, resulting in a sense of chaos tantamount to the annihilation of the self. This, he believes, arises from a failure of maternal containment in infancy: "the uncomprehended is transformed for the infant into the incomprehensible" (p. 56). The resulting *malignant misunderstanding*, as Britton termed it, is split off into a third object, which is perceived as threatening the idealized empathic link between mother and child.

In such cases, couples might attempt to maintain an idealized fusion in their relationship in which differences between them are minimized, the malignant misunderstanding being split off into the sexual relationship that threatens, in its full expression, to annihilate their sense of self. This underscores a predominantly narcissistic form of relating that attempts to deny the reality of difference and separateness, a form that Britton (2003, p. 169) has termed *adherent narcissism*, distinguishing this from *detached narcissism*.

Adherently narcissistic partners combine to make themselves extensions of the other, reinforcing their similarities while projecting any potential for misunderstanding into sex, external arenas, and the therapists themselves. By doing so, they buy into the unconscious fantasy that the misunderstanding other can be eliminated, leaving them as a couple to inhabit one undifferentiated, totally understanding mind. These couples may have understandable and historically rooted reasons for fearing separation, but remain unconscious of how this impedes the psychic separation that is needed for them to engage in creative intercourse together. Their interaction corresponds with that of the *anxious/ambivalent* infants observed in the "strange situation procedure" (Ainsworth, Blehar, Waters, & Wall, 1978) and *preoccupied* patterns of adult attachment captured by the "adult attachment interview" (George, Kaplan, & Main, 1985). Here, anxiety about being separate and feeling aggressive is managed through forming enmeshed relationships with others (although these relationships do not escape the unconscious hatred directed towards the partner whom they fear will leave the relationship if not controlled to stay in it). Clinically, it can be helpful to think about both adherent narcissism and preoccupied attachment as states of mind that become pronounced in the face of intense feelings stirred up by the threat of separation and the prospect of loss, rather than see them as classifications of fixed personality features.

Detached narcissistic partners, for whom Britton (2003) wrote "the sacrifice to be made to secure a place indoors [he is here using the metaphor of physical space to illustrate problems associated with sharing psychological space] was to be caged within the limiting framework of the other's comprehension of the world" (p. 173), similarly conflate relationship boundaries, but through attempting to make others extensions of themselves rather than themselves becoming extensions of others. Such partners are likely to show avoidant (infancy) and dismissing (adult) patterns of attachment that maintain emotional (and sometimes physical) distance to protect themselves against the fear of dependency and the associated prospect of rejection and loss. Patterns of relating in adulthood that can result from pairing together different types of insecure attachment (and, by extension, different types of narcissism) have been identified by research undertaken at the Tavistock Centre for Couple Relationships with couples seeking psychotherapy (Fisher & Crandell, 2001). They can be regarded as shared defensive systems operating to afford protection against the fear of becoming imprisoned in the mind of the partner, or the fear of being malignantly misunderstood.

Underlying these defences may be a shared impasse that has militated against the development of an internalized capacity to contain deep-seated anxieties, and thus of a sufficiently robust self capable of withstanding the threat of annihilation associated with encountering another mind. There is, then, a shared terror that the integration of separate minds will result in a return to *primordial chaos* that Britton (1998, p. 54) believes corresponds to the notion of *nameless dread* (Bion, 1962, p. 116), which he posits follows the failure of containment. The stark alternatives to the threat of colonization are either to capitulate or to colonize others.

From a psychoanalytic perspective, the therapeutic process involves creating conditions in which the uncomprehended might be understood, so that the scope for malignant misunderstanding and threats of colonization are reduced. Often, in these cases, a history of rejection or conditional attachment in the parental family can inhibit desire, sexuality, and the capacity for creative intercourse, as demonstrated by the following vignette.

A couple came for help because of the man's impotence. In the course of the therapy he also consulted a psycho-sexual therapist, was investigated by a urologist, and prescribed a PDE-5 inhibitor by his doctor in attempts to overcome his problems in maintaining an erection. Alongside supporting these investigations, the couple therapy focused on the meaning of the impotence for the partners as a couple. Simplifying a complex story, it was clear that in the sporting community, where he excelled, with friends, and in his partnership the man created an environment in which he felt under pressure to perform and comply, and then sought to retreat from that world and his anger about its demands. This dynamic was imported into their relationship as a couple. He had an on–off relationship with his partner over many years, in which their commitment to each other as a couple had become a central question. The relationship had never been sexually consummated. His partner, as a result of her own personal history, was predisposed to believe that men would reject her. His impotence, therefore, had a particular significance for her. So, for him, impotence signified anxiety about, and an unconscious protest against, a potentially engulfing world; for her, it represented confirmation of an internal conviction that bidding for intimacy would result in rejection. Understanding these unconscious assumptions made a difference to them as a couple.

As they discussed their relationship, it became possible for them to feel safer together and to risk exploring their sexuality without being too dismayed by their failure to make sex work between them. Anxiety about rejection and malignant misunderstanding reduced between them. Their gift to their therapist at the end of the therapy was to convey the information that they had, indeed, succeeded in having penetrative sex. What they felt had been important for them was the development of an increased sense of security and acceptance of each other in the relationship. This involved acknowledging feelings of both love and hate. It was as if they each needed to create the conditions in which they felt secure in their attachment to the other before they could feel desire and connect sexually. The role of therapy was to help create those conditions.

While fear of intrusion or rejection may inhibit desire, the threat of loss can activate it through mobilizing protest.

A couple came for help following the husband's affair. They were at a time in their lives when she was consumed by child-care responsibilities and on the verge of re-entering the world of paid work. He was becoming successful as a performer. Their lives had become separated with the arrival of children, and the locus of emotional engagement had shifted from their relationship as a couple towards their responsibilities to children and work. Feeling unimportant at home, the husband was vulnerable to the attention paid him by a work colleague, and he started an affair. When this was exposed, his wife was devastated.

The history of their courtship suggested a dynamic between them in which he would make the running and she would hold off until he thought she no longer wanted him and began to look elsewhere. She would then re-engage with him, as if she could only know about her desire for him at the point of his leaving. This pattern lay behind the decision to marry, leaving her husband with a question of whether it was him she really wanted, a question that resonated with his own childhood experience in which he felt displaced by siblings in the affections of his parents.

When the affair first came to light, the couple's sexual relationship became passionate and frequent, and instigated by the wife. She was desperate not to lose her husband to another woman and angry with him for his infidelity. He felt guilty about the affair, but continued to struggle with the question that had dogged him throughout their relationship about whether it was him she wanted, or whether she just feared being on her own. She was the only child of American parents who had parted when she was on the cusp of adolescence, soon after coming to this country. She had tried to look after both her parents when they separated, but felt that choosing one of them would cost her the other. While she was sensitive to the feelings she attributed to her parents, she was less aware of her own susceptibility to the pain of rejection, as well as hatred towards her parents centred on being displaced from friends in the USA and abandoned in a strange country. It took the prospect of loss to trigger her feelings of sexual desire, which then flooded her as she re-engaged with powerful feelings of longing and anger from her own childhood. Rather than hatred being manifest through withholding (with the fear that its more direct expression would drive him away) it became possible to channel it through sex when there was little left to lose; indeed, his love was potentially to be regained by its release.

In these examples it was possible for the therapists to retain a psychoanalytic focus: to engage with the feelings, both loving and hating, that underlay the disorders of desire for which the couples wanted help and to enable them to think about their experience.

Sometimes, the approach for help is couched in such concrete terms that a real question is posed about whether the consulting room of a psychoanalytic psychotherapist is the right "place" for the couple, or whether behaviourally orientated psycho-sexual therapy for one or both partners might be more appropriate. This question can be particularly acute when the request is for a change in sexual behaviour that is so focused on bodily functioning that it compromises the attempt to engage with affective states and their meaning.

Of course, when psychoanalytic psychotherapists ask themselves if the (therapeutic) relationship a couple has chosen is the "right place" for them, they are not only framing a diagnostic question but also, potentially, making a statement about their countertransference to the couple. This, in turn, constitutes a different kind of diagnostic question, one that invites therapists to review their affective responses to the couple with an eye to intersubjective processes that might link their experience to that of the couple. Such a stance complicates the assessment process, but it also holds out the hope that body, mind, and relationship can be thought about as parts of an interrelated whole when considering disorders of desire.

This reflective stance is particularly important when the presenting symptom is a product of splitting. If the countertransference reflects a failure in maternal containment, it might convey a difficulty shared between couple and therapist about being fully present with each other, or about giving full rein to feelings and impulses without triggering some unnamed catastrophe. A feature of such couples can be their request for guidance, especially in connection with diagnosis and treatment, which deflects from exploring their problem in the round. This tendency might also become manifest after breaks in ongoing therapy. It is as though they are searching for a homing device to avoid anticipated misunderstanding in the hope of gaining a sense of the other and connecting, or reconnecting, but with little faith in a spontaneous attunement process. In the countertransference there may be a strong urge to respond to this in a similarly concrete manner, perhaps replicating a practical but emotionally disconnected mother–child interaction. Prescribing alternative treatment then carries with it the risk of acting out the defence against making connections with emotional experience. For example, maintaining a sense of therapeutic potency might defend against connecting with feelings of shame, helplessness, and blame that couples unconsciously communicate through the feelings they elicit in the countertransference (see, for example, Chapter Seven).

In the two examples that follow, we track the importance of the therapists' countertransference, and its reflection in their co-therapy relationship in making sense of and working with anxieties surrounding the desire for intimacy.

A couple in their early forties, who had two children in their early teens, came for help to improve the quality of their sexual relationship, which had been perfunctory at best throughout their fifteen-year marriage. Sex was scheduled fortnightly, when he obtained physical relief and she endured the encounter with little desire and no orgasm. She said she did have a capacity for sensuality, but that it was hard to access, and she needed him to do more to arouse her, like touching her genitalia. He was reluctant to do so, deeming it unnatural. She had procured sexual self-help books that she urged him to read, but to no avail. While she wanted something better sexually, he was content with the status quo. Otherwise, their relationship was described as good and harmonious, and they took great pride in their children.

The question of whether couple psychoanalytic psychotherapy was the treatment of choice came immediately to the fore. This was discussed with them at their consultation, and information was provided about more behaviourally-orientated approaches that included sensate focus exercises. While the wife was sure they had come to the right place, her husband was less sure. The therapists felt that they were faced with a choice about whose treatment world they would inhabit, his, hers or theirs, and pondered on how they might maintain a link between all three. The therapy went ahead on an exploratory basis, in the course of which the husband expressed concern about negative feelings that were being evoked in the sessions. Some time after this, the therapists were told that he had set up a DIY sensate focus programme for himself and his wife. While they succeeded in making a more regular time to be close to each other, his wife was unresponsive to his sexual over-tures. The experiment, carried out independently of their therapists, did not work out.

This disconnection between the couple in approaching their joint project was reflected in the co-therapist relationship. Institutional and training constraints prevented one of the therapists from bringing her psycho-sexual experience directly into the work, and the potential for harnessing this with the psychoanalytic approach of her co-therapist seemed an impossibility. The possibility of drawing creatively on these differences was felt to be prohibited by the context in which the ther-apy pair was working. The dilemma was played out between them when the female therapist recommended a psycho-sexual paper to her colleague and he failed to read it. This made her feel very frustrated and overlooked by him. On deeper reflection, she recognized that her initiative constituted a defence against a more direct interaction with her co-therapist, which she subsequently took up with him and to which he was more amenable. This can be understood as an enactment of the couple's dilemma in which creative intercourse between them was inhibited by a pattern of relating that contained the rebuffing of something felt to be "unnatural" to the psychoanalytic therapeutic process, resulting in a cruel withholding by one partner and the resentful submission of the other. The therapeutic opportunity provided by this incident was to know how powerfully anxiety about negation could be raised by the prospect of working together, and the feelings this could generate. It alerted the therapists to the couple's anxiety about engaging with their differences, and how avoiding conflict in their relationship dampened down their desire.

Another couple seen in co-therapy, who were young and had no children, described their sex as having more to do with holding than intercourse.

The wife clung to her husband as though to a rock. He was driven to extricate himself from her clutches, and, in the process, found it difficult to know about, let alone implement, his own desires. He felt the only way to be in touch with himself was to detach himself entirely from her, while she sought, through physical contact, for them to be as one. Their sexual interaction appeared to embody opposing strategies for dealing with a shared dilemma: a terror of psychic separation involving intercourse between two minds, rather than one. For both, this seemed to be associated with a catastrophic coming together in which one would inevitably annihilate the other; fusion or disconnection seemed to be their preferred defences.

The therapy involved working through these dynamics in the relationship with their co-therapists. In the first phase of the therapy, the threat of annihilation seemed to come for her from the therapists as she tried to maintain a fusion with him. He, on the other hand, attempted to ally himself with the therapists as a protection against engulfment by her. In the next phase, as she felt more understood by the therapists, they were each inclined to seek reinforcement of their positions from the therapists to ward off the other's misunderstanding. In the last phase, as the couple gained a more realistic knowledge of each other and some greater psychic and physical space in their relationship, together with an attenuation in the perceived threat from each other, they combined, after a long summer break, to present the therapists with an agreement to work towards an ending. She was to come on her own for some weeks, but for the last session they would come together. It seemed that the therapists were now perceived, particularly by him, as the source of malignant misunderstanding from which it was necessary for him to disconnect.

The task for the therapists seemed to be to resist annihilation and maintain an understanding—rather than misunderstanding—mind of their own in the face of the couple's apparently united front. They explored their joint proposal that she come on her own, asking whether it resulted from an experience of one voice having been heard in the therapy at the expense of the other. The husband said he had felt heard and understood by the therapists, but questioned whether they could bear his rage. They suggested that the break over the holiday period may have stirred up angry feelings, and that he might be expressing these through wanting to leave the therapists, rather as he might have felt left by them. He rejected the interpretation, leaving the therapists with the feeling that they had no option but to bear his rage and the feeling that he just did not want to come to therapy. His wife was desperate that the therapists accept their agreement, and, while she would have preferred to continue together, their proposal was valuable in that it represented something they had been able to work out together.

The therapists were left in a quandary. Should they go along with their proposal, treating it as an accommodation of their differences, or should they refuse to accept it, facing the couple with choosing between both or neither of the partners coming to future appointments? If they did accept the proposal, would they be colluding with a defensive arrangement that avoided working with opposing wishes, and leaving nobody having what they really wanted, including the therapists? Was this another version of the familiar dynamic in which she was to fuse with the therapists while he disconnected himself from them? How could a way forward be found that did not result in someone feeling their perspective had been discounted, perhaps confirming the shared phantasy that engaging with differences would be annihilating for someone?

Accordingly, they suggested that some time was taken to think about their different positions, including those of their therapists, so that their decision was informed by a consideration of different perspectives represented in the room. They both responded to the suggestion that they might be relinquishing the opportunity to have more. There followed an uncertain period, in which the therapists could not be sure whether the couple were staying or going. Contact in the sessions displayed the same uncertainty, oscillating between moments of emotional contact, illusory connection, and sadness at the sense of opportunities foregone, or recognized only in retrospect. The therapists encountered the urge to force through a decision or, alternatively, passively comply with what was going on while attempting to process the experience. Eventually, the partners decided as a couple to end the therapy, saying that they felt better able to accept the constraints of their relationship and to consider having children together. He was no longer threatening separation, and she expressed interest in pursuing individual therapy, prepared perhaps to deepen an encounter with herself as a separate being and further develop her own sense of internal space.

In this case, our hypothesis was that the containment of loving as well as hateful feelings towards the therapists modified fears associated with the meeting of separate minds, enabling the greater psychic and physical separation necessary for creative intercourse and more spontaneous sex. It illustrates the central tenet of our argument.

Desire and the psychoanalytic stance

Of the examples we have given, two involved therapists working on their own and focusing primarily on transference aspects within the couple relationship in making sense of disorders of sexual desire. The last two cases involved therapists working together as a couple and focusing on dynamics between them and the couple, and between the therapists themselves. These are all key sites for psychoanalytic work with couples, and offer opportunities for observing and experiencing some of the "impossible conflicts" that manifest themselves as disorders of desire.

We are aware that by highlighting existential dilemmas posed by sexual intimacy, and by focusing on the interactive and inter-subjective fields that shape desire, we might be reducing explanations for sexual problems, and the implications for therapy that follow from them, to the same common denominators that we use for understanding other symptoms of couple problems. We have invoked attachment security, narcissistic patterns of object relating, and Oedipal conflicts as our key conceptual narratives for illuminating disorders of desire, much as we might have done in addressing other couple problems. But are they adequate? What about the biochemistry of the body, the cultural images of sexuality, and the phenomenon of cybersex? How do we incorporate these realities into our thinking? A therapeutic approach that is historically rooted, trades in symbols, privileges parallel process, and is attuned to intersubjective realities might be vulnerable to the charge of desexualizing desire, confusing coitus with communication and approaching intercourse and interaction as if they are interchangeable. Where, in short, is the body?

The answer that we would offer, and very much in the spirit of encouraging further debate, is to suggest that the ways we think and feel about our bodies, our relationships, and the social world we inhabit provide the key to what happens in each of these domains. That is not to imply that we ignore the physiological and biochemical dimensions of sexual functioning, or the depictions of sexuality in the wider world that can impact so powerfully on what we look for and expect from sex, but only to clarify what is an appropriate focus for psychoanalytic psychotherapy. Desire is an emotion. It is triggered by certain sets of stimuli and inhibited by others. These stimuli are, we have suggested, essentially relationship based. Contemporary psychoanalysis has dispensed with the concept of libido as instinct, and in its place instated affect and relationship. There is a debate to be had about whether a proper synthesis has yet to happen in relation to this argument. What we are proposing is that the task of couple psychotherapists is to engage with the affective component of sexual relating. This, we think, will help overcome the lure of enclosed, idealized illusions and the threat of destructive unconscious fantasies that, taken together, can inhibit and divert the expression and reciprocation of sexual desire.

References

Ainsworth, M. D. S., Blehar, M., Waters, E., & Wall, S. (1978). *Patterns of Attachment: A Psychological Study of the Strange Situation*. Hillsdale, NJ: Erlbaum.

Bion, W. (1962). A theory of thinking. *International Journal of Psychoanalysis*, 43: 306–310 [reprinted in *Second Thoughts* (pp. 110–119). London: Heinemann, 1967].

Boyd, W. (1983). *An Ice Cream War*. Harmondsworth: Penguin.

Britton, R. (1989). The missing link: parental sexuality in the Oedipus complex. In: R. Britton, J. Steiner, & E. O'Shaugnessy (Eds.), *The Oedipus Complex Today: Clinical Implications* (pp. 83–101). London: Karnac.

Britton, R. (1998). Subjectivity, objectivity and triangular space. In: *Belief and Imagination: Explorations in Psychoanalysis* (pp. 41–58). London: Routledge

Britton, R. (2003). *Sex, Death and the Superego. Experiences in Psychoanalysis*. London: Karnac.

Cassidy, J. (2001). Truth, lies, and intimacy: an attachment perspective. *Attachment and Human Development, 3*(2): 121–155.

Cassidy, J., & Kobak, R. (1988). Avoidance and its relationship with other defensive processes. In: J. Belsky & T. Nezworski (Eds.), *Clinical Implications of Attachment* (pp. 300–323). Hillsdale, NJ: Erlbaum.

Clulow, C. (1984). Sexual dysfunction and interpersonal stress: the significance of the presenting complaint in seeking and engaging help. *British Journal of Medical Psychology, 57*: 371–380.

Crowell, J., & Waters, E. (2005). Attachment representations, secure-base behaviour, and the evolution of adult relationships. The Stony Brook Adult Relationship Project. In: K. E. Grossman, K. Grossman, & E. Waters (Eds.), *Attachment from Infancy to Adulthood. The Major Longitudinal Studies* (pp. 223–244). New York: Guilford.

Diamond, D., Blatt, S., & Lichtenberg, J. (Eds.) (2007). *Attachment and Sexuality*. New York: Analytic Press.

Eagle, M. (2007). Attachment and sexuality. In: D. Diamond, S. Blatt, & J. Lichtenberg (Eds.), *Attachment and Sexuality* (pp 27–50). New York: Analytic Press.

Fisher, J., & Crandell, L. (2001). Patterns of relating in the couple. In: C. Clulow (Ed.), *Adult Attachment and Couple Psychotherapy. The "Secure Base" in Practice and Research* (pp. 15–27). London: Brunner-Routledge.

Fonagy, P. (2008). A genuinely developmental theory of sexual enjoyment and its implications for psychoanalytic technique. *Journal of the American Psychoanalytic Association, 56*: 11–36.

Fonagy, P., & Bateman, A. (2006). Mechanisms of change in mentalization-based treatment of BPD. *Journal of Clinical Psychology, 62*(4): 411–430.

Fonagy, P., Gergely, G., Jurist, E., & Target, M. (2002). *Affect Regulation, Mentalization, and the Development of the Self*. New York: Other Press.

Freud, S. (1912d). On the universal tendency to debasement in the sphere of love. *S.E., 11*: 177–190. London: Hogarth.

George, C., Kaplan, N., & Main, M. (1985). The adult attachment interview. Unpublished, University of California, Berkeley.

Glasser, M. (1979). Aggression and sadism in the perversions. In: I. Rosen (Ed.), *Sexual Deviation* (pp. 279–299). London: Oxford University Press.

Hazan, C., & Zeifman, D. (1999). Pair bonds as attachment: evaluating the evidence. In: J. Cassidy & P. Shaver (Eds.), *Handbook of Attachment. Theory, Research and Clinical Applications* (pp. 336–354). New York: Guilford.

Heard, D., & Lake, B. (1997). *The Challenge of Attachment for Caregiving*. London: Routledge.

Holmes, J. (2007). Sense and sensuality: Hedonic intersubjectivity and the erotic imagination. In: D. Diamond, S. Blatt, & J. Lichtenberg (Eds.), *Attachment and Sexuality* (pp. 137–159. New York: Analytic Press.

Kernberg, O. (1995). *Love Relations. Normality and Pathology*. New Haven, CT: Yale University Press.

Laschinger, B., Purnell, C., Schwartz, J., White, K., & Wingfield, R. (2004). Sexuality and attachment from a clinical point of view. *Attachment and Human Development, 6*: 151–164.

Lyons-Ruth, K., & Jacobvitz, D. (1999). Attachment disorganisation; unresolved loss, relational violence, and lapses in behavioural and attentional strategies. In: J. Cassidy & P. R. Shaver (Eds.), *Handbook of Attachment. Theory, Research and Clinical Applications* (pp. 520–554). New York: Guilford.

Messler-Davies, J. (2005). The times we sizzle and the times we sigh: the multiple erotics of arousal, anticipation and release. In: K. White (Ed.) *Attachment and Sexuality in Clinical Practice* (pp. 57–79). London: Karnac.

Mikulincer, M., & Goodman, G. (Eds.) (2006). *The Dynamics of Romantic Love. Attachment, Caregiving, Sex*. New York: Guilford.

Mikulincer, M., & Shaver, P. (2007). A behavioural systems perspective on the psychodynamics of attachment and sexuality. In: D. Diamond, S. Blatt, & J. Lichtenberg (Eds.). *Attachment and Sexuality* (pp. 51–78). New York: Analytic Press.

Mitchell, S. (1988). *Relational Concepts in Psychoanalysis*. Cambridge, MA: Harvard University Press.

Phillips, A. (2005). *Sane Sex*. London: Faber & Faber.

Target, M. (2007). Is our sexuality our own? A developmental model of sexuality based on early affect mirroring. *British Journal of Psychotherapy, 23*(4): 517–530.

Winnicott, D. (1971). The capacity to be alone. In: *Playing and Reality* (pp. 49–56). Harmondsworth: Penguin.

CHAPTER SIX

Sexual dread and the therapist's desire

Susanna Abse

I n this chapter I will discuss why some therapies seem to help couples re-establish their sexual relationship while other therapies cannot shift longstanding difficulties in this area. Linked to this, I will explore whether therapists need to work directly with the details of a couple's sexual relationship, as these may represent enactments of otherwise inaccessible anxieties. I will also address how the therapist's countertransference can be helpful in making sense of these body-based symptoms.

An aversion to sex?

It is commonly said that couple psychoanalytic psychotherapists do not talk much about sex. Because of developments in psychoanalytic theory since the middle of the last century, and in particular the influence of Melanie Klein, there has been a dominance of interest in early object relations and a focus on the relationship between mother and baby. This focus has made it less common for psychoanalytically informed couple therapists to be curious about their patient's sex life in the ordinary, day-to-day way that Freud and other early psychoanalysts were. Kennedy (2001) comments in his reader, *Libido*, that modern psychotherapists tend not to discuss sex much with their patients, and points out that it was from these ordinary discussions that Freud developed his thinking about many aspects of sexuality.

Some say that the British psychoanalytic movement has been suffering from difficulty in integrating Freud's genital theory with the object relations emphasis on early experience at the breast (see, for example, Budd, 2001). There has been a tendency to reduce sex to love and attachment, ignoring the expression of sexuality as a goal in itself. Bringing together a perspective that can incorporate the embodied and the relational self could be said to be an appropriate aim for those working with sexual dysfunction, but couple psychotherapists have differing views about how to approach the sexual relationship. Some refrain from enquiring into this area, preferring to wait for the material to emerge without prompting. Their view is that the sexual relationship is simply one way in which unconscious phantasies about object relations are demonstrated, and that material about a couple's eating habits are as rich symbolically of their relating and intercourse as a direct discussion about their sexual habits. This idea, together with a concern that the therapist may be experienced as unhelpfully intrusive if they address the sexual relationship directly, tends to mean that a therapy can proceed without any particular discussion of sex.

In a move away from Freud's interest in genital impulses, where sexual drives were seen to dominate the individual's psyche, the object relations tradition understood sexual impulses as profoundly influenced by early pre-genital infantile experiences. Rather than sexual drives being the bedrock of the human psyche, the infant's earliest oral relationship to mother and the breast predominates, and sexuality is seen as an arena where creative and destructive impulses can be elaborated and played out. As Royston (2001) says:

> Simply stated it is that the psychodynamics of the earlier era, the oral stage, are gathered up by the toddler and transported to the later phases where they are stamped onto all aspects of the older child's emerging sexuality. Sexuality, then, is infancy in a new erotic form, babyhood in a different jacket. [p. 37]

A consequence of this way of understanding and working with sexuality can be a belief that the sexual relationship does not hold anything particularly special or significant with regard to a couple's shared unconscious phantasy. Understanding the couple's core unconscious preoccupations is central to the work of the couple psychotherapist, who sees the analysis of these shared phantasies as key to digesting and containing, and eventually changing, unhelpful and destructive patterns of relating. Of course, shared unconscious phantasies are, by their very nature, largely unknowable, but therapists seek to find echoes from the depths of these underlying concerns to understand the deepest dynamics of a relationship. The debate is whether elements of these phantasies are uniquely available in the sexual relationship, or whether they can be observed in other aspects of a couple's life together.

In the tradition of clinical practice at the Tavistock Centre for Couple Relationships, it has certainly been true that working with a couple who come to examine their difficulties does not necessarily mean that a light will be shone on their sexual relationship. Many couples come, explore their dilemmas, cry, shout, and reflect in our consulting rooms over many years, without ever really talking at all about what goes on in the bedroom. Over time, I have indeed found that couples with, for instance, a very sado-masochistic dynamic have replicated that dynamic in their sexual relationship, and that other unconscious patterns of relating have been satisfyingly mirrored in sexual activity.

> Jean and Peter came to see me because they had married, bought a flat, and wanted to start a family, but had never had penetrative sex. Peter, a successful lawyer who drove a powerful motorbike, came to the session dressed in leathers. Jean, willowy, fragile, and dressed in florals, worked as a junior colleague to Peter. Peter appeared firm, determined, and very in control of his life and the relationship, whereas Jean seemed fearful of life and the potential impact of the therapy.

> Conversely, in their sexual relationship this pattern was reversed. Peter could not maintain an erection, felt frightened and inadequate, and avoided sexual encounters at all cost. Jean, on the other hand, wanted a full sexual engagement and, indeed, had had several other successful sexual relationships in her life. She seemed to exude sexual confidence.

In this brief vignette we can see that, although the roles reversed in the sexual relationship, the essential pattern of one partner feeling fragile and inadequate while the other felt confident and empowered was enacted both in and out of the bedroom. This shared pattern of relating meant that together they enacted their deeper unconscious anxieties about getting close and being intimate.

On the other hand, there have been times when this way of understanding sexual difficulties has been completely confounded, and patterns of relating and sexual narratives have appeared not to match up.

> Caroline and Ahmed came to therapy because violence had erupted between them during Caroline's labour. The couple, who had both suffered traumatic ruptures in care in their childhoods, resorted to violence when vulnerability and dependence threatened them. Threats of abandonment or loss brought about such unmanageable feelings in this couple that at these times their relationship would descend into verbal and physical violence. In the sessions they spat out accusations and insults, and for many months the therapy was dominated by their cruel and vicious fights. In describing their sexual relationship, however, it seemed that vulnerability and dependence was allowed, and they described to me on several occasions unexpected tenderness and openness in their frequent love-making.

This is puzzling is it not? Certainly it was to me.

Sexual behaviour and symbolism

An individual therapist colleague once asked me rhetorically whether I thought that the detail of a couple's sexual life together was the royal road to their unconscious? Freud (1900a) believed that the unconscious would make itself known in dreams, and that dreams could give the patient and analyst access to parts of the self that were otherwise not available for analysis. He also believed that the patient's unconscious was accessible through words, and could be analysed in the free associations of the sessions. Later, Melanie Klein (1926), working with children, suggested that the play of young children was symbolic of their unconscious preoccupations, and that one could reach their fears and concerns through an understanding of the meaning of their play. Couple psychotherapists do not, on the whole, actively seek dream material or encourage the kind of free associating that Freud did. However, the material brought to sessions is frequently full of stories about the couple's life together. Fisher (1999) describes these narratives as being similar to dream material, and it is certainly true that psychoanalytic therapists working with couples treat these household stories as material rich with symbolism.

> Michael said he was angry with his wife, Janine. He said she always sided with the live-in nanny, Gina, and that he had no say in the way the house ran. He felt that the nanny was not taking care of their one-year-old son, William, properly, and that he was left without one-to-one attention while the nanny did the chores for Janine. He felt strongly that William should not be left alone with his toy box. As the couple were struggling with their sexual relationship, their therapists took this story up as symbolic of Michael's feelings about being left alone without his wife's sexual attention. They also explored with Michael whether William's toy box stood for his penis and his sense of being expected to satisfy his own needs though masturbation.

In this vignette, the therapists use the symbolic material to interpret towards the body and sexuality (see Chapter Two) and, through these interpretations, hope to make Michael's own feelings of exclusion more available for thought and analysis.

The presentation of sexual difficulties in a couple is often located in a bodily dysfunction and the dysfunction (if not organic) can feel mysterious both to the couple and the therapist. In addition, both the couple and the therapist may find that these problems are often difficult to explore imaginatively. Loss of desire in one or both partners may not be accompanied by any easily accessible narrative, nor are sexual dysfunctions such as erectile problems necessarily understandable through material brought verbally to the session. Is this because these somatic difficulties are indicative of an experience that cannot be symbolized? Sometimes it seems that experience can be stuck in the body without the symbols and thoughts that would allow for its containment and metabolization. Without this capacity for symbolization, body-based symptoms might remain inaccessible through the verbal interchange of the session and might be reachable only through the sexual "play" or "enactments" of the couple.

Bion (1962), in his classic paper "A theory of thinking", described the process whereby the bodily experience (sense data) of the infant is gradually converted into the capacity for thought. This process is facilitated by the primary carer, who responds to the infant's projective identification by using her capacity for thinking to contain the projection, thereby converting frightening unprocessed experience, "beta elements", into the processed and contained "alpha elements" that make thought possible. Without this primary experience of containment, the infant is forced to take back his inchoate experience, which is now felt to be what Bion termed "nameless dread". Over time, the experience of containment allows the infant to develop his own thinking function, enabling experience to become meaningful through the use of symbols.

The therapist's countertransference

In psychoanalytic work with couples it is usual for the therapist to have to wait patiently for material that leads to understanding and insight into the couple's unconscious preoccupations. Being unable to make sense of the couple's material and difficulty is an everyday problem. However, I have had experiences of this absence of understanding when working with sexual difficulty that has particularly confounded me. While some couples restore their sex life quite naturally as the therapy makes progress, quite often sexual difficulties can remain resistant to understanding or change: the relationship might be improving and the quality of the intimacy in the sessions deepening (both between the couple and with their therapist), but the sexual relationship remains stuck and sterile. Over the years, I have found that sensitivity to the countertransference experience, both embodied and relational, is the way that I can begin to reach repressed and split-off areas of the couple's shared sexual fears that remain body-based and without symbols or words to contain them.

> Karina and Mike had been coming to see me for eighteen months. Their relationship had been fragile, but we had usefully explored many aspects. One problem that remained was Mike's passivity in the bedroom. Karina found sex unsatisfying, partly because of Mike's

premature ejaculation, and partly because Mike refused to touch, arouse, or energetically penetrate her, preferring her to be on top while he remained motionless below. On one occasion Mike came to see me alone. He told me this story. He had gone to a new hairdresser to have his hair cut. He was gowned up and taken to the basin to have his hair washed. The shampooist washed his hair and then applied conditioner and gave him a head massage. During the massage, he had an orgasm. He had not been aware of being aroused, and was certainly alarmed and taken aback at orgasming without warning and without any direct stimulation to his penis. I listened to his story, and, using my memory of previous sessions and my theoretical canon, tried to make links between infantile experience, his relationship to Karina, and his excitement at being handled like a passive baby. No doubt these were useful links, and some of them may have been psychically accurate, but I had the sense that both of us were confounded. For me, the experience was odd. I felt I could in no way relate to his experience, and my countertransference was of being in utterly foreign territory.

This sense that neither he nor I could make a link between his relational and embodied self was both curious and frustrating. Was there anyway to make sense of what my patient understood as a purely bodily experience unlinked to any thought or fantasy? Certainly my experience of mystification could be understood as the countertransference response to his deep dread of knowing about his sexual excitement.

Freud (1940a) described how the earliest experiences of sexual arousal mould sexual phantasies. These arousals can be generated through day-to-day experiences of nappy changing and similar tactile experiences. They can also come from traumatic experiences, such as sexual abuse or bodily damage. Whatever the genesis of these bodily experiences, the infant will need them contained and made manageable, and the more powerful and traumatic these experiences, the more the primitive ego will need to evacuate them through projection.

Over the years of my practice, I have had several experiences of hearing about sexual encounters that seem to leave both myself and the patient puzzled. Stories of sexual comings together that have failed, stories of the arousal of desire that has then been lost, and stories that speak to the emptiness where arousal and desire would ordinarily be found. In his novel *On Chesil Beach*, McEwan (2007),

describing a first sexual encounter, brilliantly evokes both the generation of desire and the accompanying dread that comes with it:

> When they kissed she immediately felt his tongue, tensed and
> strong, pushing past her teeth, like some bully shouldering his way
> into a room. Entering her. Her own tongue folded and recoiled in
> automatic distaste, making more space for Edward. [p. 28]

And:

> It must have been accidental, because he could not have known that
> as his hand palpated her leg, the tip of his thumb pushed against
> the lone hair that curled out free from under her panties, rocking it
> back and forth, stirring in the root, along the nerve of the follicle, a
> mere shadow of a sensation, an almost abstract beginning, as infi-
> nitely small as a geometric point that grew to a minuscule smooth-
> edged speck, and continued to swell. She doubted it, denied it, even
> as she felt herself sink and inwardly fold in its direction. How could
> the root of a solitary hair drag her whole body in? [p. 87]

And:

> Despite the pleasing sensation and her relief, there remained her
> apprehension, a high wall, not so easily demolished. Nor did she
> want it to be. [p. 88]

In my experience, such stories tend only to be brought to therapy if elicited by the therapist; they are often so fragmented and
without a coherent narrative that couples find it very hard to
verbalize them unassisted. Once elicited, however, they can present
the therapist with a particular countertransference experience
where bodily feelings and longings may be projected into the therapist. Listening to any material about a couple's life together invites
the therapist to identify imaginatively with the scenes evoked, and
this is used to empathize and get close to the experience of their
patients. Often, through projective identification, the therapist is
required to experience feelings that are split off and denied by the
patient. Listening to sexual material is, in my opinion, no different.
Just as feelings of anger, hurt, and rage are frequently evacuated
into the therapist, so also are sexual feelings linked to desire, revulsion, and dread. In addition, the more an experience is purely body-

based, the more excessive the projection is likely to be and the greater the likelihood that the therapist will experience strong feelings in the countertransference.

In the following account of a therapy, I chart the process whereby body-based symptoms move from the mysterious and unknowable, both by the couple and myself as their therapist, to something that can be articulated and thought about, and the impact this had on their sexual relationship.

From dread to desire

I had been working with Sean and Mariana for nearly five years at the point that this account begins. Their therapy had started in an unpromising way, as the couple were very late for their assessment session and, when they did finally arrive in my consulting room, Mariana immediately needed to use the toilet. Minutes passed in silence as Sean and I sat there waiting for her return. Eventually, I opened my door and found Mariana being herded towards the consulting room by one of my colleagues, like a lost child. There had also been problems with times, problems with money, and, most importantly, problems with commitment to ongoing therapy.

Their presenting problem was centrally to do with their argumentative and fractious relationship, and a lack of any satisfying sexual relationship. The couple had been together for just under three years and these problems were told to me in the context of a somewhat vague wish to settle down together and have children.

Mariana looked very young for her age, with chic short blond hair and an athletic, well-kept figure, while Sean looked somewhat crumpled, and I noticed his skin was very scarred from adolescent acne. Their dismay at the lack of a sexual relationship between them waxed and waned throughout the therapy. At first, the sessions were dominated by Mariana's dissatisfaction at Sean's failures, failures that ranged from not cleaning the bath to being mean with money. From time to time she would also bring up his lack of sexual potency, his apparent disinterest in sex, and his failure to please her in this department. This was often linked to his physical failings, where she drew attention to his poor deportment, flabby stomach, and bad skin.

Mostly, Sean would sit passively through these attacks. At times he would try to argue his case, but he largely seemed to find ways to absorb and survive the attacks through a profound withdrawal into himself. In one session he described this as the Fabian defence, a battle tactic he had read about in a business manual, which was supposed to wear the opposition down through inaction. Sean's strategy of cutting off from contact seemed to leave Mariana holding the wish both to relate and to criticize, and she would redouble her efforts to get through to him by shouting, berating, and harrying him in a way that would have been hard for anyone to bear. Sean, acknowledging his life-long capacity for withdrawal, described how Mariana's determination to try to "get under his skin" was the exact reason why he was so compelled by her.

Mariana was born in South America. At her birth, her mother became psychotic and remained hospitalized until her death, when Mariana was a teenager. Mariana had few memories of her mother, but described a fantasy of her as mad, wild-haired, and smelly. Her father, represented as cold, rigid, and unable to care for her, sent Mariana in infancy to a convent children's home and, apart from a few failed attempts to return home, she was cared for by nuns throughout her childhood. She had very few memories of her childhood, but told me of some rudimentary memory of her father touching her inappropriately as a teenager on one of her visits home. Mariana believed that experience did not lead to any physical encounter of sexual abuse, but left her feeling confused, uncertain, and wary.

Sean was born in Ireland. Throughout his childhood his mother struggled with cancer, dying when he was sixteen. For much of his childhood his mother was bed-ridden, and Sean appeared to have been her main carer (looking after her physically) and companion. Father, a primary school teacher, was largely absent from the family and had an affair with a female colleague whom he married soon after his wife's death. Sean's mother was deeply disappointed in her husband, whom she berated contemptuously at every turn. He described his mother as loving, but very demanding. She had high hopes for Sean, including ambitions that he would leave Ireland, go to Oxbridge, and achieve a glittering career.

Despite his story, Mariana was determined to idealize Sean's relationship to his parents, wanting to believe that he had inside him the kind of experience of family life that she had so longed for as a child. Her belief that he could somehow show her the way to a stable and secure emotional situation was matched by his eagerness to care for her and make up for the severe deprivations of her childhood. Sean's success and status at work reassured Mariana that she had made a good choice, but the shared hope that she could be repaired by Sean was frighteningly threatened in other areas. Sean's limitations, represented largely in his disappointing physical appearance, his poor cleanliness around the house, and his lack of sexual potency, caused Mariana great anxiety, which resulted in endless nagging and furious attacks.

We explored the link between Sean's experience of Mariana and that of his mother early on in the therapy. Like his mother, Mariana could be demanding and persecutory and, as with his mother, Sean knew that underneath her controlling behaviour Mariana was very fragile. It was striking how he repeated his relationship to his mother, feeling responsible for Mariana and for caring for her fragile and damaged parts. Mariana's feelings towards Sean veered between believing he *could* rescue and restore her and enormous disappointment and anger when this proved not to be possible. Her relationship with him seemed largely based on a narcissistic identification. In particular, Mariana's revulsion and rage at Sean's physical shortcomings seemed to represent a coming into contact with the mad, smelly mother part of herself that she hoped to repair and restore. His bad skin and poor posture were felt to be a personal affront to her, which she tried to sort out through fixing doctor's appointments and gym sessions. His inadequacies, which she constantly picked at, made her extremely anxious and controlling. In these ways, they mutually projected into each other parts of themselves that felt damaged, ugly, and inadequate.

Their sexual relationship had never really got off the ground. Early encounters had been only partially satisfactory, though Mariana was keen to assert that, before Sean, she had had robust and lively sexual experiences with beautiful, potent, muscular men. It emerged, however, that she had never orgasmed with a partner, and had been known to break down in tears in response to her own sexual excitement. She could not understand what led to those tears, and they had a mysterious and puzzling quality. Her weeping response to desire had happened in the early part of her relationship with Sean, and this, together with her angry attacks on his physical inadequacies and his tendency to withdraw, seemed to have pretty much destroyed their sex life. Sex, it seemed, was one area where neither of them could restore and repair the other, and where they came up most painfully against their damaged selves.

As the therapy proceeded and many of difficulties were better contained, the question of addressing the difficulties in their sexual life became more pressing. In one session, they described a lazy Sunday afternoon where both of them had gone to bed for a nap and woke up feeling close and sexy. They described having felt close and loving, and having tried to have sex, but the whole thing had gone wrong.

As they spoke about the events, I felt two things. First, a very puzzling sense that I could not understand what had gone wrong, which prompted my curiosity. Second, a powerful desire to help them achieve intercourse. I could at this point have interpreted their shared disappointment at the experience of being let down and then left it at that, but my curiosity to understand exactly what the mechanics of the problem were drove me to enquire further. My countertransference led me to ask for the details of what had "gone wrong". Without hesitation Mariana told me that she had noticed during the cuddling that Sean had had an erection and that had made her excited and expectant. Sean told me he was unaware of his erection until Mariana pointed it out. Mariana said, "That's weird isn't it? Surely you would have known?" They described how they had begun to touch each other intimately and how, before long, Sean had attempted to penetrate Mariana, but she had discouraged him. At this point, their stories diverged. Mariana said she had tried to stop him because he was not hard enough, and he would not be able to penetrate her without a full erection. Sean maintained that he had been hard enough, and the couple argued fiercely about this for several minutes.

Listening to their different accounts led me to a disturbing feeling of not knowing where truth or reality lay. Was Sean's assertion that he was hard enough correct, or was Mariana in touch with something that Sean could not know about? His acknowledged difficulty with even knowing at the beginning of the encounter that he had an erection made me wonder about some kind of profound split between mind and body, and I linked this in my mind with Mariana's description of her mysterious crying in response to sexual excitement. I actively wondered, though it was well out of my normal practice, if I should proceed to a body-based "hands on" intervention, such as a programme of sensate focus used in psycho-sexual therapy (see Chapter Eight). I knew that, although they wanted to return to their difficulties with sex, the sense of dread that surrounded it led to a general avoidance of the issue. I wondered about my collusion with this avoidance and how unhelpful it was. This led to my subsequently taking up a great deal of their material as sexual metaphors, which led to more news of sexual encounters that I explored with them in detail.

Around this time, Sean's level of engagement in the sessions began to change. Early on, I would notice that I would need to be the initiator of any real contact and that this unsurprisingly always had the potential for tipping over into something persecutory and intrusive. He took the initiative in talking about his childhood, and several important sessions were spent on his early years, his discovery of his father's infidelity, and, most importantly, two traumatic events. First, it emerged that, aged five, he was hospitalized and operated on for phimosis. He described how his parents had taken him to the hospital and left him there. He remembered the experience as frightening, and described his sense of being abandoned. He also talked about his feeling that his penis had never been quite right, and that he thought he had a deformity because of this early operation.

The second trauma, which he described in another session, came gradually out of discussions about bathrooms. Both Mariana and Sean would describe scenes between them that often had their setting as the bathroom. Mariana would complain that Sean left the bathroom dirty, and Sean would complain that he did not like Mariana coming into the bathroom while he was in there. In one session, Sean said that he felt that bathrooms were dangerous; they were full of hard surfaces and hard tiles, and he thought he had a slight phobia about them. Mariana said, "You don't like swimming pools either", and recounted Sean's discomfort at the local pool the previous weekend, which he said was to do with his sense of vulnerability when unclothed with water and hard surfaces around him. Sean then retrieved a memory and told us the following story.

He remembered that he was eleven or twelve years old, and was at a swimming pool on a busy weekend. He was having a good time and playing with lots of friends in the water. There was one girl he liked, and they were playing chase. He got out of the water to run after her, and in the chase slipped and went crashing though a glass window. He remembers his hand being almost severed from his body and the discussion at the hospital about whether they would be able to re-attach his hand or whether it should be cut off. I interpreted the link to his early experience of circumcision, and said that in his mind he was trying to work through powerful anxieties linked to castration and damage. I also commented on how he had linked his excitement and active pursuit of the girl with the disastrous event where he nearly lost his hand/penis.

In the following session, Sean recounted this dream: "He and I are together, and he is lying naked on his back. I am playing with his penis and he is getting erect." I wondered anxiously to myself whether this dream represented a feeling that I was titillating and seductive, and that my active enquiry into their sexual life together had prompted this response. On the other hand, I felt that this was a positive dream, and chose to interpret how the work we were doing was helping him feel more potent; not only that, but in the dream he was able to know that my actions (playing with his penis) led to him becoming excited and that this was about links being made which would allow him to know about and embrace his sexual excitement.

All through this period the couple were undergoing fertility treatment. Though on one level both of them wanted a baby, the treatment required a sustained commitment that they found difficult to meet. Gradually, however, the ambivalence lessened and treatment began to progress more smoothly. Soon after the dream session, the couple came and found a pram in the corridor outside my consulting room. The pram belonged to another patient who was seeing a colleague working next door. This event coincided with an IVF cycle and a time when the couple were waiting to take a pregnancy test to see if their treatment had been successful. Mariana was very excited and curious about the pram, and wondered whether this was a sign that she was pregnant. Two weeks later, to the couple's great joy, they had a positive test. Although the conception was not as a direct result of the couple's sexual intercourse, it was clear that their growing capacity to be a couple in a sustained, potent, and sexual way had led to the pregnancy. The couple said that the sighting of the pram had been highly significant to them, and a good omen for this successful pregnancy and the birth of a healthy baby girl.

These creative and sustained steps towards greater intimacy and potent creativity came about, I believe, through the creation of symbols and meaning. The development of images of broken glass and broken damaged bodies made it possible for the containment of dread and allowed for the birth of images of creative intercourse symbolized by the pram. The creation of symbols transformed unknown and frightening aspects of their bodily experience into something that could be thought about and thereby contained. Both Mariana and Sean were able to move away from projecting these damaged/traumatized parts of themselves into each other by using the therapy to transform unmetabolized beta-elements into alpha functioning (Bion, 1962). This in turn led to a "conception".

Isaacs (1952), in a classic paper, evolved the idea that unconscious phantasies are the mental representations of instinct, and that every bodily event is eventually accompanied by an unconscious phantasy. Perhaps the creation of symbols lifted this couple out of the world of bodily symptoms into the world of meaning, converting "raw sense data" (Bion, 1962) into thoughts. Inchoate bodily experiences that were lodged in their bodies as somatized symptoms were transformed into symbols and thought, connecting body and mind.

The therapist's desire to bring the couple together, as felt in my countertransference, also seems to me a vital part of this linking process. My countertransference wish to connect them up became most evident to me later in the therapy while watching Mariana trying to establish a feeding relationship with her new baby. As she struggled in the room to get herself and the baby comfortably joined up, while also managing her feelings about her very sore and damaged nipples, I was overtaken with a wish to put the nipple firmly and squarely into the baby's mouth. This wish, which I resisted with some difficulty, reminded me of the fantasy I had had months before, when I longed for a "hands on" intervention to help them achieve intercourse.

Disturbances in sexual functioning that have no organic basis must forever remain largely mysterious. We cannot know what the meaning of any bodily symptom really is, or how it was generated. What seems to me important is the therapist's willingness to engage in meaning-making with the couple through the use of metaphor; a process that involves the use of the therapist's embodied and relational self. Where sexual difficulties remain meaninglessly stuck, a direct and detailed examination of the mechanics of a couple's sexual life may be helpful. The resulting countertransference response may make it possible to elaborate and interpret their symptoms, which can set off the process of symbol formation and, eventually, the containment of sexual dread.

References

Bion, W. R. (1962). A theory of thinking. *International Journal of Psychoanalysis*, 43: 306–310 [reprinted in *Second Thoughts* (pp. 110–119), London: Heinemann, 1967.

Budd, S. (2001). No sex please—we're British. In: C. Harding (Ed.), *Sexuality: Psychoanalytic Perspectives* (pp. 52–68). Hove: Brunner-Routledge.

Fisher, J. (1999). *The Uninvited Guest*. London: Karnac.

Freud, S. (1900a) *The Interpretation of Dreams*, S.E., 4–5. London: Hogarth.

Freud, S. (1940a). *An Outline of Psychoanalysis. S.E. 23*. London: Hogarth.

Isaacs, S. (1952). The nature and function of phantasy, In: M. Klein, P. Heinemann, S. Isaacs, & J. Riviere (Eds.), *Developments in Psychoanalysis*. London: Hogarth.

Kennedy, R. (2001). *Libido (Ideas in Psychoanalysis)* London: Icon.

Klein, M. (1926). The psychological principles of early analysis. *International Journal of Psychoanalysis, 8*: 25–37.

McEwan, I. (2007). *On Chesil Beach*. London: Jonathan Cape.

Royston, R. (2001). Sexuality and object relations. In: C. Harding (Ed.) *Sexuality: Psychoanalytic Perspectives* (pp. 35–51). Hove: Brunner-Routledge.

CHAPTER SEVEN

Loss of desire and therapist dread

Sandy Rix and Avi Shmueli

The loss of sexual desire is a frequent symptom presented to psycho-sexual therapists, almost exclusively by women, and one that challenges the therapeutic effectiveness of those they consult. A survey carried out in Relate identified the most commonly presenting sexual dysfunctions as disorders of desire (Roy, 2004). These disorders are invariably understood as female conditions rather than relationship problems, and are capable of evoking strong responses in their therapists. This chapter describes the results of a small scale qualitative study of the experience of a group of psycho-sexual therapists working with couples where the woman reported loss of sexual desire. The study was carried out as part of a post-graduate Masters programme undertaken by Sandy Rix at the Tavistock Centre for Couple Relationships. It describes the counter-transference of the psycho-sexual therapists, including their sense of dread, and proposes that this reflected emotional problems that remained unaddressed in the partners and between them as a couple. The potency of therapists is challenged in psycho-sexual work, and it is argued that engaging with the unaddressed affect in both therapy and couple relationships is important in addressing defensive aspects of presenting symptoms and the anxiety that underlies them.

Loss of sexual desire

There is a vast research literature that attempts to define and conceptualize the experience of loss of sexual desire, which suggests that there is something elusive about the condition despite the many assertions that have been made regarding it. The studies mainly focus on loss of desire as a problem, although defining the nature of the problem itself has proved problematic. In attempting to do so, there has been a drift towards medicalizing the experience.

The Diagnostic and Statistical Manual (DSM-IV-TR) (1994), published by the American Psychiatric Association, defines hypoactive sexual desire disorder as:

> A deficiency or absence of sexual fantasies and desire for sexual activity (Criterion A). The disturbance must cause marked distress or interpersonal difficulty (Criterion B). The dysfunction is not better accounted for by another Axis 1 disorder (except another sexual dysfunction) and is not due exclusively to the direct physiological effects of a substance (including medications) or a general medical condition (Criterion C).

A number of criticisms have been made about this definition, in particular that it implies a medical disorder but one that is hard to categorize (Kaplan, 1995; Wylie, 2001). Bancroft (1983) defined sexual drive as being a subjective state that is characterized by a predisposition to seek out sexual stimuli, a state that Lieblum (2002) viewed as interchangeable with sexual desire. But can an indisposition to seeking out sexual stimuli be classified as a disorder? While most studies focus on physiological or behavioural aspects of the sexual relationship in defining desire or its absence, both men and women tend to conceptualize it as a subjective and psychological experience rather than a physiological state or behavioural event (Regan & Berscheid, 1996). Although the definition of hypoactive desire has been revised to reflect subjective aspects of sexual experience (Basson et al., 2000), a discrepancy between the ways couples and researchers understand sexual desire—between what we might call subjective and objective approaches to the phenomenon—remains, raising questions about why this might be so.

Some researchers have shifted their thinking in an attempt to address subjective and contextual aspects of sexual desire and its loss. Basson and colleagues (*ibid.*) suggest that problems of sexual desire are an indication of a lack or loss of differentiation in the couple's relationship. Leiblum (2002) investigates gender differences in sexual desire and challenges the universal stereotype that men are driven by their sexual impulses while women rarely feel desire. Despite these developments, ambiguity remains about the nature and treatment of loss of sexual desire. In the face of this ambiguity, the default response is to categorize loss of desire as a disorder: for example, "hypoactive sexual desire disorder" (Beck, 1995). Bancroft (2002) has urged caution about this response, and suggested that until a distinction between adaptive inhibitions of response and maladaptive dysfunction can be made it will be difficult to predict when pharmacological treatment can be helpful. This is important, since the pharmaceutical industry has shown considerable interest in the problem, adding a commercial dimension to the debate on definitions. Interestingly, the move into disorders seems to reflect an attempt to take control of what have been described as being among the most complex and difficult of sexual disorders to treat (Ravart, Trudel, Marchand, & Turgeon, 1996). Could this contradiction add to the discrepancies in ways of understanding loss of sexual desire to suggest a defensive dynamic operating in research and therapeutic approaches?

Two further points emerge from the studies. First, loss of sexual desire is seen principally as a female condition. Most of the clinical literature and research associated with loss of sexual desire has located the problem in the woman, relabelling the difficulty as "female arousal dysfunction". An international conference specifically focusing on female sexual dysfunction in 2000 considered papers that must have added considerable weight to understanding sexual problems as gender specific. For example, "responsive sexual desire" (Basson et al., 2000) was claimed to be one of the commonest type of female sexual desire problems. The definition of this concept has been developed in terms of it being the ability to be aroused that is lost, rather than desire itself, with the conclusion that "reasons for failures in the management of desire disorders in women are largely due to the previously held but inaccurate depiction of women's sexual desire" (Basson, 2003, p. 113).

The second point is that loss of desire is principally approached as an individual problem, and not as a phenomenon occurring within the context of a relationship. This individualistic approach has been criticized in relation to women's sexuality generally, because it ignores the extent to which sexual problems may be co-constructed in relationships (Vincent, Riddell, & Shmueli, 2000, p. 29). *Sexual and Relationship Therapy*, Britain's major journal covering this field, has not published one paper since 2000 that focuses on the problem for the couple of loss of sexual desire. At the European Federation of Sexology Congress in 2004, where several hundred papers were presented, only one focused on "hypoactive sexual desire disorder", and that concerned whether women experienced subjective arousal and orgasm (Hall, Gregory, & Ahmed-Jushuf, 2004). This was despite the opening talk that stressed the importance of integration in sex therapy, and that acknowledged not only that most sexual problems take place within a relationship, but also that they are treated within a relationship (Weeks, 2004).

It is difficult to find published papers about couples dealing with the problem of loss of sexual desire. Keinplatz (2003), in her examination of current trends in sex therapy, felt this void resulted from a focus on symptoms rather than on the intrapsychic and relationship dimensions of sexual problems themselves. Bohart, O'Hara, and Leitner (1998) suggest that clinical approaches that take account of relationship factors appear less scientific because measurement is complex. However, Riley (1998) points out the limitations of pharmacological and other medical treatments that do not address relationship problems or intrapsychic conflicts, arguing that they are frequently the major source of sexual distress. In short, there is a paucity of literature where the loss of sexual desire is not specifically located in one partner, that one partner being the woman: with one exception, no papers were found by us that reported male loss of sexual desire. The exception (Pridal & LoPiccolo, 2000) suggested that men who have low desire for sex have even *lower* desire for sex therapy.

The current emphasis may reflect the orientation of cognitive behavioural therapy, which appeared from our reading of the literature to rely on treating the symptomatic partner regardless of whether the background research referred to the couple. For example, while one intervention study did make reference to the significance of the couple, the therapeutic focus was clearly on the symptomatic partner (Ravart, Trudel, Marchand, & Turgeon, 1996).

The main objective of this study was to examine cognitive processes in women with hypoactive sexual desire. Similarly, MacPhee, Johnson, & Van de Veer (1995) conducted an outcome study that examined the effect of marital therapy on inhibited desire, but featured only female loss of desire.

Essentially, the cognitive–behavioural approach, which informs the majority of the published research, seeks to explain loss of sexual desire in terms of negative patterns. Internal negative self-talk, based on dysfunctional assumptions and their accompanying negative ways of thinking, are seen to play a significant role in reducing sexual interest and desire, consequently affecting the quality of overall sexual response (Trudel, Boulos, & Matte, 1993). Yet studies such as this recognize the quality of the couple's relationship as being one of the most important causal factors of hypoactive sexual desire. Those who have treated hypoactive sexual desire by attempting to break the sexual avoidance relationship pattern have reported this as being a most difficult problem (McCarthy, 1997), and maybe herein lies a clue.

Although loss of sexual desire in couples is presented clinically with increasing frequency, understanding the problems facing therapists in the work has not, by and large, been addressed by researchers. We found only one paper that specifically focused on this area (Polonsky, 1997). This argued that therapy success rates, as measured by sustained increased sexual activity, were not impressive. But the paper suggests the importance of understanding couple dynamics from an object relations perspective, and focusing on the meaning of the therapist's feelings while in the company of the couple. It proposes that the therapist's reactions might reflect the more difficult aspects of the couple relationship, arguing that the feelings most often aroused in therapists when with such couples were hopelessness, anger, dissociation, and boredom. The paper concludes with a plea for both couples and therapists to accept what is, rather than trying to change it. This paper evoked a strong response, which deconstructed both the therapist's experience and expertise and advised other therapists to think clearly about the problems being treated as a protection from "countertransference rage" (Levine, 1997).

From our review of the literature, we have concluded that loss of sexual desire is a difficult problem to define. Furthermore, the majority of work published on the subject tends to focus on the individual rather than the couple, and that individual is the woman. This is perplexing when sexual desire is usually generated by, and finds expression within, a relationship. The research presents us with an abundance of intellectual concern that contains little of real value for the therapist working with this problem, despite the recognition that this is a challenging area in which to work.

Exploring therapists' experiences of working with loss of sexual desire

The review of the literature raised a number of questions for us, which provided the impetus for a study that aimed to explore what happens to therapists when working with couples experiencing loss of sexual desire. We wanted to see if this might shed light on the difficulties in defining the problem itself.

The study aimed to examine the nature of the loss of sexual desire in couples through addressing the experiences of clinicians working with this presenting difficulty. In particular, it sought to understand the meaning of the observed reluctance in therapists to work with the problem in the context of the couple relationship. The research, which we go on to describe, was a small scale qualitative study carried out at the Tavistock Centre for Couple Relationships as part of a Masters degree course.

The study was of a small sample of cases, which highlighted the subjective experience of the psycho-sexual therapist subjects. Each therapist was interviewed using a semi-structured interview to examine their experiences of working with loss of sexual desire in couples. It incorporated our particular interest in the affect aroused in therapists when working with these couples. The interviews were subsequently analysed using a grounded theory methodology (Glaser & Strauss, 1967), interrogating the dynamic relationship between data analysis and data collection procedures. This mutual interrogation comprises a critical characteristic of the grounded theory approach to research. As a procedure, it has similarities with the psychoanalytic process, where sense is made of the content of the analytic session between patient and therapist in a similarly interrelated way.

The four subjects were all highly experienced psycho-sexual therapists, each of whom had worked in the field for twenty years or more. Two had been trained as cognitive–behavioural therapists, and two as psychodynamic therapists. In this they reflected the dominant theoretical underpinnings for treating loss of sexual desire. We looked for a broad consistency between self-reported theoretical approaches to practice and those identified in the Opinions of Psychological Problems Questionnaire (Pistrang & Barker, 1992), which we used as confirmation of self-rated theoretical orientations. This provided a baseline for examining what therapists actually do in sessions as compared with what they say do. The sessions were analysed in a way that allowed dominant themes to emerge, paralleling the process of psychoanalytic work that uses the concept of free floating attention (Sandler, 1976). This process has been described in the following way.

> In a situation where meaning is not apparent and facts are accumulating, the relationship of psychic particles to one another is not determined until the analyst's attention is taken by something which becomes the *selected fact,* and there emerges a *configuration* as the other psychic particles cohere by virtue of their relationship to it. [Britton & Steiner, 1994, p. 1076]

Five significant themes emerged from the analysis of interviews with the therapists that focused on their affective experience in the sessions with couples.

1. *An inconsistency between the therapist' approach to their work* as captured by the Opinions of Psychological Problems Questionnaire (OPP) *and the illustrations they provided of the actual work they were doing with the couples reported on.*
    An example of this inconsistency is provided by one therapist who identified her way of working in cognitive–behavioural terms: ". . . and although, sometimes, you can change the behavioural component, the cognitive part needs to be . . . addressed. And I would use both . . . erm . . . approaches in couple therapy". Having said this, she went on to explain the source of loss of sexual desire as the differing responses in the couple to their life stage, what she described as the "empty nest syndrome", which was an essentially psychodynamic formulation of the problem.

2. *An inconsistency between how therapists conceptualized loss of sexual desire in couples and their own theoretical orientation.*
    There were some surprising discrepancies in the therapists' accounts, given the length of experience they had. For example, one therapist identified her theoretical orientation as primarily cognitive–behavioural, but, when asked to conceptualize loss of sexual desire in couples, said, "I think in our society we see female sexuality as about being passive and losing control, and male sexuality as about being active and in control. And many of the women I see . . . do not like the concept of being out of control. And so being sexually passive is uncomfortable for them . . . I think it is a major contributory factor to their loss of desire." Another therapist talked of a couple in psychodynamic terms, despite her main theoretical orientation being cognitive–behavioural: ". . . you could say there is a theoretical framework which comes from the cognitive analytic or cognitive behavioural, where people think things about behaviours which may not be congruent with events. [But for this woman] her sexuality was much more integrated into her core personality and identity. For the man it was quite split off."

3. *Confusing sexual desire with sexual function.*
    A confusion between desire and sexual functioning was surprising for these therapists, who were among the most experienced currently working as psycho-sexual couple therapists. One therapist, who viewed herself as a clear thinker (and had a PhD to support this) gave a very muddled account of the distinction: ". . . the relationship dynamics, their learning in their childhood and so on and so forth [contribute to sexuality] so I think in essence there isn't . . . there doesn't have to be a lot of difference [between desire and function]." Similarly, another therapist showed confusion by responding to a question about the distinction by saying: ". . . I do think a certain amount of background is important. I'm thinking about a whole range of possibilities that might cause sexual problems from . . . a recent bereavement or an unacknowledged terminated pregnancy thirty years ago, to being quite upset and angry with a partner, to loss of employment."

4. *An underlying assumption that loss of sexual desire in couples is a predominantly female problem.*

   Again, this was a surprising result given the level of experience of the therapists, all of whom had been trained to think of the "client" as the relationship and not either of the individuals within it. One of the therapists referred to some research not published ". . . which showed . . . that [of] women in a relationship 46% of them never feel sexual desire. They don't feel the need for sex, they don't feel the desire. [For] women without a relationship, 25% or something like that never feel the need for sex. So in general, not feeling desire . . . can be normal." Another therapist chose two couples to discuss with the researcher, in both of which she located the loss of desire in the woman. In relation to the second couple, she said in justification, "Well, he hasn't got the loss of desire."

5. *A lack of emotional coherence associated with working with loss of sexual desire.*

   A sense of dread was sometimes experienced by therapists working with the couples, which could have a powerful impact upon their professional functioning. Curiously, asked to name the feelings experienced when working with the problem of loss of sexual desire, all therapists chose words that might have been expected to have reflected either the couple's conscious feelings or those they felt they had lost. What was interesting was that the therapists did not seem to realize or question the significance of their choice of words, even when the feelings named were "aroused and stimulated". For example, "Sadness . . . loss . . . frustration . . . anxiety" were identified by one therapist describing her feelings in response to the core couple problem of loss of sexual desire. Thinking about these feelings seemed to cause a lot of confusion for this therapist: "I guess the sadness is that they have lost the ability to do that, which then follows on with the loss because it is a loss of part of their relationship." Asked how she would think about the meaning, she replies, "Meanings is a kind of cognitive bit, erm . . . I don't really know how to answer [your question about] meanings of feelings." Another therapist seemed to be articulating feelings that might be said to have been lost by the couple: ". . . I'm aroused to alertness and vigilance." She later confused "aroused" with "stimulation" while apparently being unaware that the relevance of this choice of words might have to do with the couple with whom she was working who had lost those very feelings. "Did I say stimulation?", she asked, as if surprised by her choice of word. Another therapist highlighted her feelings of heightened responsibility and potency when she described the couple as her "number one responsibility . . . and I choose that because, quite literally, we are talking about the scenario where the couple could break up." She seemed unconsciously to be removing some of the couple's potential for potency by working with them as if they were not responsible for themselves.

Therapist experience and the centrality of countertransference

The interview used in the research project was designed to tease out the affect in the therapist when working with couples' loss of sexual desire. This aim was set alongside verifying the experience, knowledge, and theoretical framework from which the work was carried out. The inconsistencies and confusions in the results were taken as central indicators, suggesting something emotionally important happened to these highly experienced therapists during the work of which they were unaware. Significantly, the words chosen by therapists to describe their feelings when working with couples who had lost sexual desire suggested the potent affect was claimed by the therapists, leaving the couples with less potent feelings. This could happen without awareness on the part of the therapist or protest from the couple, suggesting that there might be an unspoken collusion between the parties to keep the potency where it seemed safest to lie.

It was an unexpected finding that very experienced psychosexual therapists confused sexual desire and sexual function. This was curious, since the loss of a function such as an erection or the ability to orgasm is clearly distinguishable from the desire that precedes sexual behaviour. Equally curious was confusion about the location of loss of desire. It was hard to explain why couple trained therapists should have had an underlying assumption that loss of sexual desire was predominantly a female problem. The notion that lost parts of the self are located in the partner is as central to understanding couple interaction as the lifelong quest of Hermes and Aphrodite to locate the other part of themselves in each other is to Greek legend. This kind of experience echoes that of the published research alluded to earlier, in which defining what is meant by loss of desire has proved elusive, and its relationship context is surrendered in favour of female-centred and medically-orientated diagnoses. And all this can be done in an authoritative and weighty manner, despite the disjunctions that exist between this and how couples actually experience what is happening to them.

The results raised a question as to whether the therapists' capacity to think about their emotional experience was undermined or defended against when working with the symptom of loss of sexual desire. We might also ask if this dynamic has affected research on loss of sexual desire, and whether therapists might fall back on the protective weight of published research as a defence against painful feelings. While subjecting the weight of published research in this area to such an interpretation is highly speculative and open to critical comment, from a psychoanalytic perspective it is a thought worth playing with.

Thinking of these areas of confusion as powerful countertransference communications is one way of making sense of the results. Paula Heimann (1950) was the first psychoanalyst to write about countertransference as a means of, rather than impediment to, understanding the analytic encounter. She observed that "the analyst's countertransference is an instrument of research into the patient's unconscious", which she conceived as being the result of an interaction whereby the "analyst's unconscious understands that of the patient's unconscious" (p. 81). The "patient" Heimann refers to when extrapolated to working with couples is the couple relationship. Sandler (1976) developed the concept of countertransference by focusing on what he referred to as the "role relationship" between patient and analyst. For him, the patient's transference represented an attempt to impose an interaction on the analytic relationship representative of his internal world, and the countertransference was part of this intersubjective field. Carpy (1989), among others, has pushed the frontiers of understanding further by proposing that patients can induce in their analysts states of mind that are very similar to those they are attempting to eliminate from themselves.

In the field of couple psychotherapy, Ruszczynski (1993) recounted the practical application of countertransference experiences by considering the feelings of the psychotherapist as having been projected into him by the patient for both defensive and evacuative purposes and as a means of unconsciously communicating aspects of his internal experience. The task for the therapist is then to become consciously aware of what is being stirred up in her or him, to try to make some sense of it, and to offer some understanding back to the patient through an interpretation or comment. He suggested that if this initially unconscious communication cannot be translated into the therapist's consciousness, for whatever reasons, then that which had been stirred up might be re-enacted with the patient or in some other situation.

The pressure to re-enact defensive patterns of relating is frequently a response to perceived threats to the self. The analytic encounter, akin to the sexual encounter, can generate real existential fears clustering around the unconscious fantasy that intimacy creates winners and losers: the potent and the impotent, the emperor and the colonized, the destroyer and the destroyed, and so on. Haldane and Vincent (1998) highlighted how the dynamics of threesome relationships can undermine the thinking capacity of therapists, and suggested two major difficulties inherent in threesome couple work: first, the emotional power of the couple dynamics can result in therapists feeling either overwhelmed or excluded; second, therapists working on their own may experience shame when the focus on the couple is lost and alliances with one partner are formed at the expense of the other. In both cases, they suggested that the capacity for professional self-reflection is either minimal or attacked.

In connection with feelings of desire, Mann (1994) argued that there is no difference between transference love and normal love. However, when discussing erotic countertransference, he thought this was more difficult. He suggested that the block afflicting therapists might derive from the therapeutic relationship mirroring aspects of the parent–child relationship that made open discussion difficult. He believed that "parental" guilt associated with admitting erotic feelings towards children fostered the incest taboo, which silences the parent, and also silences the analyst, because an equivalence is drawn between thinking and doing.

The results of this study pointed powerfully towards the conclusion that working with the problem of loss of sexual desire creates a great deal of anxiety that can manifest itself in the therapist's state of mind. It suggests that therapists might be concretizing their thinking about working with loss of desire, an essentially affective condition, and defending against the feelings that are aroused by it. Of particular interest was the finding that the therapists demonstrated a conscious sense, not of impotence, but of power. Perhaps this might be understood as an impenetrable defence against the sense of internal chaos that is feared if the problem of loss of desire is removed, so the role of removing the problem is ascribed to the therapist along with the feelings associated with it. The suggestion is that there is something about loss of sexual desire that cannot be symbolized and therefore thought about, but that is enacted by the therapist with the couple in ways that rob the couple of their therapeutic potency. The results showed that, irrespective of theoretical orientation, these extremely experienced therapists moved outside their familiar working framework. This raised a question about the levels of anxiety they were having to manage, and whether their conceptual framework was being used creatively or defensively in managing those anxieties. The same question might be asked in relation to the underlying push to medicalize and individualize sexual problems, and whether they represent an attempt to create something that is more potent for those treating the problem than for those experiencing it.

Thinking about loss of sexual desire as a couple phenomenon

Psychoanalytic thinking about the couple relationship proposes that problems and conflicts between partners in a sexual relationship are inevitable and normal, although they sometimes constitute a sufficient threat to the relationship for partners to want to put them out of mind. Ruszczynski (1993) described the couple relationship as a fluid interaction between two people who are simultaneously treating each other as an object of their needs, wishes, and conflicts, both consciously and unconsciously. This unconscious interrelating results in a transference–countertransfer-ence cycle operating within the couple relationship and outside the conscious awareness of each of the partners. For each of them, internal representations are manifested in the minutiae of behav-iour between them that seek to "nudge" or evoke responses in the partner that are in line with these representations. The degree to which the partners are accepting of such unconsciously driven "nudges" determines their role-responsiveness to each other (Sandler, 1976). The underlying wish is invariably to try to rework past relationships in the current relationship and resolve now what might not have been resolvable before.

However, this developmental wish faces difficulties if what is to be reworked is psychologically painful. In such circumstances, the individual will also try to nudge his or her partner into a position that defends against the wish to rework and re-experience the past. Manifestations of the developmental–defensive tension in the couple relationship form the "dance" that is unique to each couple. This mutual process relies on finding a place of resonance in the partner and plays a key part in unconscious fit (Ruszczynski, 1995). However, if too much of the self is repudiated and projected into the partner, then the remaining sense of self becomes im-poverished and the boundaries between self and others becomes weakened.

The fate of the couple relationship relies on the ability of the partners to use their relationship as a forum in which to allow both the expression and resolution of conscious and unconscious con-flicts. Colman (1993) argues that couple difficulties might be seen in terms of the struggle to make an internal marriage, which involves intercourse both as a sexual reality and as an internal symbolic union of opposites (see, also, Chapter Two). This encapsulates the capacity for intimacy, "since intimacy implies differentiation and separation and the sharing of our innermost being with another" (*ibid.*, p. 132).

The tensions between conscious and unconscious factors within each individual, and their consequent reflection and reworking in the couple relationship, lead to different presenting manifestations or symptoms. Morgan (1995) used the phrase "projective gridlock" to describe the kind of couple relationship in which partners have a problem feeling psychically separate from each other, resulting in a sense of being locked together in a defensive collusion that permits only a very limited capacity for growth. She suggests such couples come together to avoid a relationship, because the differentiation associated with being in a real relationship, where there are two separate people, is infused with anxiety for them. Fisher (1993) explored what he called "the false couple", whom he described as having "the illusion of being a fused couple". He suggested that this type of couple enact "a duet for one" in that they are unable to create together the space they need for mutual relating. He draws on Britton's account of Bion's view that "the inability of the mother to take in her child's projections is experienced by the child as a destructive attack by her on his link and communication with her as his good object" (Britton, 1989, p. 89). The infant then experiences an impermeable mother. Feldman (1989) develops the idea into that of an impenetrable couple. Fisher (1993) argues that the impenetrable couple exerts a powerful pressure on the therapists to re-enact defensive patterns of relating in therapy sessions. He adds that these couples present considerable technical difficulties for therapists as there is a constant struggle to find the space to reflect on the process between them and the couple.

What our research suggests is that loss of sexual desire might surface in couple relationships as an impenetrable defence, where potency is split so that the problem is located in the symptomatic partner rather than being thought about as a couple problem. So, what is it that is so unconsciously feared that a defence of this order must be established and maintained? What emerged from our study was evidence of inconsistencies resulting in fluctuating boundaries of professional identity, and confusion sitting alongside certainties that maintained the potency of the therapist, both of which we took to be indicative of emotional states associated with the loss of sexual desire. Within the countertransference, therapists could re-enact the impenetrable defence that operated between the partners.

Psychoanalysis may have mimicked this defence by interpreting sexual material as either the bedrock of human experience or the defence against it. It has been observed that sexual experience has gone relatively unexplored in contemporary analytic practice, in much the same way as the manifest content of a dream has been discarded in favour of latent dream thoughts. Erotic experience is unarguably intensely physical, something psychoanalytic theories have struggled to represent, perhaps leading them to depict a shadowy picture of human sexuality that is cut off from its roots in bodily experience (Budd, 2001).

Nevertheless, there has been a shift in current thinking, and an attempt to try to understand more about sexuality. The word "sexuality" has crept into recent conference titles concerned with relationship issues. At one such conference, Fonagy (2006) argued that gratifying the human sexual drive requires intimacy with another person. The key word here is "intimacy", because it is an acknowledgement of the need for physical and emotional connection with an other. The couple relationship is an accepted source for meeting this intense and basic human need.

Fonagy (2008) suggests that psycho-sexuality is close to madness, or at least inhabits the borderline spectrum. He wonders if subliminal awareness of this may underlie the tendency of analysts to describe patients' sexual feelings and behaviours in terms of primitive disturbances. His explanation and understanding of sexual feelings and behaviour is rooted within the emotional context of unfolding object relationships (see, also, Chapter Five). He argues the following points.

- The object of excitement becomes the desire for the idea of the lost object. It can never be found, but the search for it permeates human sexuality. The mother sexualizes the infant's arousal, unconsciously seducing him, leaving the infant with a sense of inaccessible meaning.
- The infant in a state of sexual tension is not met by a congruent metabolized representation of his or her emotional experience. Without mirroring, there can be no full experience of containment or, indeed, even a sense of ownership of these feelings.
- Incongruent mirroring disrupts the self's coherence. A consequence, then, is a sense of incongruence in relation to the experience of the self associated with the psycho-sexual. Sexual arousal can never truly be experienced as owned.
- Adult sexual excitement, because of its developmental roots, is by its nature incongruent with the self. Therefore, it has to be experienced *in* the other, and only as a consequence of that constraint, *with* the other.

Schwartz (2004) charts how sexuality and attachment are no longer considered as two unrelated motivational systems but as intrinsically entwined phenomena shaped by experiences in the hands of care-givers. Aggressive aspects of sexuality are thought not to be instinctual, but the result of damaging emotional experiences, and the masculine split between sexuality and love is understood to be the resolution of the Oedipal dilemma in a social climate where fathers are largely absent care-givers. Abse (2006) wonders if the missing link for attachment theorists in understanding sexual aggression is the drive for autonomy. She argues that aggressive aspects of the self are required for the individual to achieve unit status and differentiation, so that the embodied and sexual self have to manage both the need for proximity and the drive towards autonomy.

Partners within a couple relationship are often preoccupied with whether they are the same as, or different from, each other. This might be to do with gaining more knowledge about their identity both as individuals and in relation to each other. Where both partners have a well-formed sense of self, this interest in difference and sameness arises out of curiosity and a capacity to tolerate anxiety associated with the unknown. It leads to a genuine getting to know one another. However, when partners suffer from an insecure sense of self, the prospect of getting to know others can be fraught with anxiety. Rosenthall (2002) suggests that

> This state of mind [insecurity] is driven by a primitive terror which if put into words would sound something like: "I don't know where I am in the world, I might be alone and lost forever". There is a longing to defend against these unbearable feelings, and it is not uncommon to employ the help of one's partner in creating a place of safety. The existence of a partner enables individuals in this dilemma to say "I am not lost because I am stuck to you and I know who I am because I am either the same as or different to you". [p. 21]

Couples who present for therapy with the problem of loss of sexual desire seem to bring with them a sense of underlying despair about that loss. The loss that most couples are aware of is a consequent loss of closeness. This is how they describe the meaning for them of loss of sexual desire. Unconsciously, perhaps, is the countering fear of being overwhelmed by closeness. Intercourse represents actual and symbolic union with the other in the mind of the couple. At that point, each partner is, momentarily, both alone and fused with the other. In order for this to happen, each of the two individuals needs to have a solid sense of the boundary around the physical self. For intercourse to take place, this boundary is temporarily suspended, and there must be confidence that what is momentarily in abeyance can and will be restored.

It is paradoxical to think about loss of sexual desire in terms of individual issues when its existence is intricately connected with being in a relationship with a real or fantasy other. Such loss is rarely a problem for a person not in a relationship. Sexual intercourse is part of the way couples express their physical and emotional connection to each other. This is what couples mean when sexual desire disappears and they say they have lost closeness. In order to risk being fused with another in intercourse, the boundaries of the emotional and physical self have to be firmly in place. Loss of sexual desire might be thought about as a protection of those "self" boundaries for the couple when, despite conscious desires for the contrary, they are too fragile to tolerate any fusion, however momentary. An explanation of this kind is essentially a relational explanation.

If what is feared is a threat to the boundaries of the self, and the loss of sexual desire is the impenetrable defence designed to protect against that anxiety, then its significance and importance needs to be understood by therapists both in working with this problem and making sense of their countertransference experiences. Equally, if current research can shift its focus towards couple dynamics, then it, too, might be able to reflect on its own self boundaries and about the underlying interests that are protected by keeping the problem in the individual and within the medical orbit.

Couples bring the problem of loss of sexual desire to therapy both wanting and not wanting the dysfunctional partner to be cured. The couple who cannot have intercourse bring a loss of potency to therapy. The defence against being potent might protect against a sense of dread about the loss of a sense of self in becoming fused, even temporarily, with the partner. Therapists may unconsciously be invited to take up that potency, or experience its opposite, and to join the impenetrable defence against emotional connection. They may have personal and professional motivations for perpetuating the collusion, but reflecting on the countertransference experience provides a means of engaging with the anxieties of such couples, and offers the hope of helping them to break free from the deadlock that so disrupts their sexual lives.

References

Abse, S. (2006). Review of K. White (Ed.) *Attachment & Sexuality in Clinical Practice* (2005). *Journal of Analytical Psychology, 51*(1): 156–158.

American Psychiatric Association (1994). *Diagnostic & Statistical Manual of Mental Disorders (DSM-IV-TR)*. Washington, DC: American Psychiatric Association.

Bancroft, J. (1983). *Human Sexuality and its Problems;* Edinburgh: Churchill Longman.

Bancroft, J. (2002). The medicalisation of female sexual dysfunction: the need for caution. *Archives of Sexual Behaviour, 31*(5): 451–455.

Basson, R. (2003). Biopsychosocial models of women's sexual response: applications to management of "desire disorders". *Sexual and Relationship Therapy, 18*(1): 105–115.

Basson, R., Berman, J., Burnett, A., Derogatis, L., Ferguson, D., Fourcroy, J., Goldstein, I., Graziottin, A., Heiman, J., Laan, E., Leiblum, S., Padma-Nathan, H., Rosen, R., Segraves, K., Segraves, R. T., Shabsigh Sipsko, M., Wagner, G., & Whipple, B. (2000). Report of the International Consensus Development Conference of Female Sexual Dysfunction: definitions and classifications, *Journal of Urology, 163*: 888–893.

Beck, J. (1995). Hypoactive sexual desire disorder—an overview. *Journal of Consulting and Clinical Psychology, 63*(6): 919–927.

Bohart, A., O'Hara, M., & Leitner, L. (1998). Empirically violated treatments: disenfranchisement of humanistic and other psychotherapies. *Psychotherapy Research, 8*: 141–157.

Britton, R. (1989). The missing link: parental sexuality in the Oedipus complex. In: J. Steiner (Ed.), *The Oedipus Complex Today: Clinical Implications* (pp. 83–101). London: Karnac.

Britton, R., & Steiner, J. (1994). Interpretation: selected fact or overvalued idea. *International Journal of Psychoanalysis, 75*: 1069–1078.

Budd, S. (2001). "No sex, please—we're British": Sexuality in English and French psychoanalysis. In: C. Harding (Ed.), *Sexuality: Psychoanalytic Perspectives* (pp. 52–68). Hove: Brunner-Routledge.

Carpy, D. (1989). Tolerating the countertransference: a mutative process. *International Journal of Psychoanalysis, 70*: 287–294.

Colman, W. (1993). The individual and the couple. In: S. Ruszczynski (Ed.), *Psychotherapy with Couples* (pp. 126–141). London: Karnac.

Feldman, M. (1989). The Oedipus complex: manifestations in the inner world and the therapeutic situation. In: J. Steiner (Ed.), *The Oedipus Complex Today: Clinical Implications* (pp. 103–128). London: Karnac.

Fonagy, P. (2006). A genuinely developmental theory of sexual enjoyment and its implications for psychoanalytic technique. Plenary paper given at the Winter Meeting of the American Psychoanalytic Association.

Fonagy, P. (2008). A genuinely developmental theory of sexual enjoyment and its implications for psychoanalytic technique. *Journal of the American Psychoanalytic Association, 56*: 1- 36.

Fisher, J. (1993). The impenetrable other: ambivalence and the Oedipal conflict in work with couples. In: S. Ruszczynski (Ed.), *Psychotherapy with Couples* (pp. 142–166). London: Karnac.

Glaser, B., & Strauss, A. (1967). *The Discovery of Grounded Theory: Strategies for Qualitative Research.* Chicago, IL: Aldine.

Haldane, D. & Vincent, C. (1998). Threesomes in psychodynamic couple psychotherapy. *Sexual and Marital Therapy, 13*(4): 385–396.

Hall, J., Gregory, A., & Ahmed-Jushuf, I. (2004). Hypoactive sexual desire disorder: a retrospective study to assess whether women with HSD experienced subjective arousal and orgasm. *Sexual and Relationship Therapy, 19*: 12.

Heimann, P. (1950). On countertransference. *International Journal of Psychoanalysis, 31*: 81–84.

Kaplan, H. (1995). *Sexual Desire Disorders.* Bristol: Brunner Mazel.

Keinplatz. J. (2003). What's new in sex therapy? From stagnation to fragmentation. *Sexual and Relationship Therapy, 18*(1): 95–106.

Leiblum, S. (2002). Reconsidering gender difference in sexual desire: an update. *Sexual and Relationship Therapy, 17*(1): 57–68.

Levine, S. (1997). Some reflections of countertransference: a discussion of Dr Derek Polonsky's presentation. *Journal of Sex Education & Therapy, 22*(3): 13–18.

MacPhee, D., Johnson, S., & Van de Veer, M. (1995). Low sexual desire in women: the effects of marital therapy. *Journal of Sexual and Marital Therapy, 21*(3): 159–182.

McCarthy, B. (1997). Chronic sexual dysfunction: assessment, intervention and realistic expectations. *Journal of Sex Education & Therapy, 22*(2): 51–56.

Mann, D. (1994). The psychotherapist's erotic subjectivity. *British Journal of Psychotherapy*, 10(3): 344–354.

Morgan, M. (1995). The projective gridlock. In: S. Ruszczynski & J. Fisher (Eds.), *Intrusiveness and Intimacy in the Couple* (pp. 33–48). London: Karnac.

Pistrang, N., & Barker, C. (1992). Clients' beliefs about psychological problems. *Counselling Psychology Quarterly*, 5(4): 325.

Polonsky, D. C. (1997). What do you do when they won't do it? The therapist's dilemma with low desire. *Journal of Sex Education & Therapy*, 22(3): 5–12.

Pridal, C., & LoPiccolo, J. (2000). Multi-element treatment of desire disorders: integration of cognitive, behavioural, and systemic therapy. In: *Principles and Practices of Sex Therapy* (pp. 85–117). New York: Guildford.

Ravart, M., Trudel, G., Marchand, A., & Turgeon, L. (1996). The efficacy of a cognitive behavioural treatment model for hypoactive sexual desire disorder: an outcome study. *The Canadian Journal of Human Sexuality*, 5(4): 279–293.

Regan, P., & Berscheid, E. (1996). Beliefs about the state, goals, and objects of sexual desire. *Journal of Sex & Marital Therapy*, 22(2): 110–120.

Riley, A. (1998). Integrated approaches to sex therapy. *Sexual and Marital Therapy*, 13: 229–231.

Rosenthall, J. (2002). Sharing a heart: the dilemma of a fused couple. In: *Proceedings of the Conference "A World of Difference", Oxford, August 2001* (pp. 21–27). London: Society of Psychoanalytic Marital Psychotherapists.

Roy, J. (2004). A survey of Relate psychosexual therapy clients, January to March 2002. *Sexual and Relationship Therapy*, 19(2): 155–166.

Ruszczynski, S. (1993). *The Theory and Practice of the Tavistock Institute of Marital Studies*. In: S. Ruszczynski (Ed.), *Psychotherapy with Couples* (pp. 3–23). London: Karnac.

Ruszczynski, S. (1995). Narcissistic object relating. In: S. Ruszczynski & J. Fisher (Eds.), *Intrusiveness and Intimacy in the Couple* (pp. 13–32). London: Karnac.

Sandler, J. (1976). Countertransference and role responsiveness. *International Review of Psychoanalysis*, 3: 43–47.

Schwartz, J. (2005). Attachment and sexuality. What does our clinical experience tell us? In: K. White (Ed.), *Attachment & Sexuality in Clinical Practice* (pp. 49–56). London: Karnac.

Trudel, G., Boulos, L., & Matte, B. (1993). Dyadic adjustment in couples with hypoactive sexual desire. *Journal of Sex Education and Therapy*, *19*: 31–36.

Vincent, C., Riddell, J., & Shmueli, A. (2000). *Sexuality and the Older Woman: A Literature Review*. London: Pennell Initiative for Women's Health.

Weeks, G. (2004). Integration in sex therapy. *Sexual and Relationship Therapy*, *19*: S11–12.

Wylie, K. (2001). Can classification systems help the sexual therapist? *Sexual and Relationship Therapy*, *16*(1): 5–6.

CHAPTER EIGHT

Loss of desire: a psycho-sexual case study

Laura Green and Jane Seymour

The psychoanalytic approach can, at times, be an effective way of addressing a difficulty in the sexual relationship. However, the insight gained into the unconscious dynamics of the dysfunction does not always result in a change of behaviour. On the other hand, a purely cognitive behavioural approach might fail to effect a long-term recovery if the underlying causes of the problem are not addressed. The use of an integrated model enables the psycho-sexual therapist to formulate both psychodynamic and cognitive behavioural interventions as appropriate, thus addressing both the psyche and the soma simultaneously. This model was employed at London Marriage Guidance, and is now taught and practised at the Tavistock Centre for Couple Relationships.

Psycho-sexual clinicians are trained to assess a couple sensitively and thoroughly. While working with the psychodynamics of the case, the clinician will also formulate a treatment plan that may include a referral for any necessary medical intervention, a sex education programme, and a cognitive behavioural programme of exercises. This formulation will be presented to the clients in order that they may fully understand the rationale behind any proposed course of treatment and thus give their informed consent before treatment proceeds. Attention is paid to the development of a strong therapeutic relationship. This is crucial in order to acquire the couple's trust (they have almost certainly not divulged such intimate material before) and to observe and monitor the psycho-dynamic processes. Through this relationship, the therapist can eventually understand the deeper disturbances that lie beneath the presenting symptoms.

The following case illustrates the application of such an inte-grated model. A detailed account of the case is presented along with a commentary, set in normal text paragraphs within the displayed text of the case history itself (minor, "aside" comments are set in italics, within square parentheses), on both the psychodynamic and behavioural aspects of the case. Where necessary, this commentary also includes an explanation of the theory and rationale that under-pin those cognitive and behavioural aspects of psycho-sexual ther-apy that might be unfamiliar to the psychoanalytically orientated therapist.

> The couple (seen for approximately fourteen months by one of the authors) were particularly open to the process, showing both insight and bravery as they confronted some very painful and complicated issues. Tom and Charlie presented for therapy at a point when, after being together for five years, they were considering getting married and starting a family. However, although they saw themselves as best friends, they were forced to admit that the sexual relationship was virtually dormant. There had been sexual contact only six times in the previous two years, and they were now avoiding all intimate physical contact.
>
> Tom, thirty-four, was tall, good-looking and moved rather gracefully. He was a sculptor and artist. When necessary, he supplemented his income by taking on students. He seemed eager to come for therapy and at ease when speaking about the relationship. Tom had recently finished three years of individual therapy. Charlie was an attractive woman of thirty-two. She was the more direct and dominant of the two, and her job, running a prominent London art gallery, made full use of her considerable organizational skills. She, too, had ended indi-vidual therapy after two years and now wanted to focus on her rela-tionship with Tom.

During their first session, both Tom and Charlie seemed anxious. Charlie appeared to be quite guarded with the therapist, measuring her responses carefully and peering quizzically at her over her glasses. Where Charlie was reticent, Tom rushed to fill the gaps. The therapist was aware of trying very hard to engage Charlie, to put her at ease, while all the time feeling that she was not quite living up to her expectations. Tom seemed forthcoming, responsive, and charming. However, the therapist noted with some irritation that he could not tolerate any silences and would often attempt to finish her sentences.

> The couple were encouraged to describe the history of their relationship. There had been an instant mutual attraction when they first met, but both were in other relationships. Some months later, at a party, they began kissing. Charlie had "fancied him for ages". With very little discussion, they went home together and had sex. Charlie said she "couldn't believe my luck". But, within a couple of months, as they grew closer, she regularly spoke of wanting to end the relationship, although she was unable to explain why. This was a pattern in previous relationships, where after a few months she would walk away. On this occasion, however, she was unable to disappear as she and Tom met frequently through work. She felt very uncomfortable being with Tom, although she discovered that she could, temporarily, allay these feelings when they had sex. When sex was over her anxieties would rapidly overwhelm her again and she would threaten to leave. Tom always persuaded her to stay. Gradually her panic subsided, and they enjoyed a brief period where things were good between them.

When asked about this good period they both became quite defensive, unable to be specific about it and unwilling to change their view of it in any way. For the first time the therapist experienced them as a unit from which she felt excluded.

> They continued with their story. After a couple of months it was Tom's turn to question his commitment. This moment was a turning point for Charlie. They continued to have sex but she lost all desire for him. It felt, she said, as though "a switch had been turned off" for her. Tom was unaware of this, since they were not in the habit of discussing their sexual relationship. A few months later they moved in together, and it was around this time that intercourse became painful for Charlie. Although it was not mentioned, Tom was aware of Charlie tensing up at the point of penetration. Understandably, Tom's desire waned as soon as he realized that sex was painful for Charlie. Despite the fact

that they no longer desired each other, the sexual relationship continued and both regularly masturbated in private. Charlie asked her GP
about the dyspareunia (pain on intercourse) and was referred to a
gynaecologist. Tests showed that she had mild endometriosis (a condition in which tissue of a type which lines the uterus grows outside the
uterus, causing pain, irregular bleeding, and, in some cases, infertility)
and the GP also suspected she had irritable bowel syndrome (IBS).
Internal examinations were uncomfortable but not unduly painful.
Neither condition was thought to be linked to the painful intercourse.
Accordingly, the GP agreed that psycho-sexual therapy was a suitable
form of treatment. When asked, Tom confirmed that he had no medical
or organic problems of his own. Towards the end of the session, both
Tom and Charlie admitted to feeling some anxiety at the thought of
resuming their sexual contact. They were, however, in agreement that
they could not think about marriage until the sexual aspect of the relationship had been addressed.

At this point the therapist was aware of being invited in to the
couple's relationship, and that for both Charlie and Tom this carried
some degree of risk. For Charlie, the expectation of being let down
was very high, and she was, as yet, not sure whether she could trust
the therapist to contain her anxieties. For his part, Tom seemed keen
to believe that the therapist could magically fix their sexual relationship. The therapist began to sense that, at some point, she was
bound to disappoint him.

When a difficulty arises in the sexual relationship it is frequently
the source of anxiety in one or both partners. Since the arousal
mechanism is itself sensitive to anxiety, the next time the couple
attempt sexual contact, the "failure", which, in this case, resulted in
dyspareunia, might be repeated. This, of course, only serves to
increase the anxiety and, hence, the likelihood of yet another failure. Where this happens it is not unusual for a couple to avoid
sexual contact altogether. Other forms of physical contact can also
cease, since they might place the couple in a potentially sexual situation. In this way, the couple rapidly become physically estranged
from one another as a gulf opens between them.

The psycho-sexual therapist undertakes a thorough assessment
of the relationship, paying particular attention to the individual and
joint sexual history of the couple. Since organic and medical factors
can profoundly affect sexual functioning, the therapist will also

take a medical history and, where necessary, refer a client to an appropriate medical practitioner.

During the following session Tom was asked about his background. He and his older brother came from several generations of fishermen. His father was rather macho, a coarse, unimaginative man, keen for his sons to follow him into the family business. This suited Tom's older brother, but for Tom, it was different; he was adamant that he had nothing in common with either his brother or his father. Furthermore, he had no interest whatsoever in the fishing trade. Father tried to "toughen him up" but to no avail, and Tom became aware that he disappointed his father. Tom's mother had a creative flair that he admired, and he preferred to be in her company. He was very aware of his parents' sexual relationship, and discovered them having sex when he was about nine years old. He expressed curiosity, but neither of his parents offered him any sex education; this was left to the school, where he gained some basic information. As a young boy he discovered his father's pornographic magazines and used pornography himself from an early age, starting with magazines and later progressing to images on the internet. As a young man he had a series of short-lived relationships. Charlie was his first long-term partner.

At first, Charlie described her father as generous and charismatic. He had a mischievous sense of humour and was good company. Her relationship with her mother, she said, was more problematic. With alcoholism, depression, and child abuse in her background, Charlie's mother coped by denying anything that could be viewed as being negative. This was reflected in the way she parented her daughter. When Charlie's father was made redundant, his frustration found expression at home. He was quick to anger and displayed a tendency to shout at her mother. He also began to hit and kick both Charlie and her brother. Charlie told her grandmother about this and the grandmother duly confronted Charlie's mother. This led to Charlie being punished by her mother for "lying". When she was thirteen, Charlie challenged her father. He was remorseful, and from that point she viewed her father as a flawed but loving man. However, the relationship with her mother deteriorated as she began to despise her for being a "doormat". If life at home was difficult for Charlie, school was little better. Until, that is, she discovered that the key to gaining popularity was to make people laugh. Her humour, even during sessions, could be both self-deprecating and brutally sarcastic.

This use of humour made the therapist feel alternately protective towards Charlie or annihilated by her. The therapist now began to gain an understanding of her earlier experience with Charlie, the feeling that she, the therapist, may not be "up to the job"; her mother's inability to cope with Charlie's needs and fears had affected Charlie's ability to trust anyone.

> Charlie explained that her newly discovered bubbly personality attracted the boys, and so she was able to take her pick. In her early teens Charlie encountered pornography. She became sexually aware and found she could easily bring herself to orgasm through masturbation. Later, losing her virginity was more of a "rite of passage" than the sharing of a mutually pleasurable experience. There followed a series of short relationships in which she was always the one to leave. Despite her ability to bring herself to orgasm, Charlie had been unable to climax with a partner. At the age of twenty-four she had an ectopic pregnancy, which she described as being physically rather than emotionally traumatic.
>
> When asked what she had initially found attractive about Tom, Charlie replied that she valued Tom for his artistic abilities and saw him as kind and caring. For his part, Tom liked her confidence, independence, and assertiveness. Sometimes in the sessions, Tom seemed eager to please and would try to anticipate Charlie's thoughts and feelings. At other times, he appeared to be holding back from expressing himself. When listening to Tom, Charlie frequently wore a frown on her face and rarely acknowledged or agreed with anything he said.

The therapist, confronted by Tom's acquiescence, also found herself fighting the urge to challenge or contradict him. Hence the therapist was able to empathize with Charlie's attitude towards Tom, while also wondering what it was about him that triggered these feelings. On the face of it he was utterly charming and interested in the sessions, but unconsciously something quite different was being communicated.

At this point it was not clear if Charlie's dyspareunia was psychosomatic, or linked to either the IBS or the endometriosis. Alternatively, some traumatic memory from the ectopic pregnancy could still be present. It was also possible that sexual intimacy was emotionally too painful for them and was thus avoided. An obvious way to achieve this would be to cut off from the desire in the first place.

By now the couple were sufficiently relaxed in the therapeutic setting to be able to take a more detailed look at their sexual interaction. Tom explained that he preferred not to have sex at all rather than cause Charlie pain. [*There was, perhaps, a reminder here of the macho father and brother whom he had no wish to replicate.*] In a typical sexual encounter Charlie would make the first move, not because she felt desire for Tom, but because they "ought to" have sex. They would kiss for a short time, and then Tom would perform oral sex on Charlie. As soon as he thought she was "ready" he would attempt intercourse, usually from behind. When asked, Charlie asserted that often she was not at all ready and, in fact, felt quite sore on penetration. This led on to a discussion about the importance of lubrication. [*They had not connected the lack of lubrication to any increased risk of dyspareunia until the therapist discussed it with them.*] In the early stages of their relationship there had been plenty of foreplay, and lubrication had not been an issue. However, as time when on, foreplay decreased and their sexual encounters had become much briefer and with more focus on the end result of orgasm. Despite the fact that intercourse had been painful for Charlie, who described the pain as "deep inside", Tom usually continued intercourse until he climaxed. On the one hand, he claimed that he had no wish to hurt her, yet on the other his thrusting was harsh and brutal. [*Charlie seemed to brace herself against Tom's thrusting in much the same way as she had braced herself against her father's violent attacks.*] Tom was aware that the thrusting was accompanied by feelings of anger. He began to see that his anger was fuelled by seeing Charlie flinch at the point of penetration. When I asked why she did not tell Tom to stop when she was in pain, Charlie appeared confused and admitted that the thought had not crossed her mind. She went on to describe the phenomenon of "spectating" during sex; that is to say, she experienced a sense of standing outside herself and observing the action rather than being a participant.

Clients frequently report that they are in the habit of spectating. Where this happens, the client becomes detached from his or her arousal, thus making it difficult to engage with the process. During the course of psycho-sexual therapy, the couple will often be given information on different models of desire, the arousal process, sexual anatomy, contraception, lubrication, and so on. When, for whatever reason, an individual has not accessed this information in his or her youth, it can be difficult to ask questions at a later stage. For many clients, the therapy session is the first time they have been able to discuss sex in a frank and open way.

In recounting their sexual interaction they began to see how unsatisfactory it had been, and both expressed their shame and concern. Although the pain in itself had not stopped the sexual relationship, it had contributed significantly to their shared loss of desire for each other. A discussion ensued about the link between anger and shame.

The therapist explained that, in her experience with them, she, too, had experienced shame and passivity. She had felt crushed by Charlie's caustic wit and had also countered Tom's enthusiasm with a couple of quite unnecessary put-downs.

Charlie and Tom were surprised and interested that the therapist had become caught up in their couple dynamic and they began to recognize how abusive that dynamic had become. They continued to describe their sexual interaction. Sometimes when they were making love, Charlie would focus entirely on reaching orgasm, thus excluding Tom. She liked to use a vibrator as this enabled her to climax quickly. But it rendered Tom redundant and made him angry, he said, as if she preferred her "penis" to his. Charlie agreed that this was the case. It emerged that she had, in fact, never allowed him to bring her to orgasm. With the aid of a diagram depicting arousal like the steps of a ladder (see Figure 1), it was clear that Charlie was skipping over the early stages of arousal.

The diagram in Figure 1 shows two ladders, one for each partner. From ground level, the steps move up through desire, early arousal, plateau, pre-orgasm, orgasm, and post-coital intimacy. The use of this diagram can help the couple to differentiate between their own arousal process and that of their partner's. It can also help to pinpoint the stage at which things go wrong. They may, for example in the case of anorgasmia, get stuck at a certain stage and be unable to progress. On the other hand, where premature ejaculation is concerned, the client could be skipping over one or more of the steps. The ladder can also introduce the idea that it is possible to share pleasure with a partner without always having to reach the top steps.

Charlie, it emerged, felt more anxious towards the bottom of the arousal ladder and wanted to run up the steps quickly, avoiding the intimacy and sensuality of the early stages. For Tom, anxiety increased as he neared the top of the ladder, and his violent thrusting was

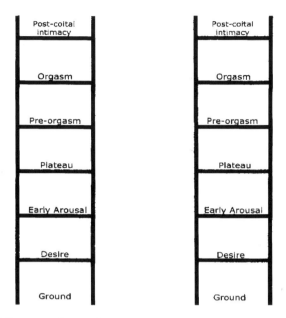

Figure 1.   The steps of arousal.

designed to "get it over with" as quickly as possible. Seeing that they were both struggling in their different ways clarified the situation and helped them empathize with each other. Both described feeling isolated in their inner erotic world, unable to connect with the other.

It was suggested that by avoiding sex they were protecting themselves and each other. Their dilemma lay in the fact that each had rejected their own gender's characteristics and chosen their partner to carry them instead. Tom was passive and almost feminine, thus allowing Charlie to be the more masculine, dominant partner. Unfortunately, they found this dynamic to be unworkable in the bedroom. In order to have intercourse, Tom would need to be thrusting and penetrating while Charlie would have to access her receptive and vulnerable qualities. Therefore sex was avoided and, outside the bedroom, Charlie could continue to be the dominant one, at times almost bullying Tom. He, meanwhile, could remain the passive and compliant partner.

After this session, Tom reported that he had felt quite emotional. Seeing this, Charlie was able to feel closer to him. They had kissed, and reported a fleeting sense of desire, which pleased them both. However, whether desire could be sustained over time was still open to question.

Perhaps Tom feared that by allowing desire into the relationship he would open the floodgates to all his needs and thus overwhelm them both. Meanwhile, if Charlie were to maintain her desire for Tom, there would need to be a degree of trust that was not, as yet, present.

Following the assessment sessions, the therapist, together with the couple, will formulate a hypothesis concerning the aetiology and meaning of the sexual symptom. The therapist then outlines the rationale for any treatment programme that might be suggested. In this case, the diagnosis given was shared secondary situational loss of desire leading to an avoidance of physical contact. (The *DSM-IV* classification for this dysfunction is hypoactive sexual desire. Since the couple had both had desire in the past, the loss was secondary rather than primary. Clearly, as they had both continued to masturbate, desire was still present, and therefore the loss of desire was situational in that it related to this specific relationship rather than a global loss of desire.) This had been exacerbated by Charlie's dyspareunia. In order to better understand the development of the sexual difficulty the contributory factors are divided into three main (and sometimes overlapping) areas: predisposing, precipitating, and maintaining.

In this case, there were several issues that predisposed or made this couple more likely to experience sexual problems. They had both rejected the same-sex parent and, thus, also rejected their own gender characteristics, and, unconsciously, chosen their partner to carry them instead. They had little experience of intimacy in their families of origin and were lacking in sex education. Both had been exposed to pornography and its attendant myths from an early age. Finally, for Charlie, her IBS, endometriosis, and ectopic pregnancy were, at the very least, experiences where her body had been a source of pain rather than pleasure for her.

Despite all of the above issues, the couple had managed a reasonably successful sexual relationship for a while. The factors that precipitated or actually caused the loss of desire were as follows. Once Tom questioned his feelings for Charlie, she began to lose desire. Moving in together for this couple represented increased intimacy and commitment, which only served to highlight the ambivalence they felt for one another. This led on to the development of Charlie's dyspareunia, which then reinforced the loss of desire for them both.

Finally, there were several factors that served to maintain the situation and keep the desire at bay. The couple were determined to keep their friendship and protect each other. This was at odds with the way Charlie bullied Tom, which, in turn, made Tom angry. Their avoidance of intimacy and commitment along with the shared fear of dyspareunia prevented them from creating a safe enough environment in which to resume the sexual relationship. There was also a striving for self gratification rather than mutual pleasure. Hence, intercourse and orgasm were prioritized at the expense of intimacy and sensuality.

Along with looking in depth at the couple's relationship, it was suggested that they would benefit from a Sensate Focus programme. This is a series of graded experiential exercises specifically tailored to fit the needs of each individual couple. The exercises are designed to bring the anxiety down to manageable levels. The focus initially is on sensuality rather than sexuality. Gradually, as the couple move through the exercises, they are encouraged to improve their communication and develop their own unique sexual style. In the first instance, the exercises were to be carried out individually, since the couple needed some self-exploration prior to being able to think about each other.

> Tom seemed quite excited at the prospect of reconnecting physically with Charlie, and checked that he had understood exactly what they "should be doing". Charlie, on the other hand, expressed doubts about the process and questioned the therapist's previous experience. Had it worked for other couples? How long would it take? What if they could not do it? For her part, Charlie could not conceive of a time when she would feel sexual towards Tom.

The therapist found herself becoming anxious about whether the programme could help them and wondered what this sudden lack of trust indicated. Later, it occurred to her that her own doubts reflected a sense of the profound difficulty Charlie encountered when placing her trust in someone else. She decided to share this with the couple and Charlie confirmed that she was, indeed, finding it difficult to believe that anyone could be trusted to help them. While reassuring Charlie that the programme could lead them to a fulfilling sexual relationship, the therapist was also mindful of how the early Sensate Focus exercises (which involve a strong element of trusting one's partner) might prove to be very challenging for Charlie.

When they left the session, Tom agreed to go home in the car with Charlie rather than on his bicycle as he usually did. They had a minor collision with another car and Tom nagged Charlie all week for the insurance details. By the weekend he was furious, and they had a screaming row in the street. This was, they said, the usual pattern. Tom traced his anger back to the fact that he had acquiesced to Charlie rather than tell her that he preferred to cycle home. They began to see that Charlie had a tendency to insist on getting her own way and Tom, having suppressed his needs, would respond by exploding over something quite minor later on. The therapist explained to Tom that she, too, felt that sometimes he agreed too readily with her remarks or interpretations. He was encouraged to feel free to be more assertive in the sessions. Not surprisingly, he agreed!

Despite the row, they had both made time to carry out their separate exercises. They had been asked, as part of the first exercise, to remove their clothes and take a look at themselves in the mirror, paying particular attention to gender characteristics. Tom had been pleasantly surprised by his masculinity, appreciating his body hair and muscular distribution. Charlie was self-deprecating and gave a humorous description of what she saw in the mirror. She was scornful of women who wore make-up and skirts and talked of the benefits of "dressing for comfort" in jeans and sneakers. Aware that she was possibly seen as a woman "who wore make-up and a skirt", the therapist confessed to Charlie that she felt torn between wanting to laugh at Charlie's witty monologue and feeling rejected and attacked. Charlie exclaimed, "Well, that's exactly how I feel; laughing about things helps me not to think about how miserable I am about everything." She continued that she found her body too masculine, her breasts too small, and her hips non-existent.

During the session, with the aid of photographs, the couple discussed their feelings around male and female characteristics. The subsequent discussion about gender identification led to both of them admitting that they enjoyed some same-sex fantasies. For Charlie, the notion of non-penetrative sex was an attractive one. In her lesbian fantasies she pictured herself seducing other women. For Tom, the fantasy was that he would find another man just like himself. This man would know instinctively what to do sexually and would also be able to withstand any amount of aggression. Both Tom and Charlie were clear that they did not want a homosexual relationship.

These fantasies could be said to reflect an urge to repair an early childhood trauma; in Charlie's case, besides the obvious attraction of physical contact without pain, she may also have enjoyed the fantasy of redressing the lack of control in her early relationship with both parents. For Tom, the fantasy was, perhaps, an expression of his desire to engage in a symbiotic relationship where difference is denied and anger can be accepted and contained—a relationship where needs are magically met. This (the therapist was to learn) was the antithesis of his childhood experience.

Photographs can help the couple to discuss their feelings around their own and each other's bodies. They are also useful where a client has a distorted body image, or where one or other partner is uncertain of genital anatomy. Before any photographs are shown, a couple will always be well prepared so they know what to expect. Their permission will also be elicited prior to the viewing of any explicit material.

> Seeing the photographs, Tom realized that he always avoided looking at his penis. Prior to meeting Charlie he had contracted several sexually transmitted infections (STIs). Neither of them had been for a checkup, and so they used condoms, despite the fact that Charlie was on the pill. It emerged that when he was twenty-one, Tom had undergone surgery after the frenulum (a thin strip of flesh on the underside of the penis that connects the foreskin to the penis) had become detached during sex. He acknowledged that this might well have been as a result of quite harsh thrusting during intercourse. Penetration had been painful for some time after this and he was concerned about damaging his penis again. He agreed that this was a contributory factor to his loss of desire. Wearing condoms gave him a sense of protecting his penis, preventing it from being torn apart.

Maybe he even harboured a phantasy of the mythological "vagina dentata", or "toothed vagina", and feared inserting his fragile penis into such a hostile environment. Tom had not felt it important enough to mention earlier. Even now, his description of the event was, like the frenulum itself, detached and free of emotion. It was interesting to contrast this with his concern at being the cause of pain both to Charlie and, further back, to his mother. When he could not be compliant and agreeable, then perhaps he felt he was the cause of their pain, both physical and psychological. He might have imagined that the therapist would not be able to take the shock of this disclosure and thought to conceal it from her in order to protect her. The more concern the therapist showed, the more the incident was played down by Tom. The therapist found this frustrating: why, when it seemed clear that Tom wanted to please her, did he find it so difficult to use what she gave him?

> The next week Charlie arrived in pensive mood. She was becoming aware of a dilemma. If she was funny, assertive, and confident did that mean she was like her bullying and abusive father? But, if she was feminine, kind, and sensitive she risked being the passive victim like her mother. She felt she was between a rock and a hard place. Charlie described an incident at a party they had been to during the week. She had walked into a room and found Tom entertaining his friends, recounting a humorous story. She had belittled him and made every-one laugh. Tom was angry, but only showed it later. On reflection, Charlie was able to see that she had felt vulnerable at the party and had projected it into him. That way she could attack the weak, "feminine" part of herself that she despised.

> The couple were due to go on holiday and agreed that, while they were away, they would not attempt to have sex. This left them free to enjoy each other without there being any pressure on either of them. They were encouraged, though, to make time to continue with their individual exercises. On their return they reported that they were becoming more physical, playful, and tactile with each other. Tom also explained that his feelings towards Charlie were becoming more "masculine". He now wanted to be the one who held her in his arms rather than the other way round. Following a discussion, the couple agreed they were ready to move on to a programme of joint Sensate Focus exercises.

The exercise programme requires the couple to focus on their individual internal experience as they are touching or being touched. This places them in a vulnerable position and, frequently, brings the deeper issues that underpin the dysfunction to the surface. Thus, the unconscious material that may be at the root of the sexual symptom becomes accessible and can be worked with alongside the behavioural programme.

In the first instance, the couple are asked not to attempt any sexual contact. They are also told that they cannot get the exercises "right" or "wrong". Rather, they are given the opportunity to physically reconnect with each other in a safe, non-demanding way. This immediately removes the concept of failure and lowers the anxiety to more manageable levels. It is important that they feel equally responsible for carrying out the programme. Therefore, they take it in turns to initiate the exercise and to make the room a pleasant environment to be in, a private haven, away from the outside world. In the beginning, the focus is on sensuality rather than sexuality, and genital contact is avoided. Gradually, the couple are encouraged to improve their communication where sex is concerned and also to develop their own sexual style, building intimacy step by step over the weeks.

> Tom was quite quiet and admitted to feeling anxious. [*Despite this, the therapist pressed on with the explanation of Sensate Focus, vaguely aware that she and Charlie were enjoying quite an upbeat banter, to the exclusion of Tom.*] It was only at the next session that Tom was able to say he had felt "ganged up on" and angry with himself for being unable to say anything else at the time. This led to a discussion about exclusion and anger. On occasion, the therapist had also felt excluded by this couple, and used this experience to encourage them to talk about their feelings of exclusion in their childhood. Tom recalled the pain of realizing, through having witnessed his parents making love, that he could never please his mother in the way that his father did. This provoked Charlie's assertion that the reason Tom had wanted to penetrate her from behind was because, at some level, he wanted to hurt her. Tom agreed that he wanted to "spike her". Once again, Charlie was puzzled as to why she had been unable to protest about this until now. It seemed that, on a day-to-day level he was unable to say "no" to her, but in the sexual relationship it was she who could not say "no" to him.

> The early Sensate Focus exercises were an emotional time for Tom. He began to experience more tender feelings for Charlie, noticing her beauty spots and her aroma for the first time. He also felt that he did not get (or take) as much attention during the exercises as Charlie. This replicated his experience when they were socializing together, that she

"took up more space" than him and, indeed, in the sessions, where he felt that Charlie was being given more attention. Charlie found the exercises difficult, since her inclination was to avoid the anxiety by skipping over the sensuality and rushing on to orgasm. Gradually, by repeating the exercises, her anxiety abated and she was able to relax. As the exercises progressed she began to enjoy being touched all over.

This part of the programme helps the couple to reconnect in a safe and loving way. The exercise requires each partner to focus on their own experience of touching and being touched in a setting that is free of demands and expectations. This is often a very powerful experience from which deeper feelings emerge.

Memories from childhood began to surface for Charlie, and she became preoccupied with the possibility of having a "real" conversation with her mother. She explained that in the sessions she now felt it was possible to say anything and rely on the therapist to be honest with her. This was in stark contrast to her attempts to communicate with her mother, who would evade any topic that required introspection. Initially, Tom was sympathetic, but he became resentful when he felt their issues were being overwhelmed by Charlie's feelings about her mother.

As the couple moved on to genital exploration, Charlie began to feel very exposed and vulnerable. The idea of allowing Tom to touch her all over made her feel extremely anxious. At one point she shouted, "It's OK for you; finding your manhood is exciting and good for you. Losing mine is very painful." The following week Charlie explained that she no longer wanted to do the exercises; instead, she wanted to go on to intercourse and try for a baby. [*Despite this being a most feminine desire, it actually felt as though she was trying to dominate the therapy in quite a masculine way.*] She was very angry when it was suggested that she was changing the agenda in order to avoid the anxiety the exercises produced. When she had calmed down, the therapist [*feeling quite vulnerable and exposed herself*] asked Charlie if that was, in fact, how she was feeling beneath her angry exterior. After a long sigh she began to sob, explaining that anger was like an "old friend" to her, without which she feared she would be lost.

She found it difficult to think about letting go of anger and receiving sexual pleasure. Sex for Charlie had always been a somewhat self-focused pursuit of pleasure in which a partner was superfluous. This in turn fed into Tom's conviction that Charlie did not need or want him (her flinching at the point of penetration seemed to symbolize this most powerfully for him). She was encouraged to continue with the exercises and concentrate on staying with the experience of touching and being touched. Subsequently, Charlie described a profound experience: as she sat in the bath in preparation for the exercise, she made the decision to let go of her resistance. She reassured herself that she would be fine and then allowed the tension to leave her body. Later, as Tom touched her gently all over, she felt tears run down her face and experienced a rush of primitive feelings: sadness, joy, and arousal. Her previous experience of "spectating" evaporated as she began to focus only on the sensual experience.

Despite Charlie's reconnection with Tom, she was still preoccupied with thoughts about her relationship with her mother. This frustrated Tom, who was now eager for them to move forward in the programme. At this point Charlie began to cry, and said she had always felt sad and worthless. She was not sleeping properly, she said, and was crying all the time. This, it emerged, was a pattern that had repeated itself throughout her life. She had told her mother about this in her teens, but her mother, true to form, had refused to see it as a problem. Charlie seemed relieved that the therapist was able to acknowledge her sadness. A visit to the GP confirmed that she was suffering from depression. She was put on medication, and, although Tom seemed concerned, he was also rather withdrawn. After a few weeks, once the medication had begun to work, Charlie reported that she had begun to feel a lot better.

It is possible that Charlie's depression was a contributory factor in her loss of desire. However, it is also the case that antidepressants themselves can have a detrimental effect on libido. Only time would tell what, if any, effect the medication would have on Charlie's libido.

What impact did Charlie's depression have on Tom? He was supportive throughout the crisis but appeared to be very detached from her. [*The therapist also felt him withdraw from her, and became concerned about his apparent lack of engagement in the sessions. It felt as if he had given up.*] The therapist commented that, although Tom had experienced Charlie's bouts of depression over the years, he had never questioned it. He shrugged, but Charlie was keen to disclose that Tom's mother had also suffered from depression. Tom began tentatively to speak about his mother. He explained that she had suffered from post-natal depression after his birth and was hospitalized for some time. He had been cared for, in those first few months, by his grandmother. Tom remembered his grandmother as a cold, unkind woman. Throughout his childhood, Tom's mother suffered from recurrent bouts of depression, as a result of which she was frequently hospitalized. He recalled "treading on eggshells" around his mother on the occasions when she was at home, trying desperately hard to please her. The illness was never referred to, as though if it were not named it could not exist.

By not recognizing Charlie's depression Tom was, of course, repeating this denial. He was also re-experiencing a longing for intimacy coupled with feelings of rejection that belonged to his earliest childhood. In her depression Charlie was as inaccessible to Tom now as his mother had been to him as an infant. Tom's response to Charlie echoed the compliant and careful response of the child to his depressed mother. Now the therapist was able to make some sense of Tom's response to her: while he searched for approval he was on the look-out for signs of rejection. This had made him too defensive to accept what was being offered to him and too anxious to risk showing emotion. For Charlie, Tom's response to her depression was a replication of her mother's defence of denial.

> When we met the following week Tom expressed his anger for the first time. Sitting on the edge of his seat, and with a raised voice, he spoke passionately about his deep regret and frustration. For Tom, his art expressed love and connection, but in real life he was unable to experience this with Charlie. In fact, he felt unwanted by her. He was tempted by the idea that he might find another woman who did want him. As the full force of his revelation hit her, Charlie declared that she would kill herself if he left her. [*Although the therapist felt alarmed*] Tom seemed quite detached and unaffected by this threat. He did indeed leave her a few days later, but on the understanding that he would still attend the next session with her. At that session Charlie was able to understand that her threats only served to confirm Tom's phantasy that he was destructive. She decided to show him that although she wanted him to return, if he decided not to she would survive. Tom failed to attend the following two sessions.

He sent no message, and the therapist had no way of contacting him, thus leaving her feeling frustrated and helpless. She wondered whether this experience echoed the feelings Tom had in response to both his depressed mother and his depressed partner.

Despite this disruption, the sessions with Charlie were fruitful, as she used the opportunity to think about how she would like to continue to think about her femininity, whether this was with Tom or not.

Three weeks later Tom returned. Charlie was surprised and a little wary. He was still conflicted, but prepared to work through his rage and confusion within the relationship and the therapy. It was important to Tom that both Charlie and the therapist had taken his departure seriously. Charlie, for her part, was able to see that she had always taken his support for granted. Now, for the first time, she wanted to discover what his needs might be.

In the weeks following Tom's return, he began to explore his ambivalent feelings for Charlie. He was now aware that his desire for her had returned, but at the same time he was very fearful of his vulnerability and neediness. He could see that these feelings stemmed from the "baby Tom" who longed for his unavailable mother.

In order to appear compliant, Tom had repressed these needs as a child. This meant they could only be expressed via his imagination and creativity; he described enjoying a vivid fantasy life where love and passion approached a spiritual dimension. His fantasy was that through making love he could escape his prosaic day-to-day existence and achieve nirvana. The crushing disappointment of his sexual relationship with Charlie simply repeated the lack of connection experienced in the early relationship with his mother. This had resulted in an even further splitting off from his needs. It followed that, if other women became the object of his desire, he could experience Charlie as a less frustrating object, one with whom he could enjoy a friendship.

By talking about this ambivalence he was able to express his anger towards Charlie. She by now was robust enough to handle it, and so Tom's fear of damaging her diminished. He subsequently experienced a powerful resurrection of his feelings and desire for her. Charlie reported being both surprised and delighted by Tom's newfound ability to confront her. [*The therapist was also able to see Tom as a more distinct, potent presence who was now prepared to risk asserting himself and was able on occasion to say when he disagreed with her.*]

They resumed the exercises and were encouraged to introduce a playful element into their relationship. They were thrilled at being given "permission" to be more light-hearted in their physical relationship;

sex had become such a serious and treacherous business. Both felt that they had missed out on this stage as teenagers, due to their early sexualization. They were now able to enjoy sensual touching and mutual genital stimulation, passing smoothly through the early stages of the exercise programme. As they moved on from sensuality towards sexuality they both became anxious at the thought of reaching orgasm. The sensuality that they had so painstakingly built up seemed to disappear. At the next session, Charlie reported that she had given Tom a "blow job". It had taken such a long time, she said, that she had developed jaw-ache. This was all to no avail since Tom had been unable to orgasm. When they swapped over, Tom had given Charlie oral stimulation and she, too, had been unable to orgasm. They had both ended up feeling disappointed and frustrated.

Initially, this was a negative experience for the couple. However, once in the therapy room it presented an opportunity to understand the dynamics at work between them. They were asked, "Why continue oral sex for such a prolonged period of time when you were not enjoying it?" Charlie replied that all men wanted "blow jobs". [*This myth was perhaps rooted in all the porn movies she had watched.*] Tom made it clear that "blow jobs" and aggressive genital stimulation were definitely not all that he wanted. However, he had felt unable to ask her to stop for fear of hurting her feelings. They began to see that they had slipped back into second-guessing each other rather than communicating their likes and dislikes. Tom was then able to tell her that he preferred the more sensual and teasing touch they had been practising. Charlie agreed that she also preferred the more sensual, leisurely touching, although she was dubious about the possibility of achieving a climax in this way. [*Once again, Charlie was looking for guarantees and demanding reassurance. This time, however, it felt less about trust and more about the therapist being able to hold on to the hope.*]

The following week they repeated the exercise but agreed to stay on the "plateau" level (see Figure 1). This freed them both to enjoy their arousal without the need to pursue orgasm as an end goal. Each felt that they could have climaxed if the other had continued stimulation just a little longer. The following week they agreed to be specific about their needs and ask for more stimulation if they required it. At their next session Tom was delighted to report that Charlie had brought him to orgasm. He had been able to ask Charlie if she was happy to continue. When she told him she was fine, he had felt free to focus on his own feelings and sensations. This was tempered slightly by his feelings of sadness at the inevitable post-coital separation. Gradually, he was beginning to see Charlie as a separate person, and this was a new experience for him. [*Likewise, the therapist felt that Tom could now see her as a separate person from whom he could take what he needed without fear of her becoming overwhelmed or depressed.*]

It took slightly longer for Charlie to feel comfortable enough to allow Tom to bring her to orgasm. In the earlier exercises she had found it very difficult to relax and trust Tom. Now, in her desire to orgasm, she felt an overwhelming need to take charge again in the old "masculine" way. She described how she had grabbed Tom's hand and forced him to stimulate her quite harshly. When this failed to bring her an orgasm she was very disappointed, and left the bedroom to watch a porn film and use her vibrator. This, she knew, would guarantee her a quick and efficient orgasm. In the following session they discussed the exercise. Charlie could see that in order to alleviate her anxiety, she had felt compelled to take control and achieve orgasm as quickly as possible. Tom, for his part, was able to tell her that she had made him feel excluded, hurt, and angry.

Charlie began to talk about her anxiety. Allowing Tom the freedom to explore her body made her feel very uncomfortable. Speculation turned to how Charlie, as a baby, might have experienced her mother's touch. [*From her own experience of Charlie, the therapist knew that Charlie sometimes experienced her as "controlling" or "demanding".*] She asked Charlie whether it was possible that she had perhaps experienced her mother's touch as intrusive and manipulative. Charlie replied that she had, in fact, been "fussed over" by her mother and had felt used as a "buffer" between her parents. It seemed likely that the panic Charlie felt when surrendering to Tom's gentle touching echoed her experience of mother's intrusive touch. This understanding helped Charlie to decide to permit Tom to touch her and focus on the sensations, blocking out distracting thoughts. When they returned the following week, Charlie recounted how she had been able to relax sufficiently to allow Tom to "lead her down the path" to orgasm. Like Tom, Charlie was very fragile afterwards, and even felt faint when she tried to stand up. Gradually, she recovered, and was reassured that she could be vulnerable without disintegrating.

By now they were ready to move on to the next stage in the exercise programme, that of vaginal containment. It was agreed that, when they were ready, Charlie would sit astride Tom and insert his penis into her and, after a few seconds, withdraw it again. Charlie reported enjoying the experience, but for Tom it provoked a lot of anxiety. He found it very difficult to feel "like a man" while in the passive, "feminine" position. He was also fearful of what might happen were he to thrust while inside Charlie. His fantasy was that there would be a resurgence of his rage and aggression.

This highlighted his dilemma: how could he be potent and masculine without seeming to be angry and brutal? Charlie was, of course, struggling with a similar dilemma: how could she be feminine and vulnerable without being passive and a "doormat"? Thus, the work on their sexual interaction now forced them to confront the issues that lay at the heart of their relationship.

They were, once more, encouraged to focus on their physical experiences when carrying out the exercises. Tom began to be able to tolerate, and then enjoy, being inside her. By using plenty of lubricant, keeping movement to a minimum and not striving for climax, they were able to try a variety of positions. There was no recurrence of the dyspareunia. Now that he was confident that Charlie would tell him if she was uncomfortable, Tom was able to relax and began to enjoy intercourse. The following week, they reported that Tom had climaxed intravaginally and Charlie via manual stimulation. They felt pleased that they could now, once more, have pain-free intercourse. They were also clear that penetration was simply one of a range of options now available to them in their intimate physical relationship.

Discovering a fulfilling sex life had a powerful impact on this couple and their commitment to the relationship. Tom began to talk of getting married. Previously, marriage had always made him think of his "unimaginative" and "dull" father. Now he began to admire his father's sense of responsibility and commitment. By integrating sex back into the relationship, Tom began to take a less polarized view of the world. Meanwhile, Charlie was discovering that she did not have to renounce her feisty personality in order to be vulnerable with Tom. Both Charlie and Tom now felt able to look to the future secure in the knowledge that they were now developing a loving and creative sexual relationship. Having at times expressed her frustration with the programme, it was to be expected that Charlie would be relieved to end the therapy. However, she was tearful at the prospect of severing the therapeutic relationship: having risked being vulnerable and taking a leap of faith, she was now loath to say goodbye.

Although the therapist also felt sad at the imminent loss, she understood and shared with Charlie that this new, good experience of a relationship with a "mothering" figure would stand her in good stead, both in her attitude towards her own mother and with her other intimate relationships.

Tom, who had feared that the strength of his needs and his anger could be overwhelming and destructive, was relieved to discover that the therapist would not collapse or push him away. This had given him a confidence in his masculinity that he was now revelling in. He was relieved that he no longer needed the therapist and was excited to be embarking on his newfound sexual relationship.

CHAPTER NINE

Power *vs.* love in sadomasochistic couple relationships

David Hewison

> "'A courtier dreamed up a new torture instrument for the tyrant of Syracuse—an iron bull in which a condemned man was to be locked and placed over a huge fire. As soon as the iron bull began to glow and the victim screamed, his wailing would sound like the bellowing of a bull.
> 'Dionysius smiled graciously at the inventor and, in order to test his work on the spot, he ordered him to be the first to be shut in the iron bull.'"

> (von Sacher-Masoch, 1870, p. 114).

Jung noted that the opposite of love is not hate, or indifference, as Bion has suggested, but *power* (Jung, 1943, par. 78). Relating through power, rather than through love, is to live in the realm of force, subservience, non-mutuality, domination, submission, and the circular dynamic of sadomasochism. The internal search of a sadomasochistic couple is for an escape from the struggles of mutually demanding and fulfilling dependency needs through an agreement that power and powerlessness shall be the emotional currency between them, allowing them a certainty that trusting in the vagaries of a loving object cannot bring. Love is too fragile to protect the couple from attack from themselves, so they enter into a relationship that attempts to master primitive anxieties by setting up physical and emotional scenarios that bind and channel their aggression in stereotypical ways. In this use of relating in the service of aggression, they become perverse (Kernberg, 1995). It is important to note that it is not aggression in relationships *per se* that is the problem, but the respective weight given to each. Where aggression is missing, erotic satisfaction is stunted or impossible (Hewison, 2005). Where aggression is used in the service of love, to get through to someone, to connect by deliberately (and rapturously) breaching the boundaries of personal space and body surface in sex, relationship has the potential to be deepened through mutual satisfying of erotic needs. Where aggression is paramount, eroticism is curtailed and becomes routine; connection between the couple is limited to particular acts and roles, boundaries (emotional and physical) are turned into objects to be used, or used by, and love dies.

There are many reasons why individuals might suffer from the replacement of love by power, and many different ways of managing this in the couple relationship. Deficits or impingements in very early relating between mother and baby is one factor; another is trauma, accidental or deliberate (including sexual abuse); and constitutional factors can also play a part, particularly in their interaction with the environment at the different life stages that our psycho-sexual selves are reworked. Repeated disappointments in love relations from adolescence onwards can also play a part in loading the balance between aggression, power, love, and hatred. Other than noting these things, the detailed study of the psychogenesis of sadomasochism is not part of this chapter, and the interested reader is directed to works by such writers as Chasseguet-Smirgel (1991), Denman (2004), Diamond, Blatt, and Lichtenberg (2007), Kernberg (1991), McDougall (1995), Ross (2003), Stoller (1986a; 1986b) and Welldon (2002), among others. It is clear, however, that the adult couple relationship offers the potential for repairing damage to the capacity for love, but it also offers the opportunity for repeating the original trauma again and again, ostensibly as mastery, but actually as servitude. This chapter explores the relationship of two different couples to sadomasochism and, in particular, the sadomasochistic contract. One couple comes from the classic novel of masochism, *Venus in Furs* (von Sacher Masoch, 1870), and the other from the award-winning but controversial film, *Breaking the Waves* (von Trier, 1996a,b).

Sadism, masochism, and sadomasochism

Sadism ties violence against others together with sexual excitement. Taking its name from the writings of the Marquis de Sade, which depict sexual and violent acts unrestrained by ordinarily accepted morality or prohibition (other than, we could say, a prohibition *against* care and concern), sadism, in its general meaning, is a state in which sexual satisfaction is dependent on the inflicting of pain or humiliation on others. *The 120 Days of Sodom* (de Sade, 1785), for example, begins with sealing its protagonists and victims away from the world in the remote castle of Silling, and there subjecting them to successively more transgressive acts, beginning in voyeurism, coprophagia, and group sex, and culminating in torture, evisceration, dismemberment, and the absolute emotional and physical destruction of the human body. Sadistic pleasure stems from total power used in a murderous way against others for the gratification of the self.

In "Destruo ergo sum: towards a psychoanalytic understanding of sadism", the Canadian psychoanalyst Arthur Leonoff comments that sadism in this sense has all but disappeared from psychoanalytic writing, despite being frequently cited as part of the compound term "sadomasochism" (Leonoff, 1997). He notes the frequent use of the term in Kleinian thinking to describe instead a form of aggression, derived from the death drive and characterized by attacks on the object, but which has no clear link to sexuality. The quality of sadism in Kleinian thought seems to be associated with hatred and envy rather than sexual excitement. Leonoff, citing others, suggests that to restrict sadism to aggression is to overly constrain its meaning and therefore its utility. As he puts it,

> sadism recruits aggression but is itself a pursuit of limitless power over another. In this regard, we might conclude that sadism's relation to aggression is analogous to that between perversion and

sexuality. As perversion recruits sexuality for purposes of aggression, so sadism recruits aggression in the service of the erotics of omnipotent power. [*ibid.*, p. 109]

That said, it is clear that it was Freud who began this under-investigation of sadism when he turned his interest to the paradox of masochism as an element in instinctual life. Freud initially felt that masochism was a state of passivity towards sexual life and the sexual object in which an excess of aggression in the form of sadism is "turned round on the subject's own self which is taken as the sexual object" (Freud, 1905d, p. 158). As a perversion he felt it was not satisfactorily explained, and that the states of activity and passivity which lay behind it were, in fact, universals of sexual life. He suggested there were a multitude of factors, such as castration anxiety and guilt, that combined with sexual passivity to produce the exaggerated and fixated sexual attitude found in masochism. It is clear that in his earlier writings he felt that masochism was the subsequent result of the actions of a pre-existing sadism (Freud, 1915c, p. 111; Freud, 1919e, p. 175), and that this was based on the operation of *opposites* in psychic life: subject–object; pleasure–unpleasure; and active–passive.

With the introduction of his theory of the death instinct, however, Freud no longer felt that masochism was dependent on sadism, nor was it a perversion like others such as fetishism, exhibitionism, and so on. He felt it had a "peculiar position" (Freud, 1905d, p. 159, fn. 3, added 1924,) and came to describe masochism as having a number of different forms:

a primary or *erotogenic* masochism, out of which two later forms, *feminine* and *moral* masochism have developed. Sadism which cannot find employment in actual life is turned round upon the subject's own self and so produces a *secondary* masochism, which is superadded to the primary kind. [*ibid.*, p. 158, fn. 2, added 1924]

Erotogenic masochism is thought to arise from the ubiquitous nature of infantile sexuality that finds any form of excitation pleasurable, including the excitation of pain. Feminine masochism is a later development of this that takes the form of identifications (in men, in Freud's original conception) with states of being castrated, being treated like a bad, dirty child, or of giving birth. Moral masochism involves a person taking up a position of being a victim from an unconscious sense of guilt, something that does not involve sexual pleasure in any direct way, but instead manifests itself in a need for punishment. Freud suggests that this is not so much a superego activity (a punitive, sadistic morality) but an activity of the ego that masochistically seeks punishment from internal or external sources, a derivative of the Oedipus complex with punishment standing in for the sexual relationship with the desired parent (Freud, 1924c).

The concept of sadomasochism takes up the idea of the opposites in psychic life, and of their inseparability: sadism and masochism are not just opposed, they are dependent on each other, and in their manifestation of activity and passivity (and reversal from one to the other) they are deeply implicated in the development of the sexual life of the individual. In this sense, in psychoanalytic thought all people are sadomasochistic; not all people are in sadomasochistic couple relationships, however. The difference is partly one of degree, but is also one of choice: the ability to choose a variety of ways of being together in an intimate couple relationship that may include elements of sadomasochism is a long way away from one in which choice is absent, with designated roles and stereotyped expressions of sexual desire. The epitome of such inflexible sadomasochism is the contract.

The sadomasochistic contract

My slave!

The conditions under which I accept you as my slave and tolerate you at my side are as follows:

Complete unconditional surrender of your self.

You have no will outside of me.

You are a blind tool in my hands, following *all* my orders without contradiction. Should you forget that you are my slave and should you fail to show me unconditional obedience in all matters, I have the right to punish and chastise you *entirely at my own discretion*, and you are not to so much as dare complain about it.

Anything pleasant or felicitous that I grant you is to be regarded as a *favour*, and must be gratefully taken by you only *as such*; I have no *obligation*, no *indebtedness* toward you.

You may not be my *son*, *brother*, or *friend*, you are nothing but my slave lying in the dust.

Just like your body, *your soul* also belongs to me, and if that makes you suffer, you must nevertheless subjugate your feelings, your emotions to my domination.

I am permitted to exercise the *greatest cruelty*, and even if I maim you, you are to endure it without complaint. You must labor for me like a slave, and if I revel in luxury while keeping you deprived and kicking you, you must unprotestingly kiss the foot that has kicked you.

I can dismiss you *at any moment*, but you must never be away from me without my permission; and should you flee from me, you grant me the power and the right *to torture you to death with any conceivable torments*.

Aside from me you have nothing. I am everything to you: your life, your happiness, your unhappiness, your torment, and your pleasure.

You must carry out anything I demand, *good* or *evil*, and if I demand a crime from you, then you must become a *criminal* in obedience to my will.

Your honor belongs to me as do your blood, your mind, your capacity for work; I am your Mistress over life and death.

If ever you can no longer bear my domination, and the chains become too heavy for you, then you must kill *yourself*—I will *never* give you your freedom.

I commit myself on my word of honor to be the slave of Frau Wanda von Dunajew, in exact accordance with her demands, and to submit unresistingly to everything that she imposes on me.

Dr Leopold Knight von Sacher-Masoch. [von Sacher-Masoch, 1870, pp. 122–123, original italics]

This contract was drawn up between the man who gave his name to the term "masochism"—Leopold von Sacher-Masoch—and his wife, Wanda von Dunajew. It was a development of a similar contract of "slavery" that Sacher-Masoch had previously had in 1869 with a young widow, Fanny von Pistor. Sacher-Masoch had written about just such a sadomasochistic relationship in his celebrated and notorious novel of 1870, *Venus in Furs*, and indeed there are similarities between his time with von Pistor and that of the protagonists of the novel. Subsequent to its publication, a young woman named Aurora Rümelin wrote to him an impassioned letter that caught his imagination—perhaps not least because she had signed herself with the name of the beloved and cruel Mistress of the novel, Wanda von Dunajew—promising Sacher-Masoch the fulfilment of his desires. The two met and married, with Aurora Rümelin changing her name to that of Wanda von Dunajew and living out her side of the bargain, albeit increasingly reluctantly if her *Confessions* are to be believed (von Sacher-Masoch, 1906). Despite the contract, and the children between them, Sacher-Masoch left her after some years in search of another dominant woman. He died in self-exile in Germany, having lost a legal fight with his publisher, fêted and condemned in equal measure for his writing, and having seen Krafft-Ebing use his name to describe the particular sexual practice of pleasure in pain when writing his *Psychopathia Sexualis* (Krafft-Ebing, 1906).

Venus in Furs concerns the relationship between a young Galician nobleman, Severin, and a beautiful, rich widow, Wanda von Dunajew, who meet in a resort in the Carpathian mountains. The young man is in love, but not with anyone human. He is in love with the Greek goddess Venus. We read of how he worships and adores her in the form of a white marble statue in the garden of his lodgings, and then we hear more about how his feelings for her are made more exciting when he comes across a photograph of Titian's painting of "Venus at her Mirror", which depicts a bare-breasted Venus, draped in red satin trimmed with fur, looking at herself in a mirror held up by Cupid. "Venus at her Mirror" becomes the Venus in Furs of his erotic imagination. The widow learns of his sexual obsession with the goddess, and constructs a scene in which she appears to him at night as such a living Venus, terrifying and overwhelming him with excitement at the same time. He runs off, berating himself as he does. The two then spend more time together and Severin professes his love for her; she returns it, but with the proviso that she is not yet ready to decide if she wants to commit herself to one man. Severin tells her that as she is a Greek goddess she must have a slave and he will be it. She gives him a year to persuade her that he is the right man for her to marry, and he accepts unconditionally, hoping that this will persuade her. Instead, it leads to a warning from her that this is a dangerous path for him to take; she enjoys playing with him. As the days go on, Severin insists that, if he cannot *immediately* be her husband, he should be her slave:

> If a marriage can be based only on equality, on compatibility, then the greatest passions, by contrast, arise from opposites. We are such opposites, almost hostile to each other. That explains this love of mine, which is part hatred, part fear. In such a relationship, only one person can be the hammer, the other the anvil. I want to be the anvil. I can't be happy if I look down on my beloved. I want to be able to worship a woman, and I can do so only if she is cruel to me. [von Sacher-Masoch 1870, p. 29]

Wanda's subsequent comment shows how attractive the other side of the contract is becoming:

> You have a peculiar way of inflaming the imagination, exciting all nerves. Making the pulse beat faster. You provide vice with an aureole so long as it's honest. Your ideal is a bold and brilliant courtesan. Oh, you're the kind of man who can thoroughly corrupt a woman! [von Sacher-Masoch, 1870, p. 34]

Severin describes his "most cherished fantasy I:

> "To be the slave of a woman, a beautiful woman, whom I love, whom I worship!"

> "And who mistreats you for it," Wanda broke in, laughing.

> "Yes, who ties me up and whips me, who kicks me when she belongs to another man."

> "And who, after driving you insane with jealousy and forcing you to face your successful rival, goes so far in her exuberance that she turns you over to him and abandons you to his brutality. Why not? Do you like the final tableau any less?"

> I gave Wanda a terrified look. "You're exceeding my dreams."

"Yes, we women are inventive," She said. "Be careful. When you find your ideal, she might treat you more cruelly than you like". [von Sacher-Masoch, 1870, p. 37, original italics]

This turns out to be exactly what ultimately happens. Despite the fact that Severin felt that he was offering himself in an unconditional way, none the less there were specific aspects to his fantasy: the cruelty had to be cruelty that he had, in a way, already imagined (and we learn in the novel that it has its roots in an incident of being tied up and beaten by a glamorous aunt, which in turn had led to his fascination with images of powerful and despotic women such as Catherine the Great of Russia, lascivious, beautiful, and violent and, importantly, wrapped in furs). In the novel, at least, unlike in Sacher-Masoch's life, the wished-for cruelty—being treated like a slave and being whipped by a woman wearing fur—was gender-specific.

When it came to writing the contract, however, the image of the relationship in Severin's mind came up against the uncomfortable fact that it takes two people to make a contract. Although Wanda anticipated his desire to have her wear furs whenever she was cruel to him, Severin had not anticipated that she might present him with two pieces of paper. On the one was the contract that he wished for—albeit that it was predicated on him remaining her slave and giving up his hopes of becoming her husband—on the other was something to be copied out and signed by him that made profound horror sweep over him. On it was written: "After years of being weary of existence and its delusions, I am, of my own free will, putting an end to my worthless life" (von Sacher-Masoch, 1870, p. 73). Severin, who had tried to motivate himself to leave Wanda several times, was still unable to do so when faced with the possibility of a shameful death. In contracting to be her slave, he had made a contract with an unknown Mistress—unknown because in his mind he was making an agreement with the embodiment of Venus in Furs—whereas in fact he was dealing with someone who had been changed as a result of his wish for her to be cruel to him:

"Dangerous tendencies lay dormant in me, and you were the first to arouse them. If I now take pleasure in torturing you, mistreating you, then it's all your fault. You turned me into what I am now, and you're actually unmanly and weak and miserable enough to blame it on *me.*" [von Sacher-Masoch, 1870, p. 109]

Wanda leaves him for a man who will dominate her as she has always wanted. But first, in order to "cure" Severin, she goes again through the process, much repeated in the novel, of pulling him close to her in loving passion only to push him away again. She had been threatening him with her relationship with a beautiful and cruel Greek man—an Apollo to her Venus—but had latterly been indicating that it is Severin, and not the Greek, whom she wants. This time, having asked that he permit himself to be tied up and whipped for the last time as a signal of his love for her, she then tells him the story of "the bull of Dionysius", indicating that his desires have had an impact on her that he had not foreseen.

Wanda goes on to inform Severin that his actions have so "inoculated [her] with selfishness, arrogance, and cruelty" that she now takes pleasure in her absolute power over him. He begs for the whip and she says he shall have it, but this time, it is not she who will whip him. Instead, she calls out and the Greek appears, beautiful, blood-thirsty, and cruel. Wanda hands Severin over to the Greek, who whips him mercilessly. At first, Severin finds this intoxicating and ecstatic; then he realizes that both of them want to hurt him, not to satisfy him. Slowly, his feelings of poetic rapture at being abused by an Apollo in front of his Venus—with both in furs—turn into a clear vision of betrayal by himself at the hands of Wanda, just as the inventor of the bull of Dionysius is betrayed by his cruel inventiveness meeting an even greater cruelty.

> It was like awakening from a dream.
>
> My blood was already flowing under the whip, I was writhing like a worm being trampled; but he kept pitilessly whipping away, and she kept pitilessly laughing away while closing the packed trunks, slipping into her travelling fur—and she was still laughing as she strode down the stairs on his arm and mounted into the carriage . . . Now the carriage door shut, the horses started trotting, the carriage rolled for a while—then everything was over. [von Sacher-Masoch, 1870, p. 117]

In the novel, Severin is cured of his slave fantasies as a result of Wanda's deliberate "therapy"—though now he wields the whip, rather than suffers it: In reality, Sacher-Masoch did not relinquish this position. Wanda von Dunajew reports in her *Confessions* how Sacher-Masoch continually sought out men resembling "the Greek", scouring personal adverts in papers and even trying to rouse her from bed shortly after she had given birth because he thought he had at last found this embodiment of Apollo. The *Confessions* show us something much more mundane and ordinary than the rarefied and compartmentalized repetitions of Sacher-Masoch's wishes: Wanda complains of having to raise the children, run the household, make ends meet and yet still, after all that, at the end of the day having to rouse herself to put on heavy furs that made her shoulders ache and flourish the whip at her (very demanding) slave of a husband when he came home. She was, none the less, hurt and enraged when he left her for someone else: the contract had been broken.

In *Venus in Furs*, it is clear that the couple entered into a sado-masochistic contract willingly, knowing what they were doing. For the central couple of *Breaking the Waves*, however, it is not so clear. Indeed, it could be said that this latter couple "contracted" sado-masochism in the sense of catching it, rather than seeking it out.

Breaking the Waves

Lars von Trier's 1996 cinematic masterpiece, *Breaking the Waves* (von Trier, 1996b), is set in a fundamentalist Christian community in the Western Isles of Scotland. Bess, a young woman who has conversations with an inner God, gets married to Jan, an older, more worldly, man from far beyond the community. She is ecstatic when she is with him, but she has to endure his lengthy absences from her because of his work on the oil rigs in the North Sea. When he goes away again, she yearns for him to return home and begs God to bring him home early as she cannot bear the waiting any more. Jan does return early, but as a result of a major accident in which he suffers severe head injuries, is paralysed from the neck down, and, despite heartening periods of apparent remission, is clearly dying. Two things then happen: Bess seeks guidance from God as to what to do, and Jan asks her to have sex with other men and come and tell him about it. Bess refuses at first, but Jan says that this is the only way he will recover, that love is a mighty power and that this reflected memory of their physical love will keep him alive. When she talks with God, God tells her, "Prove to me you love him. Then I'll let him live." She then pretends to be doing what Jan asks, but he sees through this and insists again. Reluctantly, Bess concurs. The path is then set for a spiralling increase in Bess's sexual activity and risk to herself. Her commitment to the contract she has made is tested again and again until she is rejected by family and community, and ultimately sacrifices herself for Jan. Hearing that he is now dying, despite everything she has already done, she returns to a pair of sailors who had begun to hurt her sadistically and from whom she had escaped before they could fully enter into the violent sexual scenario they had in mind. These were men whom the prostitutes of the harbour would no longer go to because of their viciousness. This second time she gives herself to them, she dies of the wounds she receives and we can only imagine the scene from the Marquis de Sade's *The 120 Days of Sodom* that she had entered into. Jan, against all the odds, recovers.

This is a sparse description of a rich and complex film, focusing on part of the relationship of the two main characters. None the less, it highlights something of the nature of the contract between Jan and Bess, and the way in which it catches them up into something unexpectedly sadomasochistic. Lars von Trier suggested, in an essay accompanying the original script of the film (von Trier, 1996a) that Bess makes a mistake in not being able to differentiate between the Jan who loved her and "another Jan" made mad by the damage to his brain, drifting in and out of lucidity as he succumbs to the toxins in his head. Jan, on the other hand, is able to see what is going on, but only during the periods of partial recovery. What had begun as an attempt to help Bess realize that Jan was never going to recover and so she needed to find some other relationship to fulfil her (the suggestion that she finds another man) becomes perverted into a sadomasochistic contract during Jan's periods of delirium and intoxication. As Jan recognizes the horror of what he is party to, he realizes how dangerous he is to Bess despite himself, and so he tries to get her beyond his reach by agreeing to her committal to psychiatric hospital. He knows at this point that he is heading towards death and that he will never see her again. He knows also that the original contract between them has gone astray, taking on a life of its own, driven by the coincidence of his relapses with Bess's refusals to prostitute herself for him. Bess takes these coincidences as *causes*, rather than accidents of timing. Jan knows that she has taken on responsibility for whether he lives or dies, and when she first turns away from the men who want only to use her sadistically—the one having sex with her while the other simulta-neously cuts her with a knife—and then she discovers that Jan's condition has seriously deteriorated, both she and Jan know that she will do more to ensure he lives. The difference between them is that Bess believes that this will happen, and Jan does not. Jan knows that it is a lie, a perversion of the truth.

What would have caused Bess not to know that it was a lie? In the film, Bess is simple, damaged, or, alternatively, so open to her powerful internal experience of God that she loses her footing in the mundane world. It seems that she had been hospitalized a few years earlier, and there are clues that this was after her brother died. It is clear that she cannot bear separation from the opening moments of the film, when she is angry at Jan for being "late, late, late", as she puts it, when she waits for the helicopter to land bring-ing him from the oil-rig for their wedding. It is also clear that she is able to be soothed by him, that she is capable of love, and that she can put another person's needs before her own. She finds sex with Jan deeply fulfilling, and she thanks both God and Jan for it. Lars von Trier suggested that Bess was a very strong character, made so by her love and her faith, and so indicates that she has something "good enough" inside her (von Trier, 1996a, p. 20). How-ever, it is also apparent that she has had to bear more than she can manage in her life, and that, had she lived anywhere else, things might have been easier for her: the harsh fundamentalism of the island community has given her so much to cope with even though it might be more understanding and tolerant of her direct experi-ence of God than another community would have been.

In a way it is this direct experience that is so damaging for her: she is unable to negotiate the difference between the black-and-white faith of her community that tells her there is a right and a wrong way of doing things, and her experience, which, ordinarily, would be open to interpretation. After a scene in which she had mistaken Jan's hallucinated ramblings about "the back of the bus" as he collapses into unconsciousness for an instruction of what to do, she gets on to a bus, sits next to a man and, without any further interaction between them, masturbates him. She then rushes off the bus and is sick at the side of the road. She has another conversation with the God inside her, calling on him for forgiveness. The reply that comes is that Mary Magdalene sinned, yet is one of God's dearly beloved. This, coinciding with a chance remark from the doctor looking after Jan's treatment that her "prayers have been answered" and that Jan is recovering from his latest relapse, confirms in her mind that there is a true contract between her, Jan, and God. She believes she *is* the key as to whether Jan lives or dies. If she can prove she really loves him, he will live; if she cannot, then, in line with the absence of forgiveness in this particular Christian denomination, he will die and she will be punished as a result. She cannot see that she is acting from a delusion, and Jan is unable to help her with it because at this point he is only rarely sane.

Jan, unlike Bess, is a man of the world beyond her religious community. He loves her in a way that allows him to tolerate her feelings at his comings and goings to and from the rig. He is able to play with her, to be sexual with her, and to help her with her new experience of this part of her. He is also willing to enter into the life of the community for her. He does not make her choose between them, despite what he can see would be the difficulties. Von Trier has suggested that he wants to settle down with someone he sees as an "angel". In the film, it is clear that he has loyal friends whom he cares about. When he is injured so badly, he does not immediately give way to despair but is able to relate to Bess and others. His suggestion that she sees someone else is not something that would therefore be expected from him, and so his motivation for making it (other than from the damage to his brain) is not really explained in the film. What we do not see in the film, however, is what is very clear in the original script: the profound impact that sex has on Bess. In the script, Bess is a much more physical person, who becomes alive and fulfilled as a result of her new experience of a mutually fulfilling sexual life with Jan. It then makes more sense that he should be concerned with this aspect of her life after his accident: he knows how much it now means to her, how complete it makes her, and how much he values her fulfilment through it. At one point, he attempts to talk to her about his fears of what is happening to him, and he even asks Bess whether she thinks people near the edge turn into different people; do they turn bad? The script makes it clear that Jan is describing his tormenting dream life, where dark things are happening and Bess is involved. The finished film, however, emphasizes Bess's promise that Jan is not going to die, and so highlights the inevitability of her final sacrifice rather than Jan's attempts to keep her safe. Both versions emphasize relatedness.

Further evidence for this emphasis on relatedness is to be found in the scene in the film where Bess returns to her church for solace and support in a place she finds deeply helpful to her, only to be cruelly rejected. At this point, she has already put herself beyond the tolerance of the community because of her sexual activities. In her mind, though, she has been following the voice of God in the service of love, and so has done nothing wrong. When she arrives at the church, a man in the congregation is giving voice as to the nature of love and perfection. She hears him say: ". . . because there is only one thing for us, sinners that we are, to achieve perfection in the eyes of God. Through unconditional love for the word that is written; though unconditional love for the Law."

Bess's response in the church just before she is cast out of the community, that she cannot understand their meaning of the word "love", is key to the difference between the film's different depictions of relating. Hesitantly, she says: "I don't understand what you're saying. How can you love a word?" She continues, seeming to be attending more and more to her own internal experience: "You cannot love words. You cannot be in love with a word." Finally, and happily, she concludes with what she knows to be true: "You can love another human being—that's perfection." As she says this, the vicar condemns her and casts her out of the community, ultimately sending her to her death at the hands of the sailors. Bess's love is both a matter of the heart and of the body; the churchmen's is sterile and empty: a rote text to be preserved rather than something to be lived.

In *Breaking the Waves*, we are left with an ambiguous picture of the relationship between Jan and Bess, though it is clear that Bess is trying to save Jan through an act of physical sacrifice, and Jan does try to limit the damage he is doing. As a result of this mix of awareness of self and care for another, it seems that, at root, the relationship between Jan and Bess is one in which both of them, had fate deemed otherwise, would have been helped to be in touch with their emotional lives in relation to each other. Bess's faith and love could have acted as a framework within which Jan could have been helped to discover just what it means to choose someone, to stick with them and try to relate over time, allowing Bess to move from being an angel to being an ordinary woman: annoying at times and delightful at others; trying to separate from the demands of her mother and the over-protectiveness of her widowed sister-in-law; trying to live life according to her relationship with a god inside her. Jan's worldliness and companionship, his delight and celebration of her physicality, and his sense of a different right and wrong (which remains, despite his part in Bess's downfall) could have helped her moderate the voice inside, forgive herself more easily, and relate as an equal. The film suggests that, despite them not having known each other for very long, they had seen something very fundamental in each other: a marriage that would be one of two souls coming together at just the right time for them both.

In terms of couple relationships depicted in the film, there is a clear contrast of the relationship between Jan and Bess with those of the law-bound, emotionally deprived relationships within the church community and with those of the purely physical, sexual commerce between the women in the harbour and the men on the trawlers and ships (which are themselves also law-bound, and emotionally deprived: you pay, you get; you sell, you give). Jan and Bess are a counterpoint to these. Even as they slip towards madness and death, what is emphasized is their thinking about, and their connection with, each other. In theory, it *could* be suggested that Jan's perversion is a version of the harshness of the church Elders, who are as happy to condemn their fellows to eternal damnation as to eternal salvation, just as it *could* be suggested that Bess's sexual activities are a version of the prostitution in the harbour. But what Jan and Bess have, that is so missing from these other depictions of relating, is a wish not to exploit, but to protect; a wish to put the other person first; a wish to remain committed at an emotional level, despite what else was going on. This is also the difference between them and Severin and Wanda.

Sadomasochism and the nature of the contract

It seems likely that Bess suffered from some degree of moral masochism prior to her relationship with Jan. Indeed, it is likely that the whole community lived under a sense of guilt and the threat of punishment. In the film, there are very few complete couples. Most appear to have suffered the death of a partner, and Bess's own father is dead, as is her brother. Only her grandfather remains, but he is under the thumb of the Elders of the Church. Bess's mother is stern, and for most of the film (though thankfully not all) she is unyielding and unforgiving. Bess's Oedipal struggles would have included trying to manage a relationship to an internal God, an archetypal figure filling her superego, a connection that her relationship with Jan would have mediated over time. Matching this tendency to masochism there may also have been something sadistic about Jan: his choice of someone so frail and so other-worldly, whom he could protect when he was with her but also abandon when he went back to the rigs, suggests that there was a part of him that needed to be in relationship to a damaged object that could be dependent on him, and whose dependency would be stimulated to a painful degree by his acts of freedom. That said, it seems that the sadomasochistic link between Bess and Jan would have been part and parcel of a sexual and relational life that was in the service of love, binding aggression and desire together, and that it would have formed part of a satisfying sexual interaction between them, providing both excitement and release in a non-perverse way. The story of *Breaking the Waves* shows this through its contrast between Bess and Jan's intentions and the tragedy of their actions. It is clear that, whatever their private fantasies, neither Bess nor Jan would have wanted what happened to each of them. For them, the sadomasochism depicted in the film is like an illness that they have succumbed to, a virus they have contracted or caught, and which has made them very ill, but has not changed their essential nature.

This contrasts with the relationship between Wanda and Severin. For the couple of *Venus in Furs*, the sadomasochistic contract was there from the start, despite what appears to be a case similar to that of Bess and Jan: of one person affecting the other more. It is clear that Severin's insistence on being Wanda's "slave" gradually corrupted her and made her take up the role of sadist with increasing gusto. She tells him that, as a result of his actions, she has developed a "taste" for the task, and she blames him for stirring up her "dormant impulses". On investigation, it is clear that there is some truth to her claim, made at the end of the book, that all she wanted was a man whom she could look up to, and not down on, like Severin. It is also clear that she had said this at different times in their relationship and that Severin could not or would not hear it. Seen like this, Severin's fate is all of his own making: he corrupted her with his insistence on what Freud would call a feminine masochism, making Wanda contract the "illness" of sadism in response to it; she, like Bess and Jan, then becomes a victim of the circumstances she found herself in. What gives the game away, however, is the way in which Wanda—at the very beginning of her contact with Severin, when he sees her indistinctly in the garden and thinks that she is the stature of Venus come alive—has very deliberately set out to enact his fantasy. She knew about his yearning for Venus in furs from his annotations on the photograph of Titian's painting of "Venus at her Mirror" that she had come across accidentally. Though she and Severin had not met, it amused her to overwhelm his senses, taking charge of his erotic life as she did even before they had so much as said a word to each other. So Wanda and Severin were not innocents in this matter; both were deliberately and mutually involved.

Of course, it is a basic precept of a psychoanalytic view of couple relationships that both partners are involved—not necessarily equally, but at least to some degree—in the construction of what goes on between them. Sadistic and masochistic couple interactions are a product of both partners, even when the natural action of the opposites of sadism and masochism in sexual life is taken into account.

What distinguishes the couple relationship of Wanda and Severin from that of Bess and Jan is that there is no attempt to escape from the danger of what they were doing in a way that demonstrated a loving relationship between them. It is true that Severin at one point attempts to escape by drowning himself, but he does this in lieu of walking out of the relationship. Attempting to kill himself because of how spurned he has been by Wanda merely confirms the nature of the agreement between them. It is the rule, rather than the exception, and it demonstrates how the sadomasochistic contract between Venus and her slave was founded on cruelty and the arbitrary exercise of a tyrannical authority. Small wonder, then, that it is *Venus in Furs* that gives voice to the story of the Bull of Dionysius, in which the murderous inventions of one person are themselves overwhelmed by the even greater deadliness of another. Setting out, as Wanda and Severin do, to have such a cut and dried sadomasochistic relationship allows no space for any development between them. They invent a relationship in which there can only be repetition, and in which reciprocal loving and dependent feelings are legislated against by the nature of their contract. *Breaking the Waves*, on the other hand, despite the horror of its story and the awful fate of Bess, is a story that focuses on the attempt to keep faith with one another; indeed, to develop a relationship of faith in one another, rather than in norms or rules, and in the face of overwhelming force. Although both stories involve sadomasochistic relating, the story of Bess and Jan, unlike that of Wanda and Severin, celebrates love rather than power.

References

Chasseguet-Smirgel, J. (1991). Sadomasochism in the perversions: some thoughts on the destruction of reality. *Journal of the American Psychoanalytic Association, 39*: 399–415.

de Sade, M. (1785). *The 120 Days of Sodom*. London: Arrow, 1989.

Denman, F. (2004). *Sexuality. A Biopsychosocial Approach*. Basingstoke: Palgrave Macmillan.

Diamond, D., Blatt, S., & Lichtenberg, J. (Eds.) (2007). *Attachment and Sexuality*. London: Analytic Press.

Freud, S. (1905d). *Three Essays on the Theory of Sexuality. S.E., 7*: 125–243. London: Hogarth.

Freud, S. (1915c). Instincts and their vicissitudes. *S.E., 14*: 109–140. London: Hogarth.

Freud, S. (1919e). A child is being beaten: a contribution to the study of the origin of sexual perversions. *S.E., 17*: 175–204. London: Hogarth.

Freud, S. (1924c). The economic problem of masochism. *S.E., 19*: 159–170. London: Hogarth.

Hewison, D. (2005). Sex and the imagination in supervision and therapy. *Psychoanalytic Perspectives on Couple Work, 1*: 72–87.

Jung, C. G. (1943). On the psychology of the unconscious. *Two Essays on Analytical Psychology C.W., 7*, pp. 3–119). London: Routledge & Kegan Paul.

Kernberg, O. (1991). Sadomasochism, sexual excitement, and perversion. *Journal of the American Psychoanalytic Association, 39*: 333–362.

Kernberg, O. (1995). *Love Relations: Normality and Pathology*. New Haven, CT: Yale University Press.

Krafft-Ebing, R. F. (1906). *Psychopathia Sexualis*. New York: Physicians and Surgeons Book(s), 1931.

Leonoff, A. (1997). Destruo ergo sum: towards a psychoanalytic understanding of sadism. *Canadian Journal of Psychoanalysis*, 5: 95–112.

McDougall, J. (1995). *The Many Faces of Eros*. London: Free Association.

Ross, F. (2003). *Understanding Perversion in Clinical Practice. Structure and Strategy in the Psyche*. London: Karnac.

Stoller, R. (1986a). *Perversion: The Erotic Form of Hatred*. London: Maresfield Library.

Stoller, R. (1986b). *Sexual Excitement: Dynamics of Erotic Life*. London: Karnac.

von Sacher-Masoch, L. (1870). *Venus in Furs*. Harmondsworth: Penguin, 2000.

von Sacher-Masoch, W. (1906). *The Confessions of Wanda von Sacher-Masoch*. San Francisco, CA: Re/Search Publications, 1990.

von Trier, L. (1996a). *Breaking the Waves*. London: Faber & Faber.

von Trier, L. (dir.) (1996b). *Breaking the Waves*. Argus Film.

Welldon, E. (2002). *Sadomasochism*. Cambridge: Icon.

CHAPTER TEN

From fear of intimacy to perversion

Mary Morgan and Judith Freedman

I n this chapter, we explore themes that emerge in psychoanalytic work with couples, particularly in those couples presenting with sexual problems, from the "ordinary" difficulties of anxiety about being intimate to the more pathological manifestations in perversion. We examine how unresolved conflict in the internal world, especially in relation to the internal couple, can lead to difficulties in the capacity for intimate relating. We suggest that intrusive projective identification and the use of "defensive sameness" and "defensive difference" serve as defences against intimacy. These defences function to obliterate the reality of the other, and it is in this sense we use the term perversion. Finally, we comment on the difficulties for the therapist who may feel drawn into a perverse arena when working with couples with sexual problems.

We use the film *Sex, Lies and Videotape* (Soderbergh, 1988) to illustrate these themes. In this extraordinary film we can observe a set of characters demonstrating the range of these difficulties, with the advantage that we do not encounter any problems about confidentiality.

Sex, Lies and Videotape presents us with four main characters, all of whom have a relationship with each other. The film witnesses the different kinds of couples they form, ranging from the marriage between John and Ann to the more transient liaison between Graham and Cynthia. John is an upwardly mobile lawyer who has just become a partner in his firm. He is married to Ann, and they have a beautiful home in a comfortable, middle-class American suburb. As the film opens, we see that he is engaged in a torrid affair with Cynthia, his wife's sister.

Ann is beautiful. She gave up work upon marrying and now occupies herself with looking after her husband and their home. She is obsessive about housework, and sees a therapist with whom she talks about guilt and anxiety that the world will be overrun with garbage. She has lost interest in sex, but realizes in discussion with her therapist that John seemed to lose interest in her before she lost interest in him. They could be a couple coming for psychotherapy.

Cynthia is everything that Ann seems not to be, and vice versa. She lives in an untidy flat and works in a bar. She is uninhibited sexually, and shows no guilt about her affair with her sister's husband. After all, as she points out to John, *she* did not take a vow to be faithful.

Graham is an old college friend of John's. They have not met for years and when they do, they stand in sharp relief to each other. Graham, in contrast to John, has not pursued a life of professional achievement. He is a loner, a drifter, introverted, with an air of innocence, as if he has been thrust into adulthood and failed to manage it. When John and Graham meet they both believe that there is a clash of values between them. John abhors Graham's non-conformity; Graham sees John as a liar.

The film revolves around these four characters, each of whom has a relationship with the others. In other words, they are a series of couples. The only other significant character is Ann's therapist, whose role is particularly interesting with regard to therapists working with sexual material, a subject to which we shall return later.

The internal couple and its impact on the capacity to relate

The presence in this film of a series of couples provokes the question of who is relating to whom. The editing of the film places this theme prominently. The interaction between the only couple who are having sexual intercourse (John and Cynthia) is overlaid with dialogue between other couples, or interspersed with interactions of other couples. We see the following: the marriage between John and Ann; the relationship between the sisters, Ann and Cynthia; the relationship between the college friends, John and Graham; the affair between John and Cynthia; the sexual encounter between Cynthia and Graham; and finally the developing relationship between Ann and Graham. Alongside these observable external relationships, we can wonder about what kinds of relationships exist inside these individuals: what kind of internal couple exists, and how this is related to.

The concept of the internal couple derives from the psychoanalytic notion that we all have an inner world, with inner objects to which we relate. These inner objects are mental representations of the way we have experienced important other people in our lives, particularly our parents. These psychic images are under the sway of infantile experiences and emotional states, so that our internal objects are not, for example, identical to our parents in real life. The most significant influences on our internal objects come from our childhood experiences with our parents, but later experiences in life can also modify them.

We carry inside ourselves representations not only of our parents as individuals, but also of their relationship with each other. This is the basis of the internal couple, the image in one's internal world of how two people relate to each other intimately. A healthy resolution of the Oedipus complex results in the introjection of the kind of internal object that we might describe as an internal creative couple (Morgan & Ruszczynski, 1998). This concept includes the capacity for mature sexual relating. It also includes, as Britton (1989) points out, the capacity to observe and tolerate others in a relationship from which we are excluded, as well as the capacity to engage in a relationship ourselves while being observed by others who are excluded. Disruptions in the resolution of the Oedipus complex result in disturbed internal couples that give rise to disordered, and maybe even perverse, intimate relationships.

Our internal world is in dynamic interaction with our external world, each influencing the other. Our inner world affects our perception of our external world; the external world shapes our inner world. The kind of internal couple we each have inside us, or the absence thereof, and the way we relate to that couple, has an impact on our own capacity for relating to others.

In *Sex, Lies and Videotape* we are taken into a world in which there is no internal creative couple, at least none that is integrated in the psyches of the individuals. Where the possibility of such a coupling is perceived, it is mercilessly attacked. The most vivid example of this interplay between the external coupling and the internal worlds of couple relationships is near the beginning of the film when John (the husband) and Cynthia (his sister-in-law) meet for a passionate sexual encounter. This scene is interspersed with another scene, that of Ann (the wife) talking to her therapist about her sexually unfulfilling and empty marriage. This second scene could easily be viewed as a depiction of the internal world (an experience of an empty relationship) that drives John and Cynthia to seek passion and aliveness in the external world and at any cost.

There is much evidence in the film to suggest that both Cynthia and John are motivated in their liaison by a wish to attack and triumph over an internal creative couple. For Cynthia, this couple is represented by her sister and John, a couple from whom she feels painfully excluded. She is unable to contain her rivalrous Oedipal feelings towards Ann, her sister, representing the internal mother, and is driven to possess Ann's husband, or any other male of inter-est to Ann, representing mother's husband. She finds herself in a desperate place in which she can never quite achieve her aim, so that the affair with John, representing the Oedipal father, is not enough. She wants to "do it" in Ann's (the mother's) bed; psychically, she wants to *be* her. She says to John after they have made love, "You know, I'd like to do it at your house sometime. I must admit the idea of doing it in my sister's bed gives me a perverse thrill. I wish I could come right out and tell everyone that Ann's a lousy lay—the beautiful, the popular, Ann Bishop Melaney." When "doing it" in her sister's bed fails to relieve her psychic turmoil, she has to have Graham, whom she quickly senses is becoming Ann's new interest. Cynthia is dominated by her internal world and her need to wreak havoc and revenge on the Oedipal couple. She is left in a lonely place without any meaningful real relationships of her own. She eventually says to John, "We don't have anything to talk about."

Later in the film there is a poignant image of Cynthia in the bar where she works with the man who does not even know her name but is always there, admiring her and wanting her, providing her with temporary respite from her usual destructive position. Cynthia's internal object relationships dominate her, so that she acts out in her external world what remains so unresolved internally. The result is extreme poverty in her relationships.

John unconsciously joins Cynthia in attacking the Oedipal couple, in his case represented by his own marriage, and perhaps also by his new partnership at work, which he treats in a similarly cavalier way. Early in the film we hear him giving advice to a friend over the phone. He says, "I'm gonna tell you a little secret. As soon as you've got a ring on your finger you start getting the most spectacular attention from the opposite gender. . . . I wish I had Super Bowl tickets for every time some filly came up to me and started talking without the slightest provocation. . . . if I'd known that (before I got married) I'd have gone out and bought a ring and saved myself a lot of time and money." For John, it is through being unavailable to all women by choosing to marry one woman that the world of women becomes freely available. In this way he is like an acting-out Oedipal father who is desired by his daughters by virtue of his position, and misuses his position to gratify his narcissism.

Neither John nor Cynthia can show any regard for, or dependence on, each other, seeming to despise such notions, and instead relating to each other as objects that can be summoned and discarded. They use each other mercilessly to deal with unbearable psychic pain, their sense of emptiness and the painful feelings of being excluded, as well as any guilt they momentarily encounter as a consequence of their destructive attacks. An example of the latter occurs when Cynthia confronts John with being a liar because he breaks his marriage vows. He makes fleeting contact with his guilt, finds it intolerable, and seeks to evacuate it immediately through sex with Cynthia.

What about Ann and Graham? Ann tells her therapist that she fears the world will be overrun with garbage. We do not hear the therapist's interpretation of this, but we might interpret it as her own fear of her messy/dirty sexual feelings. She tells Graham that in her view sex is overrated. She keeps herself distanced from her own sexuality, which she fears could easily become out of control. Instead, she projects rampant sexuality into her sister Cynthia. Her relationship to Cynthia is highly charged because they each represent a dominant internal object for the other. She is sufficiently close to Cynthia to ask her the details of her sexual encounter with Graham. This undeveloped part of her is safer in others: in Cynthia, in John, in the cruel adult world that spills out garbage. This leaves her out of touch with her own sexuality, but she feels safe and secure and identified with her mother, whom she also sees as a non-sexual woman (she buys her mother a dress that an onlooker describes as a tablecloth). We could say that Ann closes her eyes to the world of adult sexuality, including her own sexuality, because she believes this is a dangerous place. Cynthia provokes and confirms her fears. When Ann discovers the details of Cynthia's encounter with Graham, she tells her, "You're in trouble." Cynthia retorts, "You sound just like Mama."

We can postulate that both Ann and Graham share the idea of an internal couple in which sexuality is dangerous and has to be repressed or controlled. Perhaps they unconsciously recognize this in each other, in the same way that John and Cynthia recognize a shared wish to attack the parental couple. Graham tells Ann about his relationship with an ex-girlfriend, Elizabeth, subsequent to which he became impotent. He used to lie and to express his feelings non-verbally, and he scared people close to him. Here he describes a particular kind of internal relationship of a paranoid–schizoid type, in which lying is used as a defence against the other triumphing over you. Feelings are projected or acted out, instead of being owned and thought about, as would have occurred if he had more sense of an internal creative couple. Perhaps Elizabeth reacted to this by dealing him a narcissistic blow that left him impotent, or perhaps in his mind Elizabeth became the devouring sexual partner, while he disavowed any sexual interest.

In the aftermath, Graham developed a strategy to contain his sexuality through a kind of intercourse—his videotaped interviews—in which he has no physical contact with the other. The women in his films have an exhibitionist sexual experience, while Graham has a voyeuristic experience. Neither person makes contact with a real other. As Stoller (1975) points out: "Pornography spares one the anxieties of having to make it with another person; the people on the printed page know their place and do as directed" (p. 87). In this state of mind there is no sense of a real, separate other person. This seems to apply almost as much to the way Cynthia and

John relate to each other as to the way Graham relates to the women he films.

John and Ann are the only couple in the film who are socially sanctioned. The fact that they are unable to sustain an intimate relationship, in both sexual and emotional terms, tells us something important about the internal couples that exist in the minds of each of them. Yet, as we have described, they both also form quite different relationships with other people, relationships that carry remnants of their marital relationship but also differ from it. John is able to have a sexual relationship with Cynthia but, as with Ann, it lacks emotional intimacy. Ann's relationship with Graham, while emotionally open, is marked by sexual fearfulness, even thought we may feel optimistic about the possibility of her achieving a more open sexual relationship with Graham than with John.

We believe that these differences tell us about the variations that are possible when two individuals come together, bringing into contact in a unique way their internal couples. The interaction evokes different valences, so that no two couples are ever the same, even though they may share a partner.

Intrusive projective identification vs. intimacy

We have been describing intimacy in relationships and using the term to refer to both its sexual and emotional aspects. The film raises implicit questions: what is the nature of relating? What is a sexual relationship as opposed to sex? The relationship between Ann and John lacks both sex and intimacy. When Graham asks Ann if she likes being married, she responds by saying she likes the security and the house they have, and that John has just been made a partner in his firm. Her response might, in part, be a reaction to being put on the spot by an overly intimate and intrusive question from a stranger. One also senses that she lacks an intimate relationship with another, something she might not question if she lacks inside herself an internal creative couple.

On the face of it, Graham has endless intimate experiences with women. He persuades them to reveal their most private thoughts and fantasies as well as describing their actual sexual experiences. However, Graham actually has no real intimate contact with the women as he transforms them through the medium of the video camera to images on a screen. It is like living a lie in which both self and object are deceived. Graham's women may feel that they are being intimate when they talk about their sexuality and sexual experiences, but they do this in relation to a camera, and Graham watches them on film, each engaged in an autoerotic activity. Ann challenges this narcissistic relating in a scene towards the end of the film, when she confronts Graham with the fact that he exists in a world of real other people and has an effect on them. She says, "Anyone that comes into contact with you becomes part of your problem. You've had an effect on my life."

In this film, as in some couple relationships, intimacy and intrusiveness are confused. Ann and Graham attempt intimacy when they share something personal with each other: Ann her belief that sex is overrated, Graham that he is impotent. It is by trying to get inside or intrude on women's experience of sex that Graham gets aroused. In the case of Ann and Graham, what they experience as intrusiveness by the other gradually becomes transformed into a genuine curiosity *about* the other. Fisher (1995) describes mature intimacy as a "state of mind marked by humility in the face of the infinitely unknowable mystery of the reality of the other" (p. 103). After an exchange in which they each turn the camera on the other, Graham switches it off, a gesture that makes way for a genuine intimacy to emerge.

Sex can look and feel like intimacy, but John and Cynthia, who do have a real sexual relationship, show that their sex may not be intimate. They are not so much relating to each other as relating to an internal object. In the end, they discover that they do not know anything about each other. This confusion between sex and intimacy is often present when one partner in a couple has an affair. Like John, faced with a lack, or possibly fear, of intimacy in their own marriage, they look to a sexual relationship with another to provide this missing intimacy and then find they mistook sex for intimacy.

Perversions: hatred of intimacy

Thus far, we have considered problems that couples may experience when they are afraid of intimacy. For some couples—those who present with perversions—problems with intimacy may actually have hatred at their core. In this film we see a range of perverse activities, including Graham's voyeurism and autoerotism, Cynthia's exhibitionism, and Cynthia and John's incestuous acting-out. Perversions become evident because of their sexual manifestations, but their internal basis is a turning away from reality and truth. It seems apt that "lies" is included in the title of this film. The lies that characterize perversion begin as a turning away from the truth of one's early experiences, usually because these were traumatic and overwhelming to a young child. The person elaborates a perversion as an effort to master childhood trauma, and a central feature of this is the hostility involved in taking revenge by doing to someone else what was done to oneself.

We suggest that, within a couple, the individuals may resort to perverse interactions as a defence against the anxieties they would experience if they were to engage in true intimacy. These are not anxieties about normal openness and self-exposure. For the perverse individual, intimate relationships present the prospect of a repetition of an overwhelming childhood trauma. The perversion is a behavioural attempt to contain this anxiety and give vent to the hatred without succumbing to psychotic decompensation.

An important aspect of perversions is that they require the presence of another person to be enacted. The other is always present, at least as a fantasized object, and usually as an actual external object as well. Graham needs a Cynthia to film, and Cynthia needs a Graham to look at her. Cynthia and John need each other to engage in the incestuous relationship that has quite personal meanings for both of them. Although the partners in these couples are in a relationship with each other, they relate in a way that diminishes them as people. Their perverse activities rob the other person of the uniqueness and fullness of their experience. The other is required to become just what the partner wants him or her to be. If the other complies, it is at the price of becoming much less of an individual. This deadening constriction, we suggest, is the effect within the couple of the hatred that is at the core of the perversion.

We find the notions of "defensive sameness" and "defensive difference" helpful in this context. We mean by these an insistence that the other is completely the same as, or completely different from, oneself. These beliefs are maintained with certainty for defensive reasons, when a true reckoning of what is the same and what is different threatens to expose the separateness and independence of an individual's existence. The other person is dismissed as entirely the same (so there is nothing to get to know) or as entirely different (and therefore unknowable).

The perverse act often represents an attempt to obliterate differences, whether between the sexes, as in cross-dressing, or between the generations, as in incest, or by exploring differences in a controlling way. The characters in this film seem to have very much in mind their differences from one another. John says, early on, "Graham? We were very close many years ago, but I think we're very different now." Graham agrees, and says a little later, "John and I were very much alike." It is interesting that neither of them says which one supposedly has changed. When Graham asks Ann to describe her sister, the first thing she says is that she is very different from Cynthia. Cynthia pointedly seems to live her life as differently from Ann as possible, but then she wants to take over her sister's husband and marital bed.

We come to know that these characters are expressing defensive differences from each other. As events in the film proceed, the defensive process is revealed as the four characters gradually transform their self-images into what, previously, was their hated other. Thus, Cynthia wants most to have sex in a marital bed and ends up withdrawing from her promiscuous relationship with John. Ann reveals herself as interested in sex and begins a new, presumably sexual, relationship with Graham. Meanwhile, Graham steps into John's position as partner to Ann, while John becomes the odd man out, as Graham was at the beginning of the film. Ann tries to keep interest in sex located in Cynthia, while Cynthia tries to keep fear of sex located in Ann. But already this distinction is breaking down. Ann's obvious excitement and interest in the details of what happened belie her insistence that "I don't want to talk about it." What we are seeing here can be thought about as aspects of perverse internal relationships enacted in couple relationships. In other words, at the beginning of the film, each character invokes projective identification to rid themselves of internal parts that they cannot face. Cynthia carries Ann's sexuality. Ann carries Cynthia's identification with their mother. John is the potent man and liar for Graham. Graham is the sexual and professional failure for John.

This splitting up of internal experience is a central aspect of perversion. Couple relationships present an arena, particularly for more disturbed couples, in which the partners can divide between themselves aspects of their internal lives and evade the reality of who they are. Knowing that this is happening leaves us, as observers, with an ill-at-ease sense that something unpleasant is being done by each character to another, something that rigidly constrains both themselves and the other. Hence, we might construe the frequent accusations about lying as a reference to what each character is unwilling to face about him or herself. It is only with the resolution at the end of the film that Ann can admit this. She says, "I hate it when I have feelings she has. It bothers me when I have feelings about men, because I know it's how *she* thinks."

Through most of the film, the characters insist that they are different from each other, even though the differences seem not to hold. Real difference requires knowledge about oneself, in the context of relations with others, which is true and can be painful. Opposed to this are defensive sameness and difference, both of which are constraining to the self and to the other person. The various portrayals in this film of so-called differences between the characters represent attempts to take revenge on another person by denying his or her uniqueness and unknowableness. At the same time, seeing the other as just different, or just the same, protects the perverse individual against not knowing who the other person is and might become. This is protection born out of a need to control the other lest one becomes exposed to anxiety about being separate. Paradoxically, it is the ability to bear separateness that is the precursor to establishing an intimate relationship.

Voyeurism and its connection to therapy

Work with couples who bring profound difficulties with intimacy might expose the therapist to experiences that feel uncomfortable, and maybe even perverse. Watching this film may bring this vividly to our awareness as an experience of voyeurism. In *Sex, Lies and Videotape* we are invited to observe intimate and sometimes sexual behaviour between people that would be unusual and even perverse were the celluloid absent. In the therapeutic encounter, particularly with couples, and particularly when they are sharing their intimate and sexual experience, we can approach something close to this.

In the film, we are given the uncomfortable experience of feeling that we, too, are behind the video camera, witness to something that we are not sure we should be seeing. We might even feel as if the camera is on us when it seems that the director deliberately attempts to stir up erotic excitement in us. This dynamic of feeling voyeuristic and then exposed to excitement, abhorrence, or perversity, could exist in work with couples and individuals who are sharing their sexual experiences, particularly when we encounter more perverse or enacted sexuality.

The therapist in the film is depicted in a way that makes most therapists' hearts sink. It seems quite acceptable to therapist and patient when he sits on the couch with his patient! On the other hand, we could take this, as well as the intrusive questioning of Ann about her sexuality, as an enactment of countertransference that most therapists are able to process inside themselves and make use of, for example through interpretation. Thus, what appears as his curiosity about Ann's sexuality and prompts him to enquire whether she masturbates, could be thought of as *her* split off curiosity about her own sexuality which gets projected into others, notably Cynthia, and perhaps also Graham, who finds himself, like her therapist, asking her to share intimate details about herself.

We want also to consider another enactment of this perverse mechanism. We are referring to the way that making a videotape becomes equivalent to psychotherapy. The film opens in a psychotherapy session. Ann is sitting on a couch while her therapist sits in the adjacent chair. Sex is a prominent and embarrassing issue in the session. Later, Graham and Ann draw therapy into their discussion about intimacy. Graham says that you should only take advice from someone with whom you have been intimate. Ann says that she is intimate with her therapist. Graham asks whether she means she has sex with him "Oh, no!" Ann replies, in the same giggly embarrassment with which she met her therapist's question about whether she masturbates.

Compare this to a later episode. Cynthia has arrived at Graham's house and they are discussing making a videotape. This encounter could be seen as a version, albeit a perverse one, of the beginning of a therapy. Graham assures Cynthia that they will just be talking and that he will keep her tape confidential. Cynthia is intrigued, and perhaps excited by her intuition about what the tapes mean to Graham. "Is this how you get off?" she asks him. "Yes," he replies. The scene ends with a question that is familiar to us. Just as our new patients ask, "Do I sit or lie down?", Cynthia asks, "Do I sit or stand?" In the event, she sits in the middle of the couch, just as her sister sat in the opening scene with her psychotherapist.

In this sequence, therapy and making a videotape are forced to be the same thing. Their real differences cannot be tolerated. Thus, Graham's perverse aim in making the videotapes is equated with the aim of psychotherapy. In reality, there is an important difference between psychotherapy and videotapes. Videotapes in this film stand for what cannot be said in any other way, unlike psychotherapy, which is a process of increasingly facing and even speaking the truth of one's existence. In this film, Ann does not tell John about her dissatisfaction with her sexual relations with him or about her emerging sexual relationship with Graham. Instead, John *sees* these things on video. The fact is that not only do John and Graham watch videotapes, but we do, too. Watching this film forces us to enter into the perverse sexual worlds of these four characters, just as working with a couple forces us to enter into their sexual world. We take up various stances about doing this. We might be reluctant, or we might be avoidant. We might even feel excited, and then guilty. As Cynthia asks Graham, "Is this how you get off?"

In the therapeutic encounter, the therapeutic relationship and the setting is the medium within which intimacy has to be managed. This can be difficult, both for the therapist, who sometimes has to manage disturbing countertransferences, and for the patient, who might wish for a different kind of relationship with the therapist and feel perplexed about what kind of relationship it is (see, for example, Ann's discussion with Graham about her therapy). These are very real concerns for therapists and patients. This film asks us to question our and their motives for inviting disclosures. The answers might not always be very comfortable.

References

Britton, R. S. (1989). The missing link: parental sexuality in the Oedipus complex. In: R. Britton, M. Feldman, & E. O'Shaughnessy (Eds.), *The Oedipus Complex Today* (pp. 83–101). London: Karnac.

Fisher, J. (1995). Identity and intimacy in the couple: three kinds of identification. In: S. Ruszczynski & J. Fisher (Eds.), *Intrusiveness and Intimacy in the Couple* (pp. 74–106). London: Karnac.

Morgan, M., & Ruszczynski, S. (1998). Psychotherapy with couples: in search of the creative couple. Paper presented to the Tavistock Marital Studies Institute 50th Anniversary Conference, "Towards Secure Marriage", London, 3–4 July.

Soderbergh, S. (1988). *Sex, Lies and Videotape*. Film: Outlaw Productions.

Stoller, R. J. (1975). *Perversion: The Erotic Form of Hatred*. New York: Pantheon [reprinted London: Karnac, 1986].

CHAPTER ELEVEN

Perversion as protection

Joanna Rosenthall

T he term "perversion", in everyday usage, carries with it moral overtones and also a sense of deviation from a norm. However, it is used in the psychoanalytic field as a technical term, and many authors attempt to address and challenge a judgemental attitude in order to make room for understanding and exploring a complex area of human experience. It is true to say that perversion continues to defy a simple description and explanation because it encompasses physical acts, conscious compulsions, and underlying unconscious mental states in different combinations, a complex scenario that cannot be pinned down, but that nevertheless has produced extremely interesting clinical elaboration and debate. The concept has also developed over time. Because of the resulting complexity, it is often the case that each author writing about it seeks also to define it, yet the term "perversion", perhaps more than any other in the psychoanalytic field, defies definition. In my view it continues to carry enormous significance, not only because it explores a disturbing element of human experience, but also because many authors have attempted to shine a light on it from different standpoints.

Three broad, overlapping areas have been described to give the term meaning. The first explores an object relationship in which one of the individuals is explicitly or tacitly denigrated, including sexually. Much of the psychoanalytic literature is taken up with this focus, attempting to explain unusual and compulsive behaviour

> in which the person afflicted does not feel free to obtain sexual genital gratification through intimate contact with another person. Instead he or she feels "taken over" by a compulsive activity which is subjectively experienced as inexplicable and "bizarre" but provides a release of unbearable and increasing sexual anxiety. [Welldon, 1996, p. 273]

It is frequently argued that these kinds of inexplicable actions contain aggression and an unconscious wish to hurt the other person (Stoller, 1975).

The second area points to a familial constellation in which there is often an overly collusive mother who both seduces the child and also rejects the father, and thereby fosters in the child "an illusion that he has neither to grow up, nor to reach maturity . . . in order to be her satisfactory sexual partner" (Chasseguet-Smirgel, 1985, p. 2). The frequent presence of this constellation suggests that it might play an important part in the formation of perversion (Bak, 1968).

The third area focuses on perversion as a distortion of reality, or as a perversion of the "truth". This approach does not necessarily look at specific behaviours, but explores aspects of the underlying object relationships. Chasseguet-Smirgel (1985) describes how, when the process of separation from the mother's body cannot be achieved because of a lack of a containing object, there are phantasies of annihilation, an experience of intolerable psychic pain, and regression towards a sexually undifferentiated anal world. All intergenerational differences may be denied in phantasy. She becomes more specific about what this means when she says that the perversion involves an attempt to "replace genitality by the phase which normally precedes it" (ibid., p. 1); it involves a kind of sham or confusion, trying to pass one thing off as another, and this quality can be observed as an important element in perverse relating.

It is probably true to say that in the literature there is a lack of consensus and an ongoing debate about what perversion actually means. However, it seems to me that all the authors are interested in what is meant by perversion in the context of a relationship. In this chapter, I ask questions about what elements of experience, external as well as internal, would tend to attract an individual into a perverse relationship, as well as what sort of couple relationship will be formed when partners are each engaged, possibly in different ways, in perverse psychic activity that affects their interpersonal relating as well as the nature of their sexual encounters. While exploring this area, I have attempted to bear in mind the three areas delineated above. However, I have taken the nature of the connection between the partners as my main focus to explore perversity in a specific couple relationship.

The couple I am about to describe came for therapy for six years, once weekly, conjointly. They conveyed to me at the start of therapy that there was something very wrong. It was clear that they had created such an emotional tangle together that on the one hand it was suffocating to be stuck within it, but on the other it was life-threatening to attempt to unravel it. They were both in a state of terror, feeling that something very serious was at stake. This was not an "ordinary" neurotic couple difficulty that needed some development of communication or shift in the capacity for understanding the other, but a relationship in which the partners had clearly recruited each other to protect their very precarious internal selves; a shift in any direction threatened their sense of survival. They were visibly controlling, hurting and preventing development in each other. They had reached a crisis point where they could not go on as they were, but neither could they contemplate change.

The couple

Denigrating object relations

When they came for therapy, Rosa and Sam agreed something was dramatically wrong, although they could not put it into words. Previous to the therapy, they were both confused about emotions and relationships and often flooded with anxiety. They were quick to tell me that they tended to enact quite violent sado-masochistic sexual games in which he was "the master" and she "the slave". It was essential that he felt he was totally in charge and could introduce new ways of domi-nating or humiliating her, which sometimes involved equipment and doing things that really did hurt or control her: for example, using a whip that caused red wheals on her body. At other times he would tie her up and command her to get into humiliating positions. Although both of them were uncomfortable with this they were "driven to it". At the start, it was the combination of this declaration and the sense of life or death emergency and fear they expressed that alerted me to the thought that the relationship was taking place in the perverse realm. I understood their sharing of this as a need for me to know how deep their difficulties were. I understood later that the crisis they were in at the point of seeking help was intensified by her wish to withdraw from sex altogether, something she actually did about one year into the therapy.

Rosa spoke a lot, but was confusing to listen to, sharing convoluted details that appeared unconnected to a "story" she might have been telling. She seemed unable to prioritize a main element in her commu-nication. She presented herself as ill-defined and frightened of others, which made sense, because her confusion and neediness did indeed make her vulnerable to the attempts of others to control her. There was the feeling of her throwing herself at me with her eyes closed, hoping that she might have found someone trustworthy, but having no way to judge this for herself. At this time, my main function was to understand and bear a fragmented, terrifying experience. Only much later was she in a position to put into words that at this time she had been bewil-dered and frightened and could not discern or name one feeling or interaction from another: "everything was in a muddle". For several years into the therapy it seemed as if she kept her distance; although she needed me she used me in a rather objectified way, as if allowing me to get closer would feel too dangerous. It took much longer for her to allow real contact with me, which involved a wider range of emotions and recognition of a real dependency.

Sam had a harder, more defined feel to him. Sometimes his face looked set and unmoving, and I could imagine him being harsh and cruel. At other times, especially if I expressed something that made him feel understood, his eyes filled with tears that flowed down his face. His need, too, was expressed at a distance, as if he knew he needed me but this was too dangerous to acknowledge, because getting close was confused with losing control, something he could not risk. He did also convey a longing, sometimes expressed seductively, to have contact with a me that could be fair, warm, and robust.

I gradually learnt that sharing and separateness were extremely uncomfortable matters. They raised enormous levels of anxiety because Rosa was feeling so claustrophobic that she felt she could not survive in the relationship and needed to leave. She sounded as if she was unsure what her own thoughts and feelings were: in fact, unsure of her own identity. While believing that her only solution was to leave the relationship, she felt equally unable to behave in an adult and independent way. For example, she could not function at work without his constant input, nor did she have an awareness that it was necessary to keep an eye on how much money they had in the bank. Because she was the only earner, she felt she had the right to be the spender, regardless of the size of their shared resources or his needs. She felt outraged when Sam conveyed that their finances were diminished and that she should limit her spending. Simultaneously, she seemed to be divesting herself of the knowledge or desire to be separate, experiencing it simply as a burden that he was forced to carry for them both, while protesting vigorously about the cost of this to her sense of individuality and freedom. As far as I could tell, they did everything together, and their concern and positive feelings for each other seemed indistinguishable from need and control.

While Rosa felt she was suffocating, maybe even dying, Sam, although deeply ashamed, seemed to feel the opposite: that he could not survive without her. In this early phase the relationship felt extremely precarious, and the sessions were like walking on eggshells. I was the one who had tentatively and carefully to give words to the positions they felt themselves to be in, and to introduce the idea that, although they appeared to be in extreme opposite positions, they might, in fact, share a fear that they were losing essential parts of themselves as a consequence of the nature of their contact. In addition, they might both long for the feeling that they could be separate people but still remain in a close relationship. It was a great relief for them to hear me give voice to the possibility that these dilemmas were psychological, thereby implying that it was possible to resolve them in psychological ways. Nevertheless, I deduced from my experience with them that a great deal of development would need to take place inside each of them for it to become possible for them to move apart *psychically*, even by a small amount.

It was well over a year into the therapy before Rosa was able to give words more clearly to some of her thoughts. She spoke about how disappointed she was with Sam. She recognized that she had needed him to be there for her sense that she could survive in the world, but their positions had also somehow changed, and now she experienced him as extremely dependent and also controlling. For example, having been unemployed for many years, he continued to say he would get a job and share the responsibility with her to earn a living, but only if she promised to put all her earnings in a "shared pot" and not buy anything again without his agreement or permission. In this way, she felt burdened by having to be the sole breadwinner for the family, and also provoked and controlled by the unpalatable "deal" he was offering. It was possible that this "deal" was one to which he knew she would never accept, as it was an invitation for her to become a non-person. This scenario enabled him to maintain a position of justified righteousness about his dependence on her to earn, as if her intransigence was the only thing that stopped him going out and earning some money. This was the kind of entanglement that left her feeling trapped and controlled, and left him unable to develop and act as a separate individual. From my point of view, it became clearer and clearer that the sado-masochistic excitement and pleasure associated with this kind of relating needed to be addressed. It was momentous for them to discuss these issues together, as for many years this had been taboo, while each of them sacrificed the chance to develop and grow, either separately or together. In consequence, the relationship, and each of their lives, had become stagnant and deathly.

As far as the external world of work was concerned, and as the one earning the disposable income, Rosa was dominant and in charge. However, when it came to their sexual activity she became subservient and masochistic. He had a similar pattern, in that while he was dominant sexually, he reverted to a very vulnerable and diminished position when it came to the possibility that he might get a job or be active in any way in the external world.

Exploring this situation led to a greater awareness of their internal phantasies. Rosa seemed to have an unconscious picture of relationships in which one person longs for freedom but is owned and cruelly controlled by the other, who is too vulnerable to survive alone, but also gains pleasure and reward from the resulting power this provides. For her, sexually and in her overall demeanour, this had an overtly masochistic flavour, while in a more covert way she shifted unconsciously into a dominant, sadistic position: for example, by making decisions which affected them both without consulting him. For Sam, while he was able to enact being a rather cruel dictator in the bedroom, he was entertaining being in charge of an even bigger empire in his mind. He eventually confided, with a great deal of shame, that he felt

himself to be the ruler of an island in which he was extremely success-
fully running an international business empire, in charge of those
around him, but also of world renown. His mind was engaged in phantasies of being elevated and successful, and looking down on others
from a very great height. It was very difficult at first to address the gap
between this and the reality of his life, which was isolated, restricted,
and involved avoidance of contact with others almost completely.

Around this time, when we were exploring more openly the sado-
masochistic elements in their contact, Rosa withdrew from sex altogether. There was recognition that this "left Sam in the lurch", because
the elements of his personality that were bound up by the sexual activity now had to be managed in a different way.

Vulnerable family constellations

As the therapy deepened, I built up pictures of their early experiences,
which had contributed to the formation of their internal phantasies.
Both described coming from families in which they had been in
extremely close relationships, caring for vulnerable mothers, while
fathers were in a more distant or unreachable position, either oblivious
to, or else forcibly supporting, this mother–child fusion.

Rosa had two older sisters and a younger brother. She laughed when
she talked about this, as if they provided obvious reasons why her
mother had not been "properly pleased" with her. Her mother had
longed for a boy. She remembered her parents as laying down the law.
They always said "no" harshly, and without discussion. She remembered feeling that her mother could not negotiate life without someone
to hold on to, and had chosen her as a "crutch child", not with a special
feeling of love, but more to soothe a desperate need. During one session
when she was trying to describe the relationship between herself and
her mother, she told me, "It was like having one foot nailed to the
floor." It was not that love and concern were totally missing, but more
that they were offered to her in a toxic mixture of care and control. Rosa
was left with a suffocating terror that her mother would never let her
go, and she remembered wanting freedom from both of her parents at
a very early age.

On one occasion, aged about twelve, she had been part of a small group
invited to stay with a friend after a birthday party. She knew before
asking that her mother would not want her to go. When she asked, her
mother replied that she could not say: it needed father's permission.

However, mother never sought father's permission, so that each time Rosa asked her mother she would be fobbed off. There was a cruel, tantalizing quality to it, and a sense that if she were to do anything direct, like ask her father herself, or ask them both when they were together, she would get a definite "no". There seemed to be no concept of discussing something that was difficult or conflictual. Instead, there was a blocking, cruel quality to the contact, where she did not get a yes or a no. Hence, she suffered under their cruel regime and felt that her own development and separate life had to be a secret affair, like a betrayal.

Sam also had a difficult start. He described his father as a cold disciplinarian; he remembered being shouted at so loudly and suddenly as a child that he just could not continue functioning. He said that if he had been a computer, he would just have "got unplugged". His mother also seemed cowed by father, and unable to nurture and protect her child. However, she did seek shelter and solace with Sam. He had memories as a pre-adolescent of his mother taking him out to restaurants and whispering to him intensely that she loved him more than anyone in the world. This, not surprisingly, made him feel he was being asked to be a substitute husband. When Sam described the romantic quality of this relationship, he said that it had made him "feel sick". In the therapy, he started to work on the secretive part of him that also relished and maintained the special, elevated position that was implied.

In the perversion literature, a particular constellation is frequently described of a mother with a seductive and collusive attitude towards her child (Bak, 1968), so that a very intense relationship develops between mother and son, "which seems to occur in a closed circuit from which the father is excluded" (Chasseguet-Smirgel, 1974, p. 349). What is so important about this is that the child is invited to believe that he is already in the father's position and that his infantile sexuality and his penis are as good as, or even better than, the father's. Hence, it is an invitation to erase reality: the little boy does not have to bear the pain of being small, or of not being mother's partner. Through this distorted view of reality, he can instantly achieve pseudo-adult status and be mother's special partner. Part of this process involves an idealization of the child's infantile sexuality, which then becomes absolutely compelling because it is needed in order to foster the illusion and fend off the desperately painful reality.

Distorted realities

There seems to be widespread agreement that facing and knowing about reality provides a firm, reliable base to the personality, and that the development of either specific perversions or a more subtle kind of object relating, which involves perverse elements, is connected to obstructions in facing reality. There are specific areas of reality whose apprehension during a child's development provokes intense amounts of psychic pain, and it is these that are relevant to this debate: recognizing the realities of the difference between the sexes and the difference between the generations. Knowledge of these form the basis of the child recognizing not only that he is small while the parents are big, but also that they each have different genitals, which fit together during sexual activity, and this, by its very nature, excludes him. Bearing the psychic pain attached to this knowledge involves a crucial developmental step, which constitutes a strong basis for the development of his personality and implies that reality can be faced and borne even when it is painful. Perversion has been understood as something that can be put in the place of facing these realities when they are experienced as threatening the survival of the self. For certain couples, like Sam and Rosa, attempts are made to construct a relationship that achieves this denial of reality for them both.

Sam's family seem to fit into the classical scenario of an over-close relationship between mother and son. However, in a different way, so do Rosa's. She, too, had an overly needy, demanding mother who attempted to use her child to shore up her own vulnerable sense of self, giving Rosa the message, albeit ambivalently, that she was a very special child who was not really small and needy like a child, but instead had the capacities of an adult care-taker. When they met, Sam and Rosa seem to have recognized these attributes in each other, and been drawn by an unconscious shared experience, which left them seeking a particular kind of relationship that would shore up these phantasies. They had each developed pseudo adult personas, but at a deeper level they were terrified of "standing alone", each in different ways feeling ill-equipped to face adult life and the contact with reality that it requires. They seemed to have developed a relationship that helped them to manage and avoid the pain associated with becoming and being an individual, relieving them of the burden of having a separate mind and having to face unbearable realities. Each could maintain the special position status they had achieved with vulnerable mothers, as someone elevated and "knowing", while at the same time they could cling together in a stuck, undifferentiated way as if they never needed to continue the painful process of becoming a person. They shared the need to keep unprocessed, early experiences at bay: for example, facing the truth of feeling small and needing someone to understand. As a result, not only were they stuck in an unchanging, deadly world, which replicated the ones that each had suffered with their mothers, but they were also engaged in a relationship that prevented knowledge and development. Neither of them knew the difference between care and control.

When they first met, Rosa was lost and directionless. The only thing that was clear to her was that her survival meant leaving home. Rosa's mind was dominated by enormous guilt that her presence was needed for her mother's survival and a terror that she herself could not survive alone. Meeting Sam solved her crisis. She did not have to stay at home with parents who threatened to crush her as an individual forever, and she did not have to face life as a separate individual—she could join forces with him. For several years they related with a "babes-in-the-wood", stuck-together quality. They both believed that she was the vulnerable, needy one, while he appeared to be the "adult" care-taker. Differences or conflicts did not arise, and, on the whole, they managed to negotiate a shared life as if neither of them had separate wishes, ambitions, or desires. Each felt life to be a painful and humiliating obstacle course where they were in constant danger of being swamped with bad feelings, which they could only manage by returning to the superior, but ultimately isolated, position that had become familiar to them both. It is important to recognize that they were treating each other as parts of their own selves, as if they had absolute knowledge of, and rights over, each other. There were times when it was more openly revealed that their contact had an exciting sado-masochistic quality. There was pleasure in taking the superior, in control stance, and thwarting or causing hurt to each other. To perpetuate this situation meant that real exploration and understanding were not possible, because they would have been experienced as too threatening. They were denying "the basic postulate of otherness" (McDougall, 1986, p. 69).

However, this stasis could not last forever. With time Rosa, perhaps feeling enabled by the protection that the relationship had given her, started to long for development and change, but felt unable to achieve it. She was unable to attain enough distance from Sam to know what her own experience was. The relationship that had been her saviour was now exposed as crushing and imprisoning her. It was at this point that the couple came for help.

Some of the material I have described so far points to a relationship that is perverse, and some of it does not. Even as I was writing, and also during the course of the therapy, the idea of perversion was one that slipped in and out of focus. I have come to understand this as relevant to the nature of the couple's relationship: they were attempting to join together to manage shared unconscious terrors, some of which were neurotic, while others had a psychotic quality. Largely, they maintained a shared defence against these terrors by keeping their relationship in a restricted zone, where one person frequently felt dominant and the other reduced and controlled. These roles were interchangeable. At times, this seemed to contain the threat of unbearable experiences that could be psychotic in nature and intensity; at other times, when these terrors threatened to break through, the partners became more and more controlling of each other and eventually needed a vigorous activity to "bind up" their anxiety, and for this they resorted to enacting sado-masochistic scenarios in their sexual life. These always took the form of them enacting phantasies in which Rosa belonged to Sam and he could hurt or control her.

When Sam and Rosa came for help, they were living a kind of limbo half-life, in which internally they were stymied by an engulfing but vulnerable internalized object (mother) that was sometimes experienced as within each of them, and sometimes located in the other. It is possible to understand their sado-masochistic enactments as attempts to protect this object. But it was at a huge cost to them, because neither robust contact nor development was possible in their relationship. They both experienced any small adjustment or change as life-threatening. Their relationship replayed the paralysis that both partners had lived out in earlier relationships. Movement or development had been felt to threaten the survival of their parents, and now to threaten survival of a partner.

Later in the therapy, when they had started to bear some separation and were beginning to benefit from a greater sense of individual awareness and potential for development, Sam started a session in clear agitation. His mother had come round without telephoning first, letting herself in with a door key he had previously given her. She had bought a replacement bulb for the fridge light, which, without discussion, she replaced. After replacing the bulb, she had marched through the kitchen into the garden and started mowing the lawn, again with no discussion, behaving in Sam and Rosa's house as if she were the legitimate owner and part of the primary couple.

He felt hounded and angry, and yet quite unable to speak out. He was in a conflict. He wanted to be an adult man and protect his adult life with his partner, but at the same time this felt like too high a price to pay for giving up his elevated, special position as parent–lover to his mother. On this occasion he remained more preoccupied with how vulnerable his mother was, how hard it would be to be angry or to reject her by telling her to go away, or by retrieving the door key that he had willingly given her. His mind was filled with a relationship in which one person is humiliated and demoted and the other is in control and on top. The only way he could imagine talking to his mother was cruelly turning the tables and giving her the humiliating experience that she often gave him, and he was terrified she might never recover from that.

During another session, Rosa remembered how she would spend many hours sitting back against the wall, hugging her knees, in a small cupboard under the stairs that her father had converted into a darkroom. It was the one place where she felt she could think. She remembered the way she would go over events, actually feeling very alone "as if the world was all grey", but at the same time trying to secure herself into a superior position, dreaming of escaping and of her lofty ambitions for the future when she would achieve a state of utter freedom. Having described this experience, her voice dropped with sadness, and she said, "The curious thing was that even though my dreams were of success and great things, in fact I felt very lonely, time was heavy on my hands, and I was aware of having no resources and no one who could help or understand."

Perversion and the "core complex"

These two stories seem to represent two positions. On the one hand there is a relationship that is suffocating, where there is no room or space in which to develop, the mother's needs are paramount, and the child must fit in. On the other hand is a picture of parents who are oblivious to the child, who is left entirely alone and desolate in a bleak landscape with no resources. In the psychoanalytic literature, Glasser (1979) has described and explored the meaning of such pictures as internal scenarios that an individual might flip between. In a couple relationship like Sam's and Rosa's, we are more likely to see an interaction where each partner represents one of these scenarios and the relationship between them is dominated by incessant movement between claustro- and agoraphobic positions.

Schopenhauer, the German philosopher, described the porcupines' dilemma on a cold night as they tried to huddle together for warmth. As soon as they got too close they would cause pain and damage to each other, and so would move apart, only to suffer again from the threat of the cold. In this situation they were condemned to constant motion and repeated unresolvable conflict and pain, never able to find a position of comfort or satisfying contact. Glasser has taken this old story as a starting point and elaborated an internal and relational scenario, called the "core complex" (1979, 1998), which he placed at the centre of the psychopathology of perversion and fundamental to it. This picture has become an important element in starting to make sense of "inexplicable" and "bizarre" perverse activities.

First, Glasser describes the ordinary dilemma of the human infant, who longs for such intense closeness with the mother that it amounts to "merging" or a "state of oneness". This longed-for state, akin to a return to the womb, implies complete satisfaction and security. However, it holds its own dangers. Such closeness, by necessity, implies a loss of self. Glasser suggests that there are two options open to the individual as a defence against the threat of engulfment. The first is a flight from the object into a defensive narcissistic withdrawal; the second is a self-preservative, intense aggression. Flight brings its own dangers, like those facing the porcupines, that is, of being cold, utterly isolated, alone and abandoned. Relief from this state is ultimately sought by seeking proximity to the object. Similarly, the second option, self-preservative aggression, faces the subject with the potential destruction of the object, which in itself raises the terror of abandonment. Like that of the porcupines, this situation is made up of an unresolvable dilemma, moving backwards and forwards between the danger of engulfment or impingement and that of isolation. This describes the interaction between Sam and Rosa, in which they each had an arena where they attempted to control and possess the other, engendering the need for escape and freedom.

The emotional attitudes and phantasies that Glasser describes are part of normal infantile development. However, certain individuals are unable to develop beyond this stage, and continue to experience closeness as threatening annihilation or engulfment, and separation as desolate isolation. They become fixated at a very primitive stage of functioning in which the anxieties are of a life and death order. It appears that sexualization is a successful way of defending against anxiety of the loss of self "by creating the phantasy that rather than engulfment or abandonment there is an interpersonal relationship" (Ruszczynski, 2007, p. 29), even though in reality this is not achievable.

The sexualization of aggression results in sadism or masochism. In a state of narcissistic withdrawal the aggression tends to be directed against the self, and when this is sexualized it becomes masochism. On the other hand, the sexualization of self-preservative aggression results in sadism. Sexualization seems to act as a binding, organizing force in the internal state of affairs, enabling defensive measures to be effective and a certain stability to come about. In other words, the aggression is controlled, it no longer threatens destruction and loss, and the dangers of separateness and pain are also averted. It is this form of relating, which Glasser so clearly defines as a replay of an earlier paralysis with the parents, that is helpfully understood as perverse.

In his discussion of sado-masochistic and violent relationships Ruszczynski (2006) finds it essential to keep the idea of violation in mind. "The perpetrator's sense of being violated, physically or emotionally, is at the core of the violent state of mind, activating the violent behaviour towards the victim, who thus becomes the one to be violated" (p. 113). What I discovered during Sam and Rosa's therapy was that, even putting their sexual relationship to one side, they continued to live out a sado-masochistic contact with each other in other areas, sometimes switching the sense of who was dominating and who was the more vulnerable "victim". At times, I felt that the sado-masochistic elements that resulted in an experience of violation were mixed together with concern for each other in a confusing way, and it would be a distortion of their experience to describe these elements as entirely separate. Working with this couple and others who find themselves stuck in sado-masochistic enactments, sometimes actively sexual, sometimes not, I have come to recognize the importance of the idea of "a spectrum of perversion". In other words, it seems helpful to understand perversions as a dimension of the human psyche in general, "a temptation in the mind common to us all" (Chasseguet-Smirgel, 1985, p. 1), or as an element in the fabric of the mind whose presence does not preclude the simultaneous existence of neurotic or psychotic strands (Sanchez-Medina, 2002).

It is not unusual to see couples who repeatedly enact hate-filled scenarios with each other, which often cause pain in their most vulnerable area, and yet these couples are unable to part. It is tempting to think that the partners can be categorized as either the sadist or the masochist, and perhaps at the more extreme end of perverse relationships this is true. However, in my experience, many couples who come for help are in relationships where roles are more subtle than that. For example, a partner who might be sadistic in one area will become a masochistic victim in another area of the same relationship. This lends support to the notion that the primary aim of sado-masochism is to bind up and protect the individuals from unbearable primitive experience, and partners may move in and out of the two positions in achieving it; what is crucial to them is that they both "play ball", so to speak.

McDougall (1986) provides a useful parallel when she describes individuals who cannot manage to apprehend the facts and details of their lives and resort to externalizing their inner conflicts by various means, for example, by relying on substances like drugs or food, or else on other people. She describes this vividly as a "transitional theatre" in which the individual plays a part and chooses others in the external world to enact other parts that cannot be borne psychically. She explains that the wish behind such complicated dramas is to "try and make sense of what the small child of the past, who is still writing the scripts, found too confusing to understand" (p. 65). These individuals, instead of forming symptoms, are dominated by "action symptoms", which perform a similar function, neutralizing or binding up psychic experiences that cannot be borne or known about. In a couple relationship, the partners share this need, and both derive relief from externalizing early and unresolved mental pain. At the same time, this defensive strategy means that the couple relationship can only take place in a very restricted zone, which might look deeply unhappy, even hate-filled, to the observer. Here, the sado-masochism is performing a defensive purpose, while the relationship continues to hold the promise of something deeper and more fulfilling.

Mitrani (2007) likens this to a situation in which patients may "freeze up" in order to attain a sensation of solidity, this icy barrier has an impact on others and often leaves them cold, getting in the way of what Tustin (1986) refers to as "healing emotional transactions". This kind of shared defence (Clulow, Dearnley, & Balfour, 1986) means that the relationship can only survive if it stays within very rigidly defined boundaries. For Sam and Rosa, the need for an icy, hard-edged experience eventually meant no affectionate touching, no talking from an individual perspective, and no sharing thoughts and feelings. Emotional or physical touching was felt to be so destabilizing as to be almost traumatic. However, they became increasingly aware that something more sustaining and fulfilling was being missed, and they longed for it.

In this chapter, I have described a couple relationship in which clear violations were taking place, mixed in with the capacity for nurturance. When there was intense pressure to keep unbearable experiences at bay, the couple did resort to perverse sexual enactments. However, I believe I have described a perverse relationship fuelled, on the whole, not by the more obvious quest for excitement by aberrant means, but as a couple's last effort to protect themselves "from anticipated psychological breakdown, in which excitement serves as a smokescreen hiding the internal terror" (Bonner, 2006, p. 1549). As a result of this desperate quest for survival, neither of them were able to experience each other as the people they really were, but instead only as players in an already fixed, repetitive, and defensive scenario. This view encourages us to think about a shared need to pervert reality, which exists to some extent in all couple relationships.

References

Bak, R. (1968). The phallic woman: the ubiquitous fantasy in perversions. *Psychoanaytic Study of the Child*, 23: 15–36.

Bonner, S. (2006). A servant's bargain: perversion as survival. *International Journal of Psychoanalysis*, 87: 1549–1567.

Chasseguet-Smirgel, J. (1974). Perversion, idealisation and sublimation, *International Journal of Psychoanalysis*, 55: 349–358.

Chasseguet-Smirgel, J. (1985). *Creativity and Perversion*. London: Free Association.

Clulow, C., Dearnley, B., & Balfour, F. (1986). Shared phantasy and therapeutic structure in a brief marital psychotherapy. *British Journal of Psychotherapy*, 3: 124–132.

Glasser, M. (1979). Some aspects of the role of aggression in the perversions. In: I. Rosen (Ed.), *Sexual Deviation* (2nd edn) (pp. 278–305). Oxford: Oxford University Press.

Glasser, M. (1998). On violence: a preliminary communication. *International Journal of Psychoanalysis*, 79: 887–902. .

McDougall, J. (1986). *Theatres of the Mind*. London: Free Association.

Mitrani, J. (2007). Bodily centred protections in adolescence. *International Journal of Psychoanalysis*, 88: 1153–1169.

Ruszczynski, S. (2006). Sado-masochistic enactments in a couple relationship: the fear of intimacy and the dread of separateness. *Psychoanalytic Perspectives on Couple Work*. London: SCPP (p.107–116).

Ruszczynski, S. (2007). The problem of certain psychic realities: aggression and violence as perverse solutions. In: D. Morgan & S. Ruszczynski (Eds.), *Lectures on Violence, Perversion and Delinquency*. London: Karnac.

Sanchez-Medina, A. (2002). Perverse thought. *International Journal of Psychoanalysis*, 83: 1345–1359

Stoller, R. J. (1975). *Perversion: The Erotic Form of Hatred*. London: Hogarth.

Tustin, F. (1986). *Autistic Barriers in Neurotic Patients*. London: Karnac.

Welldon, E. V. (1996). Contrasts in male and female sexual perversions. In: C. Cordess & M. Cox (Eds.), *Forensic Psychotherapy*. London: Jessica Kingsley.

CHAPTER TWELVE

Intimacy and sexuality in later life

Andrew Balfour

From a train window, I recently spotted an advertising hoarding for life assurance that showed a face made up of two halves. On one side it was youthful, and on the other it was aged. I thought that this captured something essential about a psychoanalytic view of old age, the sense of the older and younger faces so closely linked, the older one containing the stamp of the younger one. It is, of course, a developmental model, and sexuality and its vicissitudes are a central part of that development. What, then, of the changing face of sexuality as we get older? When thinking about this topic we need a complex view of sexuality, linked to our psychic development and to the development of our capacity for sustained intimacy with other people, something that has been a central concern of psychoanalysis since the inception of Freud's revolutionary thinking, which began with sexuality, and with infantile sexuality in particular, more than a century ago. The question I want to address in this chapter is whether sexuality is subject to particular developmental pressures in later life.

Louis Noirot, a French physician, observed in 1873 ". . . in old age, like our hair, our desires should wither" (quoted in Stearns, 1979, p. 243). Ruth Rendell, a novelist now aged seventy-six, said in an interview published in the *Guardian* (16 September, 2006), "With age a lot of things go that one loved. Sex, of course, but I think its departure is proper and natural and not to be mourned". Contrast this with a poem written by Thomas Hardy when he was an old man, which conveys the persistence of sexual longing in later life:

I look into my glass
And view my wasting skin
And say, "Would God it came to pass
My heart had shrunk as thin!"

For then, I, undistrest
By hearts grown cold to me,
Could lonely wait my endless rest
With equanimity.

But time, to make me grieve,
Part steals, lets part abide;
And shakes this fragile frame at eve
With throbbings of noontide.

Changes associated with ageing

As ever, in regard to matters related to ageing, Freud himself was pessimistic. In a letter to Lou Andreas-Salome, dated 10 May 1925, he wrote:

As for me, I no longer want to ardently enough. A coat of indifference is slowly creeping around me. It is a natural development, a way of beginning to grow inorganic. The "detachment of old age" I think it is called. It must be connected with a decisive turn in the relationship of the two instincts postulated by me. The change taking place is perhaps not very noticeable; everything is as interesting as it was before . . . but some kind of resonance is lacking; unmusical as I am, I imagine the difference to be something like using the pedal or not. [Freud, Freud, & Gubrich-Simitis, 1978, p. 237]

Freud confided quite a lot in his letters to her about his feelings about his ageing and the physical illness that accompanied it. For example, when he wrote to her to acknowledge her congratulations on his seventy-fifth birthday, he commented that he found it wonderful that she and her husband could still enjoy the sun. He added, "But with me, the grumpiness of old age has moved in, the complete disillusionment comparable to the congealing of the moon, the inner freezing" (Gay, 1988, p. 525).

There are inevitable losses associated with ageing. There can be a loss of role or status in society, the deaths of peers, and the coming into view more sharply of the end of one's own life, as well as the loss of youthful attractiveness and sexual potency. In addition, the threatened or actual experience of what Hess (1987) has described as the "catastrophes of old age", particularly stroke or dementia, impinge as possibilities even if they do not become realities. They threaten to bring increased dependency on others and loss of the autonomy of younger adulthood, threatening, at least in phantasy, if not necessarily in reality, a return to the dependency states of earliest infancy. We also see how for older couples—unable to use work or career and the structure this has afforded them to disperse difficulties, or to contain projections of parts of themselves—an equilibrium they have found earlier on can be upset. As retirement arrives, there is a sense for some couples of being thrown back upon themselves, and of the relationship having to bear or contain things that it had not had to before. Couples can experience this as a demand for increased intimacy and contact with aspects of themselves (possibly experienced as residing in their partner) that have been avoided earlier on. The return to "two-some-ness", and the loss of a wider circle of professional activities and colleagues, can bring a return of claustrophobic anxieties associated with the most intimate relations between mother and infant, of early babyhood and childhood. I shall return to this theme shortly in the clinical material that follows. But, lest this sounds too negative, emphasizing only what is lost in ageing, "Getting older", by Elaine Feinstein (2001, p. 53), strikes a different note:

> The first surprise: I like it.
> Whatever happens now, some things
> That used to terrify have not:
>
> I didn't die young, for instance. Or lose
> My only love. My three children
> Never had to run away from anyone.

> Don't tell me this gratitude is complacent.
> We all approach the edge of the same blackness
> Which for me is silent.
>
> Knowing as much sharpens
> My delight in January freesia,
> Hot coffee, winter sunlight. So we say
>
> As we lie close on some gentle occasion:
> Every day won from such
> Darkness is a celebration.

What is likely to influence whether ageing brings "sharpened delight", as Feinsten puts it? What factors help to allow a creative engagement with the developmental challenges of old age that will affect whether experience continues to be engaged with in a lively way (which links to the capacity to sustain intimacy later in life)? Freud's early view was that less sexual expression, a decline in genital sexuality, left a problem of undischarged libido, leading to anxiety and other difficulties in old age. In 1895, he wrote about "the anxiety in senescent men at the time of their decreasing potency and increasing libido" (p. 102), referring to his view that libidinal energy could no longer be discharged via genital sexual activity in the same way any more, and that this would lead to anxiety and other psychological problems. This was developed by Deutsch (1984), focusing on female sexuality, and the menopause in particular. Like Freud, she believed that in later life the libidinal motor of development essentially goes into reverse gear, bringing psychological problems consequent upon a pathogenic damming up of libido, leading to regression. Deutsch, for example, saw depression as an inevitable feature of the menopause (Bemesderfer, 1996). However, subsequent psychoanalytic thinkers have instead taken the view that the impact of such changes will depend upon the individual's capacity to bear loss and the extent to which losses are experienced predominantly in depressive or paranoid–schizoid states of mind. This, it is argued, will determine the extent to which experience can continue to be engaged with creatively and intimacy, including sexual intimacy, can be sustained. This links the capacity to adjust to inevitable age-related changes in sexual functioning, and the ability to bear the grief that time, in Hardy's words, "part steals, lets part abide". The ageing process, with its physical signs, such as changes in sexual functioning, taxes the defences that may have been used throughout a lifetime to protect against the spectres of vulnerability, need, and dependency awakened by the experience and prospect of loss.

A common loss for men, for example, can be erectile ability. King (1980) points out the importance of the fear of impotence and the impact this may have on relationships in later life. In a review commissioned by the Pennell Initiative for Women's Health, and carried out by the Tavistock Centre for Couple Relationships (Vincent, Riddell, & Shmueli, 2001) it was pointed out that Havelock Ellis's view in the early twentieth century regarded the menopause as a cut-off point in the sexual life of women, and that in many ways society's attitudes to sexuality in later life have moved on very little since this time. In fact, a number of large-scale research studies have been carried out in recent years showing that, although sex may decrease in frequency in old age, older people remain sexually active. These studies highlight how many people adapt to changes in physical health and functioning, sustaining a sexual intimacy that may be expressed in different ways. So, an over-emphasis on genital sexuality would give a distorted view of sexuality in old age. The importance of the capacity to adapt and adjust to the changes and losses of old age and to sustain intimacy is highlighted in research that shows that marital closeness moderates the negative psychological impact of functional disability in later life in terms of depression, anxiety, and self-esteem (Mancini & Bonanno, 2006).

The passage of time, which presages mortality, is a profound loss to be borne. To paraphrase Hardy, time makes us grieve. Freud's view was that we cannot really conceive of our own death, that in the unconscious there is no reference to time, and at an unconscious level we all believe we are immortal; even as we try to imagine our death we are there as observers of our own funeral. However, Money-Kyrle (1971) suggests how, while we might not be able to imagine an abstraction such as death or non-existence, we might nevertheless inherit a "pre-conception" of it, to use Bion's (1962) term, and we can therefore recognize instances of it. He shows how temporality, the fact of things not lasting, which is a fundamental dimension of all of our experience from the beginning of life, faces us with the threat of the death of our objects and ourselves, and is for everyone an instance of the experience of mortality. This fact of life, that nothing good (or bad) lasts forever, is difficult to accept. It is the capacity to face depressive anxieties that influences our ability to tolerate this, and ultimately affects whether reality is retreated from, with consequent damage to our capacity to engage in a truthful way with our own experience and to sustain intimate relationships with others. Clinically, we can see individuals for whom the mental pain of loss and vulnerability associated with facing the passage of time, and ultimately death, seems impossible to bear. There can be a retreat into rigid and paranoid states of mind, which in couple relationships can present as two partners living in a world peopled by their own projections into one another, resulting in polarized and rigid ways of relating. I shall illustrate what I mean by this in the following clinical example.

The "no-change couple"

He was a successful lawyer, the senior partner in a commercial law firm. She had been an architect. Things had been bad since her retirement two years previously. He was still working, running his firm. They had bought a retirement house and came up to London during the week, staying in their flat while he worked and she tried to occupy herself with charity work and trips to galleries and theatres. Their retirement plans had stalled: he had kept working despite promises to the contrary, and they had never properly moved into the beautiful retirement home in the country that they visited at weekends. What they vividly conveyed to my co-therapist and me when we first met them was how they could not move into and inhabit together the territory of their old age.

At the Tavistock Centre for Couple Relationships, we send self-report forms to each partner before their first appointment. When this couple came, they told my co-therapist and me how neither of them had read the other's forms, which were sitting, out of sight, side by side on our desk, "in parallel", so to speak. These forms, each one unknown to the other, sitting like this on the desk, seemed to reflect the parallel lives that the couple lived. This was echoed in the way they each took it in turns to address us in the session, having no direct contact or exchanges with one another. On their forms, each had complained that the other was depressed; she, in particular, had emphasized her worry about his depression.

We had expected, therefore, to meet up with a withdrawn man. In fact, he presented initially as a rather chipper, quite commanding figure, and we were struck instead by her considerable grief and sadness. She was tearful and aggrieved, and it was our feeling, much to our surprise, that she was the depressed one, left waiting for him and frustrated by his unavailability. We thought that feelings of grievance and depression had been lodged in her, and this had been partly provoked by his behaviour and withdrawal into the world of work. He seemed to be keeping a distance both from her and from the depressed part of himself in her through projective identification, such that she was carrying a "double dose" of depression, his feelings as well as her own. What was striking, as we worked with them over time, was how this depression could move between them, with first she and then he appearing to be the depressed one.

At this early point in our work with them, we wondered about the timing of their seeking help, and in relation to this we wondered about the role of retirement as a trigger. It seemed to us that retirement might have threatened a defence that they had previously maintained between them—their parallel lives—where work could function to provide for their need for distance from each other. It was as if, in retirement, they feared being left only with one another, as though their relationship now had to contain all those aspects of themselves that they feared being overwhelmed by, and that they had previously managed by dispersal, in their parallel tracks, taking care that they were never both at risk of being depressed when they might "both go under at the same time", as they later said.

It was against this background that he presented their dilemma to us: that he felt empty of feeling for his wife. He cared for her, but his feelings of love had vanished. He could not force them to come back, and now he felt tortured. He was, he said, on the brink of separating from her, and yet, for some reason, was unable to do so. She seemed to be in an equally tortured position, endlessly waiting for him to make up his mind and to commit to her. The situation was bleak and, as they put it, ". . . the past is grim, the present is grim and the future is grim". We referred to this active process of keeping things stuck and unmoving as the act of "grimming" their experience. The therapy often had a timeless quality, with no sense of urgency or need to sort things out. Although there might be a bit of liveliness or a hint of movement in one session, this would be lost by the next, and we were constantly faced with the complaint that things were just the same, they were stuck in the same old groove. They could not separate and they could not come together. Feelings seemed to be emptied out, particularly spontaneous feelings, and especially any expression of aggression.

Interestingly, things were a little different when one of them was unable to come to a session and the other came alone. At such times each of them would comment on how much freer they felt than when they were together, that they could say things that they could not say when the other one was present for fear that they would be devastated if they were to hear it. While their revelations never felt particularly remarkable, what was striking was their mutual attribution of vulnerability and devastation to the other one. On one such occasion, he commented on what he felt was his difficulty in "speaking from the heart" to her. I felt there was an echo here, in the way he talked of having to be careful with her, of his treatment of my co-therapist and me. For example, we noticed that when he was angry with us he would comment, quite out of the blue, that it was not that he felt furious, not that he felt he was going to explode . . . when no one had said that he was. This negation was often our first sign that this was precisely what he felt. When we took this up with him he said that he could easily devastate my co-therapist and me. We put it to him that he tended to think of himself always as potentially devastating, never devastated. It then emerged that he had been very upset recently when she had been the one to comment angrily that they should split up. He said that he had been surprised by a comment of his son's, that he thought his mother would manage if they split up, but not his father. This was not how he thought of himself. Then, for the first time, he commented on his uncertainty about himself and what he really felt. It was at this point, when he seemed to glimpse some of his own vulnerability, that his feelings about retirement emerged for the first time. This material led us towards an understanding of their shared underlying fear, or anxiety, that emotional contact could lead to a devastating explosion. It also captured how the fear of a destructive explosion seemed to be closely linked to an underlying fear of loss and separation. It seemed that at some level there was a phantasy operating: that if nothing changed then nothing could be lost.

After a lot of work, it emerged very painfully, and with great difficulty, that he had recently had an illness that had left him with sexual difficulties. This was something they found very difficult to speak about. The problems themselves could have been ameliorated by medication, but this would have entailed a reliance upon "artificial" means to enable sexual intercourse between them, and this was too shameful. His response to his loss of functioning was to feel that he had to work harder than ever. There seemed to be an accusation in his own mind that he was not "up to it" any more. He struggled ever more desperately to prove his potency as a manager at work, while avoiding the issue of potency in the sexual relationship. He had withdrawn into an idealization of self-sufficiency, away from his vulnerability and dependency. He nurtured fantasies of being off on his own. His only imagined future was of himself as a kind of existential anti-hero, on his own in some romantic foreign city. He could not envisage a future where they were together. Increasingly, it became evident how unreal these fantasies were. In reality, he could not achieve any separation at all, not even to go away for a holiday, something that she gradually had become able to do. For him, the only separation that was possible was into the world of work, to which he felt equally shackled. Indeed, what we noticed over time was how, when she moved away from her position of being the one who "wanted" the relationship, and became, in his words, "more negative", he became "more positive". And so they kept themselves in what he termed a zero-sum situation, in which any movement in one direction or another was quickly cancelled out.

How could we understand this situation, where he threatened to leave but where it seemed that no separation at all was possible? Keeping themselves apart in this way seemed to us to be an attempt to obviate any knowledge of the losses that they had already experienced, and that might be facing them. There could be no real discussion of the loss it was clear that at some level he feared if he did retire. This was unthinkable. His response was to work ever more frantically to ablate any knowledge of the reality of his impending retirement. It was very difficult indeed for him to recognize his limitations and the point he had reached in his career, with others expectantly waiting for him to cede his power in the firm to them. He was being asked to give up his potency in his managerial role at work at the same time that he felt he was losing it on so many other fronts.

In our work with this couple, who had for many years been such high achievers, we had a painful sense of the difficulty for them in giving up a lifetime of striving, and moving together into retirement, of realizing that the baton, so to speak, is to be passed on now to the next generation. Of course, generational differences and their recognition are central to the story of Oedipus, and this leads us to the question of whether there are particular qualities of the Oedipal situation as it is encountered in later life.

Oedipus and ageing

The *New York Times* (25 November, 2007) ran a piece describing an increasingly familiar scenario: a former Supreme Court Judge found that her husband, who had Alzheimer's disease, was having a relationship with another woman. The judge was reportedly thrilled ". . . and even visits the new couple while they hold hands on the porch swing, because it is a relief to see her husband of 55 years so content". The story explores what the paper called "Old Love", illuminating the relationships that often develop amongst patients with dementia and how the desire for intimacy persists even when dementia takes so much else away. The film *Away from Her*, based on a short story by the Canadian writer Alice Munro, portrays a man watching his wife slip away from him as she is over-taken by the depredations of Alzheimer's disease only to have to witness, as she moves into residential care, her romance with a male patient in the nursing home. As he struggles with this, he eventually moves to a position of accepting the relationship, and arranges for his wife's new love to return to the nursing home after he sees how devastated she is when he is not there. The meaning of this "acceptance" is understood in relation to his own affairs earlier in the marriage, to his expiation of guilt and remorse, and the rework-ing of a familiar dynamic in the marriage with him now having to bear the pain of being the excluded one, the witness to the coupling from which he is left out. Here, of course, we are touching on the Oedipal situation, the lifelong struggle to tolerate exclusion, origi-nally from the parental coupling, to recognize that one is not at the exclusive centre of mother's mind but in a position of "linked sepa-rateness" to the parents and their relationship with one another.

The Oedipus complex is never "resolved" once and for all; we encounter it at different points in the lifespan.

> Mrs Jones, a woman in her late eighties, had lost her husband of many years. He had looked after her at their home for some time following her diagnosis of dementia. What had been striking at the time was how she experienced his death. She became convinced that he was not dead at all but that he was alive and seeing another woman instead of her. The delusion that he was still alive but betraying her with another woman might be seen as reflecting unresolved infantile oedipal struggles,

underlying difficulties which re-emerged as Mrs Jones's adult cognitive capacities deserted her.

Our current understanding is that earlier problematic emotional constellations do not "grow old" in the sense of diminishing or fading away, but persist and become more powerful as dependency increases and adult coping falls away, ". . . because the unconscious does not participate in the process of growing older" (Grotjahn, 1940, p. 97).

Ageing is a powerful site for Oedipal anxieties, with the inversion of the earlier Oedipal configuration: for the young it is the parental couple that is procreative, for the old it is the younger generation; the envied object moves from the parents' intercourse to that of the next generation. Something of the challenge that watching children develop into young adults can present for parents is conveyed by a man in late middle-age describing the experience of an attractive young woman calling at the house to see his teenaged son:

> At that moment I realised with envy that this young woman hadn't come to see me, she had come to see my son. That was a bit of a shock. A feeling of loss and nostalgia descended on me. I acknowledged to myself that my own days of sexual exploration were over . . . If I do allow myself to compare my body with his, I feel more of a sense of loss. Often, it feels like a loss of energy. I can't play football like he does, I feel worn out a lot of the time. [My wife says] I am a grumpy git, so that may well be my unexpressed anger around all of this. [*The Guardian*, 16 December, 2006]

What is being described here is the experience of one generation's displacement by the next, and the reworking of Oedipal anxieties that accompanies experiences of loss and displacement in later life. Klein (1959) comments that identification with the younger generation can help to mitigate these anxieties in older people, just as for the infant identification with the parents' happiness can help to mitigate the painful Oedipal anxieties that are stirred up by the recognition of the parental sexual relationship that excludes the child. She writes,

> This attitude becomes particularly important when people grow older and the pleasures of youth become less and less available. If

gratitude for past satisfactions has not vanished, old people can enjoy whatever is still within their reach. Furthermore, with such an attitude, which gives rise to serenity, they can identify themselves with young people. For instance, anyone who is looking out for young talents and helps to develop them . . . is only able to do so because he can identify with others; in a sense he is repeating his own life, sometimes even achieving vicariously the fulfilment of aims unfulfilled in his own life. [p. 250]

The Riddle of the Sphinx that Oedipus must solve is the task of recognizing generational difference, which so often we can try to escape from or triumph over. Shakespeare gave dramatic representation to the Oedipal issues involved in growing older in *King Lear*. At the opening of the play, Lear brings together his three daughters and the Court to hear his announcement of his retirement, "handing over the baton" to the next generation:

> To shake all cares and business from our age
> Conferring them to younger strengths . . . [1.1 (39–42]

But there is a catch: this is not a gesture born of the serenity that Klein describes. Before they can inherit a third each of his kingdom, his daughters must make a public declaration of their love for him. However, this is not just any declaration of love; they must tell him that they "love him all". He must be reassured that he is at the centre of their world and of their affections, rather like the Oedipal child seeking evidence that he is at the centre of his mother's world, wishing to disavow the Oedipal reality that she has other concerns or interests, and a relationship, ultimately, to his father, that excludes him. Cordelia, Lear's youngest daughter, refuses the pressure to repudiate generational differences:

> Why have my sisters husbands, if they say
> They love you all? . . . Sure I shall never marry like my sisters
> To love my father all. [1.1: 96–104]

Lear rejects the triangular situation in which his truthful daughter faces him with the reality that she loves him, but she also loves her husband to be. This Oedipal situation cannot be managed by Lear, at this point in his life, and so the tragedy of the play unfolds. A place in a triangular relationship is rejected and hated by Lear, and he takes refuge in the delusional appearance of love, an apparent acceptance of increased dependency and loss of power, but "giving space for younger generations" in an attempt to triumph over and control it.

The play becomes an increasingly nightmarish world of fathers being plotted against by the next generation who wish to displace them. As Edmund, the illegitimate son of the Duke of Gloucester puts it: "The younger rises when the old doth fall" (III. 3–4: 23). What is ushered in is a version of painful loss and relinquishment from one generation to the next that is coloured by the anxieties of the paranoid–schizoid position, devoid of gratitude and serenity. The more benign and mature version of the older generation handing over and identifying with the younger, which Klein describes as another developmental possibility, is absent. Lear takes refuge in a delusional world, with a collapse into narcissistic, paranoid, and, ultimately, psychotic states of mind, following on from the point where the reality of generational difference and boundary cannot be recognized. One could see the fears of older figures in *King Lear* of murderous attacks to be a projection of hatred at their own displacement, at the reversal of the original Oedipal configuration, the older generation now giving way to the young, and having to recognize their youthful potency and face a sense of exclusion from the world that goes on without them at the centre any more. The universal theme of the play is testimony to how painful and difficult this "passing on of the baton" can be, and how much can go wrong at this developmental phase.

Such dramas are not, of course, confined to the stage, but appear in the consulting rooms of psychotherapists working with couples, as my final clinical example illustrates. There are some similarities with the first couple that I described, and, indeed, I find that couples frequently come for help in later life when they can no longer use sexuality and work as they did in younger days to manage difficulties in sustaining intimacy between them.

When a couple's familiar defences no longer hold up

The couple were just entering later life, and facing depression as lifelong defences were wearing thin, he having had affairs throughout the marriage and now confronted by impotence as a consequence of treatment for prostate cancer. Ostensibly, the couple came for help because of his affairs over the course of their forty-year marriage. However, pretty quickly it became clear that it was not the affairs, so much, that were the reason for their seeking help at this point. They had made a lifelong defensive use of sexuality, he through his numerous affairs and she in both tolerating the situation and, at the same time, investigating and seeking to expose them. And the experience of prostate cancer triggered a response in the husband that was the same as at other points in his life when he had had difficulties: he had another affair. It was short-lived, and, though it re-ignited the compelling drama between them (which, in reality, did not seem to need an actual "other woman" to sustain it), it also exposed their difficulty in facing the loss, vulnerability, and dependency brought into prospect by the beginning of old age, a prospect that for each of them threatened a traumatic return of the dependency of their infancy and childhood where each had, in different ways, lost their opposite-sex parent.

The couple had met when they were both very young, and had come to the UK as adults, where they had raised a family. They rarely returned to their country of origin, though spoke, on occasion, about moving back to live in the "mother country". He was a man who had barely seen his mother for the first seven years or so of his life, as she had constantly been ill, hospitalized in isolation wards for fear of infection. She had lost her father at the age of eight, and subsequently the family home had broken up and the children were sent away to boarding school.

In the marriage, each partner showed a profound difficulty in tolerating their dependency on the other, a fear of dependency that had worsened with age and his experience of a failing body. His prowess, both on the sports field and in his capacity to attract women sexually, were very important to him. Yet, with the onset of old age, he had had two hip replacements and prostate cancer in quick succession, the treatment of which had left him with erectile difficulties: "I am old from the waist down," he explained to me.

His wife was always kept guessing, worried about where he was, fearful of abandonment by him, so reversing his early childhood situation of abandonment by mother. Now, he was the desired object of attention and she the abandoned one, never able to trust in his dependability. Even with the rugby teams he played for he would agree to appear in two or three matches on the same Saturday afternoon, and at the last minute he would let them down, feeling himself to be the indispensable, much-wanted player, with all the teams vying in his mind's eye to have him. When I first saw them he was still going on three-mile runs, trying to prove to himself that he could do the same things as ever, even though he had been told that this was damaging his hips and causing him serious physical problems. Later life had faced him with a very difficult readjustment. Defences that he had used throughout his life—his use of sexuality and manic activity—could not be sustained in the same way any more. Between them, they repeatedly enacted a very familiar situation of accusation and cover-up, investigation and exposure. This had a timeless quality, and together they would go around and around this well-trodden ground. The situation in the therapy seemed to be one where each made representations to me, as though I were the judge in a courtroom investigating their respective accusations of the other. More contact with need and dependency quickly got turned into an investigation that would expose one or other of them: he as having been "caught at it", exposed as a liar and cheat, she as being "mad" and pathologically jealous. This seemed to be an excited dramatization of their painful Oedipal struggle. Consciously, they hated it, but at the same time there was a triumph in this state of mind over more painful feelings.

They started to recognize the pattern, and a different picture of him began to emerge from the self-confident "Casanova" that both of them had encouraged me to see. When this was taken up, he would quickly get into a superior, contemptuous position. Indeed, they would join together to position themselves as the couple with all the resources, a triumphant, omnipotent state, where they felt envied by other people of whom they were contemptuous, "people who drive old cars". They joked about their contempt for people with Clarks' shoes, a symbol of being old and sensible, they said (shoes that I was clearly wearing), that they were not ready for yet. He commented that he needed to be different from his parents' flat and nothing life. In this omnipotent state of mind he reduced his parents to flat and lifeless figures, in the same way as he denied the existence of the vulnerable aspects of himself by triumphing over his need and dependency on his internal good objects and his therapist.

As time went on, he reported feeling more depressed, and she spoke of feeling more trusting of him. It felt to me that he was able to be in a more truthful contact with himself. On one occasion she described how she had tried to touch him affectionately and he had not responded. This quickly turned into an argument between them in the room, but the atmosphere shifted when he became able to talk about his fear that more intimate contact between them might lead to sex. "I have to get this bloody thing—the pump—out, it's a bloody great thing, not very attractive. It's not like me, not to try things to help myself," he said. But it faced him with what had changed, and with having to depend on something else for help, and to acknowledge his need for it. I thought that this linked to his sense of shame and exposure in recognizing his need for the therapy, and for his younger therapist.

He then commented on how he could not use the pump at home because his (grown up) children would see it, and spoke of how the onset of his feelings of depression were linked to envy of a younger couple who did not have to work so hard, and who seemed to have it all. In the transference, I thought he was communicating something important about how it felt to be showing me his fears and what was failing him, and his envy of my relative youth. When I took this up, he spoke of his fears that if he did try these aids they might not work, and then he would be left feeling that there was nothing that could help him. What he conveyed was how he no longer had access to defences he used to rely on, and that he feared he would be left with nothing in their place, exposed by his sense of need and dependency, which I thought were linked to feelings of shame. He imagined using the pump, and it taking half an hour or more to have an effect. He said he could imagine her getting fed up. He was anxiously looking at her while he talked, scrutinizing her face for her reaction. And then he spoke movingly about his fears about what she felt about the changes in him. It was very difficult for him to put these into words, but when he did so there was a glimpse of an emotional contact between them, which they found very difficult to sustain. Towards the end of the session, when I took up how they moved away so quickly from the point of contact between them, he commented, "They are losses aren't they, it's like a bereavement really, losing your potency."

They described going for a walk together on a beach, on holiday. As they got to the beach they had had an explosive row, something that came on very suddenly and violently. She had gone off in the other direction, away from him. The row had been sparked by her trying to look after him, telling him they should get out of the wind, and he had felt controlled by her. It was a poignant image of the possibility of inti-macy between them, of being able to look after one another, but, in the face of this, an explosive row, each moving off in opposite directions, sitting far apart from the other, on different rocks, looking at the sunset. They conveyed the difficulty in facing the evening of their lives together, in helping each other and allowing an intimacy with one another in which they would have to face their own and the other's ageing and losses, the changes in themselves also reflecting the changes in the other.

In such couples, who have encountered profound difficulties in facing the passage of time, it is as if they find themselves living with images of themselves in their partner that they find increasingly difficult to bear. In this way, the partners in the couple reflected to one another the reality of their ageing, literally represented by the older body now in front of them that contains the truth of time passing, confronting them with all the difficulties of facing this "fact of life".

Ageing, oppression, and opportunity

I shall conclude this chapter by returning to my starting point, to the poem by Hardy, and his sense of being oppressed by the changes of age, "wasting skin", the difficulty of still having a full heart and desires and at the same time knowing about the changes and losses of age. It is, as Hardy puts it, the "part stolen/part abiding" that brings forth grief: the continued life of the body and the mind, the awareness of desires and, at the same time, of physical changes such as the loss of youthful physical attractiveness and potency. A solution can be to wish away the desire, to "shrink the heart", in Hardy's words, to withdraw from bringing to life sexual desire or involvement and intimacy, which also then brings to life the grief at what is no longer. This was frequently the solution of the couples I have described, reflecting lifelong difficulties with intimacy that were compounded by the developmental pressures of later life, the difficulty in mourning the losses that were facing them.

In his marriage, Hardy had "frozen" his heart for many years before the death of his first wife (Tomalin, 2006a). It was his wife Emma's death, at the age of seventy-two, that produced an outpouring of poems about her, and established his reputation as a poet. These poems work and rework his feelings about the marriage, which seems to have become an increasingly estranged one with the passing of the years. In them, one glimpses the pain of his attempts to make reparation to her after she has gone, with the memory of early love and intimacy between them that has become hard and cold in their withdrawal from one another in later life. This poem he entitled *Penance* (in Tomalin, 2006b, p. 134):

> Why do you sit, O pale thin man
> At the end of the room
> By that harpsichord, built on the quaint old plan?
> It is as cold as a tomb,
> And there's not a spark within the grate:
> And the jingling wires
> Are as vain desires
> That have lagged too late.
>
> Why do I? Alas, far times ago
> A woman lyred here
> In the evenfall; one who fain did so
> From year to year;
> And, in loneliness bending wistfully,
> Would wake each note
> In sick sad rote,
> None to listen or see!
>
> I would not join, I would not stay,
> But drew away,
> Though the fire beamed brightly ... Aye!
> I do to-day
> What I would not then; and the chill old keys,
> Like a skull's brown teeth
> Loose in their sheath,
> Freeze my touch; yes, freeze.

Hewison (2006) has pointed out how, in this poem, Hardy conveys the painful recognition of his retreat from the possibility of emotional warmth with his wife, and his guilt for killing her off, in his heart, many years before her actual death. What strikes me is how Hardy describes his own "inner freezing", as Freud put it, recognizing the part of himself that withdrew from the life between them, and which now becomes linked to the chill thought of both her life that is gone and his own death to come. As the reader, this puts us in vivid contact with the difficulty of facing what we have done with the possibility of intimacy and life in our relationships, a struggle that we all have throughout our lives, and one that is given a particular quality and intensity in old age when faced with finality and the limits of reparation, of the years having passed, and with actual death. How difficult it can be to allow insight, to take responsibility for our own destructiveness, and to face depressive anxieties when the scope for actual repair may be gone: when these difficulties, which we all encounter at significant points of change or loss in our lives, cannot any more be dealt with by projecting into the future the thoughts of what we will do differently, reassuring us of our potential for reparation. While this may make for great difficulty and challenge in later life, born of the fear that now it is "too late", it can also be the case that an awareness of the limits of time passing, and of time remaining, can bring an urgency and motivation to the wish to work through past losses and to face future ones.

Hardy's poems, written late in his life, bring home with great poignancy how, although the opportunity for real repair of his relationship with his wife had passed, the work of internal reparation was given its greatest urgency, and he is brought into sharper contact than before with his inner situation, and with his need to face this, his reparative wishes bringing the flowering of a creative lyrical outpouring in his last years. Needless to say, sexuality, with all of its vicissitudes and significance in relational terms, continues for us throughout life, with familiar age-old conflicts as well as the demands of adjusting to changes in functioning and tolerating the waning of capacities. These painful realities, particularly Oedipal ones, as I have tried to show, have new coinages in old age, yet they reflect what at heart we struggle with all of our lives.

References

Bemesderfer, S. (1996). A revised psychoanalytic view of menopause. *Journal of the American Psychoanalytic Association, 44S*: 351–369.

Bion, W. R. (1962). A theory of thinking. *International Journal of Psychoanalysis, 38*: 266–275.

Deutsch, H. (1984). The menopause. *International Journal of Psychoanalysis, 65*: 55–62.

Feinstein, E. (2001). Getting older. In: W. Cope (Ed.), *Heaven on Earth: 101 Happy Poems*. London: Faber & Faber.

Freud E., Freud, L., & Grubrich-Simitis, I. (1978). *Sigmund Freud: His Life in Pictures and Words*. Harmondsworth: Penguin.

Freud, S. (1895). On the grounds for detaching a particular syndrome from neurasthenia under the description "anxiety neurosis". *S.E., 3*: 87–120. London: Hogarth.

Gay, P. (1988). *Freud: A Life for Our Time*. London: Pan Macmillan.

Grotjahn, M. (1940). Psychoanalytic investigation of a seventy-one-year-old man with senile dementia. *Psychoanalytic Quarterly, 9*: 80–97.

Hess, N. (1987). King Lear and some anxieties of old age. *British Journal of Medical Psychology, 60*: 209–215.

Hewison, D. (2006). Thoughts on creativity and the internal couple. Freud 150th Anniversary Seminars, Maudsley Hospital Psychotherapy Unit, 7th December.

Klein, M. (1959). Our adult world and its roots in infancy. In: *Envy and Gratitude and Other Works 1946–1963*. London: Hogarth.

King, P. (1980). The life cycle as indicated by the nature of the transference in the psychoanalysis of the middle-aged and elderly. *International Journal of Psychoanalysis, 61*: 153–160.

Mancini, A., & Bonanno, G. (2006). Marital closeness, functional disability and adjustment in late life. *Psychology and Ageing, 21*(3): 600–610.

Money-Kyrle, R. (1971). The aim of psychoanalysis. *International Journal of Psychoanalysis, 52*: 103–106.

Stearns, P. (1979). The evolution of traditional culture toward ageing. In: J. Hendricks & C. Davis (Eds.), *Dimensions in Ageing: Readings*. Cambridge, MA: Winthorp.

Tomalin, C. (2006a). *Thomas Hardy, the Time Torn Man*. Harmondsworth: Penguin.

Tomalin, C. (2006b). *Poems of Thomas Hardy*. Harmondsworth: Penguin.

Vincent, C., Riddell, J., & Shmueli, A. (2001). *Sexuality and Older Women—Setting the Scene*. Pennell Paper No. 1, Pennell Initiative for Women's Health. Huddersfield West Yorkshire.

INDEX